# RESEARCH AND PRACTICE IN SOCIAL STUDIES SERIES

Wayne Journell, *Series Editor*

---

Teaching Data Literacy in Social Studies:
Principles and Practices to Support Historical Thinking and Civic Engagement
TAMARA L. SHREINER

Place-Based Social Studies Education: Learning From Flint, Michigan
ANNIE MCMAHON WHITLOCK

Teaching Villainification in Social Studies:
Pedagogies to Deepen Understanding of Social Evils
CATHRYN VAN KESSEL & KIMBERLY EDMONDSON, EDS.

Civic Engagement in Communities of Color:
Pedagogy for Learning and Life in a More Expansive Democracy
KRISTEN E. DUNCAN, ED.

Developing Historical Thinkers: Supporting Historical Inquiry for All Students
BRUCE A. LESH

Toward a Stranger and More Posthuman Social Studies
BRETTON A. VARGA, TIMOTHY MONREAL, & REBECCA C. CHRIST, EDS.

Critical Race Theory and Social Studies Futures:
From the Nightmare of Racial Realism to Dreaming Out Loud
AMANDA E. VICKERY & NOREEN NASEEM RODRÍGUEZ, EDS.

How to Confront Climate Denial: Literacy, Social Studies, and Climate Change
JAMES S. DAMICO & MARK C. BAILDON

Racial Literacies and Social Studies: Curriculum, Instruction, and Learning
LAGARRETT J. KING, ED.

Making Classroom Discussions Work:
Methods for Quality Dialogue in the Social Studies
JANE C. LO, ED.

Teaching Difficult Histories in Difficult Times: Stories of Practice
LAUREN MCARTHUR HARRIS, MAIA SHEPPARD, & SARA A. LEVY, EDS.

Post-Pandemic Social Studies:
How COVID-19 Has Changed the World and How We Teach
WAYNE JOURNELL, ED.

Teaching History for Justice: Centering Activi~~
CHRISTOPHER C. MARTELL & 

# Teaching Data Literacy in Social Studies

## Principles and Practices to Support Historical Thinking and Civic Engagement

Tamara L. Shreiner

*Dedicated to my students, who have challenged
and inspired me throughout my career.*

Published simultaneously by Teachers College Press,® 1234 Amsterdam Avenue, New York, NY 10027 and National Council for the Social Studies, 8555 16th Street, Suite 500, Silver Spring, MD 20910.

Copyright © 2024 by Teachers College, Columbia University

Front cover design by Edwin Kuo. Images by Merfin, Chusakul Natchanon, and mydegage / Shutterstock.

All rights reserved. No part of this publication may be reproduced or transmitted in any form or by any means, electronic or mechanical, including photocopy, or any information storage and retrieval system, without permission from the publisher. For reprint permission and other subsidiary rights requests, please contact Teachers College Press, Rights Dept.: tcpressrights@tc.columbia.edu

*Library of Congress Cataloging-in-Publication Data*
Names: Shreiner, Tamara, author.
Title: Teaching data literacy in social studies : principles and practices to support historical thinking and civic engagement / Tamara L. Shreiner.
Description: New York, NY : Teachers College Press, 2024. | Series: Research and practice in social studies | Includes bibliographical references and index.
Identifiers: LCCN 2024005575 (print) | LCCN 2024005576 (ebook) | ISBN 780807786260 (paperback) | ISBN 9780807786277 (hardcover) | ISBN 9780807782675 (epub)
Subjects: LCSH: Social sciences—Study and teaching (Elementary) | Social sciences—Study and teaching (Secondary) | Social sciences—Data processing. | Information literacy—Study and teaching (Elementary) | Information literacy—Study and teaching (Secondary) | Information visualization—Study and teaching (Elementary) | Information visualization—Study and teaching (Secondary)
Classification: LCC LB1584 .S49 2024 (print) | LCC LB1584 (ebook) | DDC 372.89—dc23/eng/20240403
LC record available at https://lccn.loc.gov/2024005575
LC ebook record available at https://lccn.loc.gov/2024005576

ISBN 978-0-8077-8626-0 (paper)
ISBN 978-0-8077-8627-7 (hardcover)
ISBN 978-0-8077-8267-5 (ebook)

Printed on acid-free paper
Manufactured in the United States of America

# Contents

### PART I. INTRODUCTION

**1. What Is Data Literacy?**     3
    Calls for Data Literacy     5
    The Many Faces of Data Visualizations     6
    Data Visualizations as Human Choices     10
    A Look Ahead     14

### PART II. WHY TEACH DATA LITERACY IN SOCIAL STUDIES?

**2. The Importance of a Data-Literate Citizenry**     21
    Data as Evidence: A Brief History     23
    Data as Evidence for Decision-Making     28
    Common Ways Data Visualizations Can Mislead     32

**3. Data and Data Visualizations Across the Social Studies Disciplines**     41
    Standards, Assessments, and Resources     43
    Data Literacy for Disciplinary Literacy     51

**4. Primary Source Data and Data Visualizations**     57
    Maps as Worldviews     59
    Census Data and Data Visualizations     65
    Data and Data Visualizations Used as Tools of Oppression     71
    Data Visualizations in Social Movements     75

5. **A Special Role for Social Studies Teachers: Teaching Critical, Humanistic Data Literacy** — 85

   The Importance of Social Studies Teacher Content Knowledge — 88

   The Relevance of Historical Thinking Skills — 90

   Taking Data-Informed Action — 92

## PART III. HOW CAN DATA LITERACY SUPPORT STUDENT LEARNING IN SOCIAL STUDIES?

6. **Timelines as Tools for Historical Thinking** — 97

   Supporting Chronological Understanding — 100

   Understanding Historical Narrative — 105

7. **Maps for Spatial Thinking and Problem Solving** — 111

   Thinking About Maps — 115

   Thinking With Maps — 121

   Thinking Through Maps — 127

8. **Telling Stories With Graphs and Charts** — 133

   Making Sense of Graphs and Charts — 136

   Teaching Graph Comprehension — 139

   Telling Stories With Graphs — 143

9. **Producing, Wrangling, and Transforming Data: Pathways to Critical, Humanistic Data Literacy** — 151

   Producing Data — 154

   Wrangling Data — 155

   Visualizing Data — 157

## PART IV. INCORPORATING DATA LITERACY INTO THE SOCIAL STUDIES CURRICULUM

10. **Teaching Data Literacy Across Grade Levels** — 165

    Kindergarten Through Second Grade — 166

    Third Through Fifth Grade — 170

|  |  |
|---|---|
| Sixth Through Eighth Grade | 173 |
| Ninth Through Twelfth Grade | 179 |

**11. Helping Students Comprehend and Critique Data Visualizations** — 187
- Slow Analysis Technique — 188
- Slow Reveal Technique — 191

**12. Using Technology to Manipulate and Visualize Data** — 199
- Data Visualization Tools — 200
- Minimal Manuals — 205

## PART V. CONCLUSION

**13. The Data Stories Students Will Tell** — 213

**References** — 216

**Index** — 238

**About the Author** — 248

# Part I

# INTRODUCTION

CHAPTER 1

# What Is Data Literacy?

In October 2019, President Donald Trump tweeted a 2016 United States county-level election map nearly covered in red, with relatively small blue areas mainly peppered along the coasts and around recognizable urban centers like Detroit and Miami. Across the map were the words, "Try to impeach this" (see Figure 1.1). It was a powerful image—the striking sea of red sending to viewers a clear message that presumably needed no further explanation. Why bother trying to impeach a president who had nearly the entire country behind him?

The problem was that the map was both factually inaccurate and misleading. First, several counties that Hillary Clinton won, including Orange County, California, and Lake County, Minnesota, were colored in red when they should have been blue—an inaccuracy that can perhaps be traced to the point at which the map was made in the vote-counting process. What was more misleading was the way that election data was visualized on the map. As several Twitter users and news outlets were quick to point out, the map showed election results *by county*, and given that many U.S. counties are in rural areas with low population density across large areas of land, of course the map would look overwhelmingly red (Lybrand & Dale, 2019). The map masked both the numbers of people voting red or blue across the country, as well as the weight of electoral college votes that would ultimately determine the winner. While Donald Trump did indeed win the presidential election, it was not the landslide that the county-level data map would have one think. This did not stop supporters from sharing the image on their social media feeds, or from putting the image on t-shirts or book covers. It did not stop them because it was an effective data visualization for communicating the message they wanted to convey.

*Data visualizations* such as timelines, maps, graphs, charts, and tables are a potentially impactful means for communicating important, complex information in efficient and meaningful ways (Kennedy & Engebretsen, 2020). Data visualizations are visual representations of *data*, observed and quantified facts that we typically view not as individual elements, but as a body of information to aggregate and organize, drawing attention to patterns, trends, or connections (Friendly & Wainer, 2021). Given the ease

**Figure 1.1. "Try to impeach this" meme**

*Source:* Lybrand and Dale, 2019.

with which computing technologies now allow us to store, organize, and manipulate data, it is little wonder that we are surrounded by data visualizations. We see them when we watch or read the news, scroll through social media, open a utility bill, visit the doctor's office, or—as became painfully clear throughout the COVID-19 pandemic—track infection rates within our communities. However, the meaning of a data visualization can only be effectively judged by a data-literate population.

What does it mean to be data literate? Simply stated, *data literacy* is the ability to comprehend, analyze, interpret, evaluate, create, and argue with data and data visualizations (Carlson et al., 2011; D'Ignazio & Bhargava, 2015). It involves knowing what facts can be extracted from a representation of data, such as that the map in Figure 1.1 provides information on which presidential candidate won the most votes in each U.S. county, with red representing a Republican or Donald Trump win, and blue representing a Democratic or Hillary Clinton win. And it involves being able to draw accurate conclusions from data and data visualizations, like recognizing that Trump received more votes in a greater number of U.S. counties than Clinton. However, data literacy also involves recognizing when data are being used or visualized in misleading or inappropriate ways, such as knowing that winning more counties does not equal winning more votes across the United States, as well as simply recognizing what cannot be concluded from the data or data visualization alone. In short, the concept of data literacy is much more complex than can be captured in a single definition, or even in a few sentences.

This chapter begins to lay out the full scope of what data literacy entails, to establish the importance of teaching data literacy in schools, and especially in social studies. Calls for a more data-literate citizenry are widespread, and several scholars, journalists, and policymakers (e.g., Engebretsen & Kennedy,

2020; Leetaru, 2016; Independent Expert Advisory Group [IEAG], 2014) have already pointed out how essential data literacy is in a world where we are inundated with multimodal sources of information containing both verbal and visual elements. But helping people become data literate is no simple task. Only by first establishing the conceptual complexity of the term *data literacy* can I build the core argument of this book: That to ensure people are equipped with data literacy skills essential for informed, competent citizenship, we must commit ourselves to teaching students how to make sense of data visualizations, not only in math, science and other STEM courses, but also in the disciplines of social studies.

## CALLS FOR DATA LITERACY

In 2014, the United Nations released a report on the "data revolution," arguing that new technologies were "leading to an exponential increase in the volume and types of data available, creating unprecedented possibilities for informing and transforming society" (IEAG, p. 2). We now live in a data-centric or "datafied" society in which we are both constantly producing personal and behavioral data through our computers and smart phones, and constantly inundated with data related to politics, social conditions, our health, and more. These data exchanges have transformed the nature of electoral politics, our consumer habits, and even our interpersonal relationships (Kennedy & Engebretsen, 2020).

Yet there is widespread concern that few people know how to make sense of or use data (IEAG, 2014; Norman, 2023; Rogers, 2016; Qlik, 2023). While many of the loudest alarm bells about data illiteracy have been sounded by employers acutely aware of the power of data in the marketplace, scholars (e.g., Leetaru, 2016; Pawluczuk, 2019; Perez, 2019) have raised concerns about how such illiteracy underscores a power differential between so-called data influencers and data consumers that threatens the very bedrock of democracy. For example, Pawluczuk (2019) has argued that the interconnected and datafied world in which we live has resulted in a division between what she calls the data oppressed and data oppressors, creating "new power structures and new forms of inequality which extend the traditional patterns of class, gender, wealth and education" (n.p.). Indeed, the 2014 UN report on the data revolution makes data literacy a matter of national and global sustainable development, calling on governments, civil society, academia and the philanthropic sector to work together to strengthen the data literacy of citizens, thereby "ensuring that all people have capacity to input into and evaluate the quality of data and use them for their own decisions, as well as to fully participate in initiatives to foster citizenship in the information age" (IEAG, 2014, p. 18).

Building such capacity for data literacy in the citizenry is complicated. First, data literacy must be more agile and adaptive than other forms of literacy. Data are typically communicated through data visualizations, and, as I will address in the next part of this chapter, there is a seemingly endless variety of data visualizations to learn how to read. Not only that, but the history of data visualizations reveals that they have evolved over time, suggesting that we may yet discover new ways to visualize data. Readers must be able to move fluidly between different types of data visualizations, recognizing the significance of their different forms and functions to make sense of them as efficiently as possible.

Secondly, data literacy requires a fundamental understanding that data and data visualizations can be valuable as sources of information, but that they are both limited and limiting—limited in what information they can convey, and limiting if one tends to view them as absolute fact. Readers of data and data visualizations must recognize that they are always manifestations of a series of human choices, and that these choices are inevitably bound up with motivations and biases that must be accounted for when making meaning from them. Such understanding will not arise from superficial encounters with data visualizations, but comes from repetitive exposure and instruction, and from opportunities to work with data in multiple contexts. These contexts include not only those that are strictly mathematical or scientific, but also those that are more closely aligned with the humanities and social sciences. If we are to build a truly data-literate society, we must look beyond STEM, expanding our vision of where and how data literacy is taught.

## THE MANY FACES OF DATA VISUALIZATIONS

Although I have used the term *data visualization* as an all-encompassing term in this chapter and will continue to use it throughout the rest of this book, using a single term can mask the vast array of forms and functions that data visualizations can take on. Designers of data visualizations can formulate them in multiple ways, choosing from a range of graphical elements such as points, lines, or icons to represent data, and multiple aesthetic attributes such as color, shape, and size. Furthermore, designers can apply multiple combinations of titles, legends, and explanatory text to provide context for a data visualization (Börner et al., 2016; Börner & Polley, 2014; Hunter et al., 1987; Tufte, 2001; Wills, 2012).

Different forms of data visualizations are commonly categorized as charts, tables, graphs, maps, and network visualizations (Börner et al., 2016; Börner & Polley, 2014; Hunter et al., 1987; Knaflic, 2015). *Charts* are data visualizations with no inherent reference systems, such as pie

# What Is Data Literacy?

charts or word clouds, whereas *tables* are row-by-column matrices, with cells that can be color-coded or sorted and can contain graphic symbols or miniature icons (Börner et al., 2016; Börner & Polley, 2014; Knaflic, 2015). *Graphs* can be distinguished from the other types of data visualizations by their well-defined reference system, such as horizontal or vertical axes on which data are plotted (Börner et al., 2016). There are sequential graphs, which show movement, causal relations, or organization, such as timelines and time series, and quantitative graphs that have conventional presentations of numerical data on *x*- and *y*-axes, like line graphs, bar graphs, and scatter plots (Börner & Polley, 2014; Hunter et al., 1987). *Maps* are another type of data visualization, using a latitude and longitude reference system overlaid with physical or political markers. They can also be overlaid with one or more layers of data that provide quantitative statistics, or information about connections, movement, spatial expansion, and more (Börner & Polley, 2014; Hunter et al., 1987). Finally, *network visualizations* show relationships between different entities and include social networks and migration flows (Börner & Polley, 2014).

These categories fail to fully capture the variety of data visualizations that exist. Consider, for example, the data visualization shown in Figure 1.2. Created by Charles Minard in 1869 to tell a story of the losses of Napoleon's troops on their 1812 march to Moscow, it is regarded as one of the greatest data visualizations of all time (Friendly & Wainer, 2021; Tufte, 2001). It consists of six variables, encoded in different ways. One variable is the changing size of the French army, which is represented by the width of the tan (departing) and black (returning) bands with 1 millimeter equaling 10,000 men. The army's march begins on the left, where the band is thickest, representing 422,000 men. When they begin the return journey there are only 100,000 men so the band is much narrower. Location is another variable, indicated by the labels and symbols for cities and rivers on the geographic base. For example, the army's journey starts near the Polish–Russian border, and you can see cities they pass and rivers they cross. Two other variables are distance traveled by the army, which is indicated by the scale representing 50 leagues (or about 150 miles) at the right side of the visual, and the direction, which corresponds to the direction of the band, as well as its offshoots, where some troops left for different posts. A fifth variable is the dates of travel on the return trip, from October 18 to December 7, labeled along the line at the bottom of the graphic. The changes in the line correspond to changing temperatures on the return trip, the sixth variable, which you can trace to the labeled vertical axis. Values on the vertical axis range from zero degrees Celsius at the start of their return trip to the lowest point of negative thirty degrees Celsius by December. By the time the army completed their return march, fewer than 10,000 men remained.

**Figure 1.2. Charles Minard's 1869 graphic, *Figurative Map of the Successive Losses of Men of the French Army in the Russia Campaign, 1812–1813***

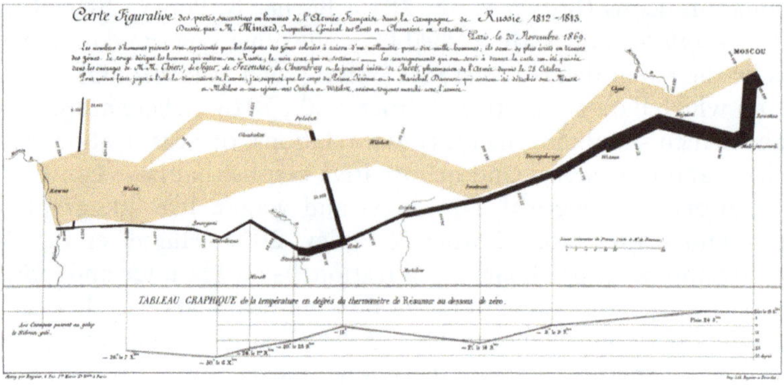

*Source:* https://commons.wikimedia.org/w/index.php?curid=297925

Minard's data visualization defies common typologies. It is probably best described as a combination flow map and time series graph, but even these labels fail to fully capture the ways in which all the variables are connected. Minard drew the visualization of Napoleon's disastrous Russian campaign before conventions for visualizing data had been long or firmly established. William Playfair had invented the line graph, bar graph, and pie chart less than a century before, and the prime meridian would not be established on maps until 1884. Indeed, it was only with Playfair's publication of *The Commercial and Political Atlas* in 1786 that many of the graphical conventions we know today, including gridlines, labeling of axes, and use of time-period indicators to show patterns over time were first established. People would continue to experiment with graphical elements as more data and improved computational technologies became available throughout the 19th century (Friendly & Wainer, 2021).

Of course, in the 21st century people use computers to reinvent or reimagine graphical conventions, creating storytelling infographics made of multiple types of data visualizations, as well as 3-dimensional, animated, and interactive data visualizations (Friendly & Wainer, 2021). Advancements in data visualization techniques and formats became glaringly obvious in 2020 during the COVID-19 pandemic, when people regularly turned to complex data visualizations, such as Johns Hopkins' COVID-19 dashboard (see Figure 1.3) to receive near real-time information on the transmission and impact of the virus. Such computer-based data visualizations can be updated regularly, and can feature dynamic and multifaceted displays to satisfy multiple inquiries among people with varying technological savvy and areas of interest.

What Is Data Literacy? 9

**Figure 1.3. Image of the Johns Hopkins COVID-19 Dashboard from June 18, 2020**

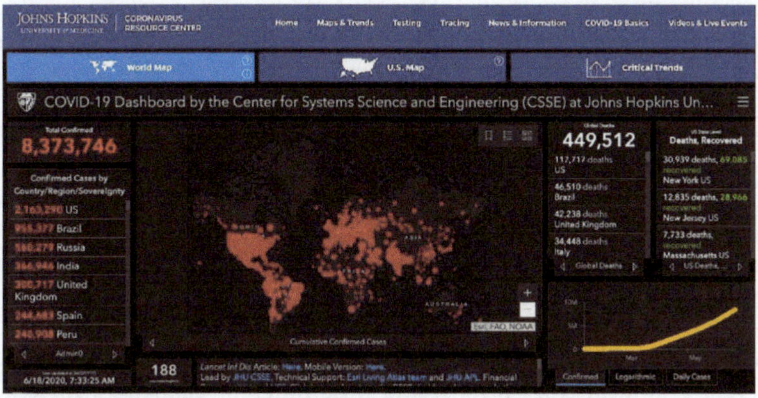

*Source:* Swenson, 2020.

Because some data visualizations of both past and present defy simple categorization, it can be useful to group them by the questions they address, labeling them temporal, spatial, spatiotemporal, topical, or network. *Temporal* data visualizations, for example, answer "when" questions, functioning to show us how data have changed or been distributed over time. They allow us to visualize when events occurred, as well as how they are temporally related to when other events occurred. They help us understand the sequence and duration of events, how events overlapped or were separated in time, and how things may have changed or remained continuous over time. Timelines are the most obvious form of temporal data visualizations, but line graphs, area graphs, and bubble graphs often show change over time as well.

*Spatial* data visualizations answer "where" questions. Maps are the most common type of spatial data visualization, allowing us to discover and visualize spatial relationships and to make large-scale movements or patterns—those normally outside of human perception—contained and visible. We use choropleth maps, connection maps, and dot maps to visualize spatial patterns and distributions that cannot be observed with the naked eye, or connection maps and flow maps to show movement of people, goods, diseases, and languages. Maps can show the whole world and parts of the world at the same time, making it possible for us to make comparisons or see how events in one part of the globe relate to the whole. There are also *spatiotemporal* visualizations, which are complex, multilayered displays with data indicating growth, movement, or other sorts of changes over time. They help us answer "where" and "when" questions simultaneously. Minard's data visualization in Figure 1.2 is an example of a spatiotemporal data visualization.

*Topical* data visualizations are more focused on helping us answer "what" or "how" questions. They include bar graphs, area graphs, pie charts, and population pyramids, helping us make comparisons, observe relationships, or notice patterns at a particular time or in a specific setting. Finally, *network* visualizations help us answer "with whom or what" questions. They show relationships between data elements, whether people, places, or even words in a text.

Such a variety of forms and functions for data visualizations requires a degree of flexibility in skills for making sense of them. In Figure 1.3, for example, reading the temporal line graph that focuses on changes in the number of confirmed cases over time is not the same as reading the spatial bubble map showing the distribution and quantity of confirmed cases across the world in the same display. They encode data differently, use different graphical conventions, and pose different challenges for readers. Comprehending and integrating multiple modes of information, whether moving from verbal to visual or across different visual formats, requires strategy shifts that can only be developed with practice (Schnotz et al., 2014; Serafini, 2015).

In spite of the so-called datafication of society, school curricula often deemphasize the reading of data visualizations, giving short shrift to data literacy in favor of verbal literacy or the acquisition of content knowledge (Schnotz et al., 2014; Shreiner, 2020; Tønnessen, 2020). Of course, verbal literacy and content knowledge are important too, which is why one teacher in one grade level cannot do it all. This is particularly true if we conceive of data literacy as more than just comprehending the meaning of data at a surface level. Even the creators of the Johns Hopkins COVID-19 tracker expressed concern that the public and policymakers were failing to fully comprehend the meaning of the data and their implications for policy. They noted that numbers can be "wrong for lots of different reasons" (Swenson, 2020, n.p.) and that the numbers could fail to provide the context necessary for recognizing the differential impact of the disease on different communities. Such deep understanding of data visualizations, including what they can and cannot tell us, comes only with an understanding of the nature of data visualizations and the human choices they embody.

## DATA VISUALIZATIONS AS HUMAN CHOICES

Though data themselves are often seen as equivalent to facts, the data that we read or use are human constructs, and from collection through visualization, they are never neutral and objective. Data and data visualizations are socially, politically, and materially created and, therefore, embody culturally mediated human choices (Gillborn et al., 2018; Hullman & Diakopoulos, 2011; Irgens et al., 2020). A data-literate person is aware

# What Is Data Literacy?

of the influence of these human choices and will take them into consideration when determining the evidentiary value of data or when making data-based decisions.

Consider, for example, the U.S. Census Bureau data from 2021 on educational attainment displayed in Figure 1.4. This relatively small and seemingly uncontroversial dataset embodies a multitude of choices. For example, someone has made a choice that the "education" one can attain is defined as formal academic school or university instruction. The dataset does not include vocational training, wisdom passed down from parents or grandparents, or knowledge gained through independent reading or life experiences. Furthermore, it does not include people who have earned two master's degrees, nor does it differentiate between people for whom "some college" is one semester versus three years. In addition, someone has made seemingly arbitrary decisions about how to parse the data about educational attainment into age groups, with 25 years at the lower end of the age range. If they chose to display education attainment of people, say, 23 years and older, the numbers could change considerably.

The survey used to collect the data embodies yet another set of choices—choices the survey designers have made about which questions to ask and in which order to ask them, as well as choices the respondents have made about whether and how to answer the questions. The data in Figure 1.4 come from the Census Bureau's American Community Survey (ACS), which has been administered on an annual basis since 2005, and is meant to provide the same demographic, housing, social, and economic data that were previously collected only once per decade with the U.S. census. The Census Bureau provides not only annual data collected from the survey but also 3- and 5-year average estimates (Maier & Imazeki, 2013). Like all surveys, the ACS is imperfect because it depends on people selected for the survey to complete it, and to do so accurately. Furthermore, despite the fact that it is legally required (Title 13, U.S. Code) for selected households to complete the survey, people from minority and low income households sometimes do not respond, and this non-response bias can be exacerbated by events like the COVID-19 pandemic (Maier & Imazeki, 2013; Villa Ross et al., 2021).

The 2021 ACS that provided the data in Figure 1.4 is a 48-page document consisting of a first section with a series of questions on the demographics of each member of the household, a second section on the family's housing, and then a much larger section with seven pages of questions dedicated to each household member. In this latter section, which begins on page 12 of 48, the survey asks about each individual household member's education. The education question associated with Figure 1.4 immediately follows a series of questions on the person's citizenship status and time in the United States, and asks, "What is the highest degree or level of school this person has COMPLETED?" The questionnaire then directs the

Figure 1.4. Dataset on educational attainment of the population 25 years and over as it appears on the U.S. Census Bureau website

Both Sexes

Educational attainment

| Characteristic | Total | None – 8th grade | 9th – 11th grade | High school graduate | Some college, no degree | Associate's degree | Bachelor's degree | Master's degree | Professional degree | Doctoral degree |
|---|---|---|---|---|---|---|---|---|---|---|
| Total | 224,580 | 7,936 | 12,118 | 62,547 | 33,455 | 23,487 | 52,805 | 24,059 | 3,443 | 4,730 |

*Source*: U.S. Census Bureau, 2022.

*Note*: Numbers in thousands. Civilian noninstitutionalized population.

What Is Data Literacy?

respondent to mark (X) in one box from a list that begins with "No schooling completed" and ends with a subsection on post-bachelor's degrees including a master's, professional, or doctoral degree. It does not specify if the schooling needs to have been completed in the United States, which may be confusing for people who moved to the United States when they were of school age, given that the question of education was immediately preceded by one on when the person moved into the country. The survey designers could have chosen to ask questions about education before questions about citizenship status or provided the choices for level of education in a different order, or even allowed the respondent to write in the highest level of education received. This is not to say that the selection or order of questions is wrong—only that questions and their sequencing represent choices, which may in turn influence the choices respondents make about how to answer them.

Then there are the choices people working for the U.S. Census Bureau made about how to display the data on the institution's website. The bureau's resource library holds, among "census infographics and visualizations," a webpage with a simple infographic titled "A Higher Degree," centered on a stacked bar graph (see Figure 1.5). The stacked bar graph visualizes the data shown in Figure 1.4, but focuses only on bachelor's degrees and higher, while also comparing degree attainment in 2021 to that of previous years.

Relative to the table in Figure 1.4, the graph in Figure 1.5 is easy to read. It allows for simple comparisons and could lead the viewer to draw quick conclusions about how highly educated U.S. residents 25 years and older are, and about how the number of people with at least a bachelor's degree has steadily increased since 2001. It might lead the viewer to conclude, then, that we are doing something categorically right with respect to higher education access in the United States—a conclusion they might unknowingly feel to be substantiated by the happy cartoon graduates in the infographic. However, while the visualization gives you the number of people with a bachelor's degree or higher, it does not tell you what percentage of people in the population hold these degrees and how this percentage has changed over time. As the population has also increased over the period displayed, percentages instead of numbers of people might tell a different story. Furthermore, the visualization creators chose not to visualize data highlighted in the press release (https://www.census.gov/newsroom/press-releases/2022/educational-attainment.html) and showing that, for example, over a third of the population over age 25 has no college education at all, and that 28% of Black people and 21% of Hispanic people hold a bachelor's degree compared with 61% of the Asian population and 42% of the non-Hispanic White population. The visualization also does not tell you that foreign-born people who recently came to the United States were more likely to have a college education than foreign-born people who arrived in

**Figure 1.5. Infographic displayed on U.S. Census Bureau site**

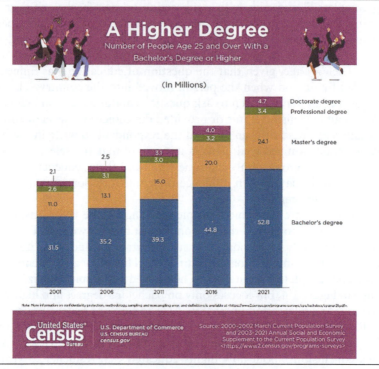

*Source:* U.S. Census Bureau, 2022; A Higher Degree (census.gov). https://www.census.gov/newsroom/press-releases/2022/educational-attainment.html#:~:text=In%202021%2C%20the%20highest%20level,college%20but%20not%20a%20degree

the 1990s or earlier, or the native-born population (https://www.census.gov/newsroom/press-releases/2023/educational-attainment-data.html).

Attending to this additional information, as well as recognizing that data and data visualizations are as much (if not more) about choices as they are about facts, might lead you to draw different conclusions about college education in the United States. This, in turn, might lead you to make different decisions about policy proposals related to college funding and access than you otherwise would. Most, if not all, data used as information have consequences, and so do our data-informed opinions and decisions.

## A LOOK AHEAD

We are surrounded by data and data visualizations in our everyday lives. Data and data visualizations typically exist not only to inform, but also to help people make decisions about policies, their finances, and even their health. But data and data visualizations can also deceive. They can obfuscate information just as easily as they can reveal it. It is for this reason that scholars and policymakers largely agree that data literacy is an essential competency for citizenship. However, being data literate is more complicated than simply knowing how to comprehend data and data visualizations. It requires a multi-faceted and flexible skillset, and the inclination to look beyond what we see at a surface level, recognizing that data are not "just the facts." This cannot and should not be accomplished in STEM classes alone. To help students become truly data literate—to ensure that they can not only read data and data visualizations, but also critically analyze them and use them for social justice—we must recognize how social studies content and skills can enhance data literacy, and how data literacy can enhance our understanding of social studies. We must commit to teaching data literacy in social studies classes.

Right now, such a commitment to teaching data literacy in social studies does not exist. Research suggests most social studies teachers—especially relatively new teachers with less than five years of experience—do not teach data literacy as part of their curriculum, and only a narrow majority feel it is important to do so (Shreiner & Dykes, 2021). Furthermore, many social studies teachers fail to recognize data visualizations as authored and constructed sources of information that should be critically evaluated rather than accepted as absolute fact (Myers, 2022). Part II of this book addresses this issue, building the argument that teaching data literacy, particularly a critical, humanistic form of data literacy, in social studies is crucial. In Chapter 2, I focus on how teaching data literacy helps fulfill the central, civic mission of social studies in the schools. I examine the role of data and data visualizations in the media and politics, arguing that one important reason to teach data literacy in social studies is that data visualizations are often used to influence our social and political beliefs and decisions. In fact, data visualizations were developed to address social and political issues, and over their relatively short history, pioneers and innovators in data visualization have honed them to be powerfully persuasive tools. However, anything with power to inform also has the power to misinform. Because social studies educators are in the business of preparing students for their roles as citizens, they must also prepare them to identify when data visualizations are being used to mislead them.

The fact is, as I will argue in Chapter 3, social studies teachers are probably already exposing students to data and data visualizations in their classrooms, even if they are not teaching students how to make sense of them. Data and data visualizations are mentioned across state standards documents, and social studies textbooks and other curricular materials are full of them. Data and data visualizations also play an important role in the core disciplines that make up the social studies—that is, in civics, economics, geography, and history. Therefore, teaching data literacy is essential for helping students learn the disciplines of social studies.

Admittedly, as the subtitle of this book suggests, I focus most attention on the role of data literacy in the discipline of history. History is the discipline students likely spend the most time studying, and data visualizations are an important, but too often underappreciated, part of history. For these reasons, Chapter 4 focuses on primary source data and data visualizations students might use to study different topics in world and U.S. history. I conclude Part II with an argument about the special perspective and skills social studies teachers have to offer by teaching data literacy. I place particular emphasis on the role social studies teachers have in teaching a critical, humanistic form of data literacy.

Part III of the book considers the benefits and challenges of teaching familiar types of data visualizations. In Chapter 6, I focus on timelines, a common temporal data visualization in social studies. I argue that teachers should provide more deliberate instruction around timelines, using them to support students' historical thinking, including their understanding of historical time, chronology, and narrative. In Chapter 7, I concentrate on maps. Borrowing a framework proposed by Liben (2001), I argue that we should be teaching students to think about maps, with maps, and through maps in social studies. This approach goes beyond teaching map-reading skills or using maps merely to show the location of places being studied. Rather, it takes fuller advantage of all the benefits to spatial reasoning and learning inherent in maps, while also helping students see maps as authored objects to be critically analyzed and challenged. Chapter 8 focuses on graphs and charts, which can be temporal, topical, or network visualizations. I argue that despite their reputation for being easy to read, making sense of graphs and charts is a complex process that should be explicitly taught. Furthermore, I make a case for data-based storytelling with graphs and charts, drawing on research to establish this as a best practice in both data literacy and social studies more generally. Finally, Chapter 9 addresses the value of having students work with data before they are visualized—producing their own data, creating databases, or working with existing databases to clean, cull, and otherwise make data more useful.

In Part IV, I distill arguments from the bulk of the book into some practical advice for teaching. Chapter 10 suggests a scope and sequence for teaching students to comprehend, use, and create data visualizations. These recommendations might be used to flesh out advice offered through social studies standards, to prompt conversations among teachers in a school or district, or to guide the development of social studies curricula. Chapters 11 and 12 then describe some general instructional techniques for teaching about data and data visualizations, with the former focused on helping students decompose and make sense of existing data visualizations, and the latter focused on helping students create data visualizations. I conclude the book with a vision of how a commitment to critical, humanistic data literacy might empower students to become data influencers, rather than just data consumers, and thereby empower them to reshape data stories about the world in which we live.

Part II

# WHY TEACH DATA LITERACY IN SOCIAL STUDIES?

CHAPTER 2

# The Importance of a Data-Literate Citizenry

Disinformation and misinformation plague our society. Often referred to collectively as "fake news," *disinformation* is false information created and shared with the intent to mislead, manipulate, or harm, while *misinformation* is false information shared by people who believe it is true and have no intention of causing harm (Wardle & Derakhshan, 2017). Although disinformation and misinformation arguably have been around since the printing press (Bergstrom & West, 2021; Posetti & Matthews, 2018), in the modern age of the internet, the complexity and scale of these information pollutants are unprecedented (O'Connor & Weatherall, 2019; Rid, 2020; Wardle & Derakhshan, 2017). Digital technologies and networked computers have made it easier, cheaper, and faster to generate and spread false or misleading information, while social media platforms have made it easier for people to tailor their social networks to consist of trusted, like-minded people among whom belief-confirming information will go unchallenged (Bergstrom & West, 2021; O'Connor & Weatherall, 2019; Rid, 2020; Wardle & Derakhshan, 2017). A 2021 poll conducted by the Pearson Institute for the Study and Resolution of Global Conflicts at the University of Chicago and the Associated Press-NORC Center for Public Affairs Research indicated that 95% of Americans believe that misinformation is a problem, and that 75% or more worry that family, friends, and they themselves have been exposed to misinformation through social media platforms (The Pearson Institute & The Associated Press-NORC Center for Public Affairs Research, 2021).

Concerns about the spread of misinformation are certainly not unfounded. As just one example, in the three months before the 2016 U.S. presidential election, the top 20 legitimate news stories from reputable media outlets were shared, liked, or commented on 7,367,000 times on Facebook, while the top 20 false election stories from hoax sites and hyperpartisan blogs were shared, liked, or commented on nearly one and a half million more times (8,711,000) in the same period (Silverman, 2016). Moreover, several studies indicate that people of all ages are bad at spotting false information for a variety of cognitive, psychological, and sociological reasons, and that people who are most confident that they can spot false information are most susceptible to it (Breakstone et al., 2021; Calvillo et al., 2021; Lyons et al., 2021).

Unambiguously false information from fake news websites is not all that should worry us. News consumption accounts for only a small fraction of people's overall media consumption, and online news consumption—which has raised the most concern over the spread of false information—is a fraction of people's overall news consumption, which also includes television, radio, and print (Allen et al., 2020; Watts et al., 2021). Therefore, it is important to consider the full constellation of misleading information that can contribute to people's unfounded beliefs and erode the integrity of civil discourse. As Watts et al. (2021) have argued, "Misinformation is a much broader phenomenon than outright falsehoods. There are many ways to lead a reader (or viewer) to reach a false or unsupported conclusion that do not require saying anything that is unambiguously false" (p. 2). These methods include presenting partial or biased data, quoting sources or experts selectively, omitting alternative explanations or context, conflating correlation and causation, or simply writing titles or headlines to lead a reader or viewer. Such sources of misleading information are more prevalent and, in some ways, more insidious than outright fake news. They can be propagated by reputable news sources, and they present with a thicker veneer of believability, making them more likely to go undetected.

Given all these issues with false and misleading information, social studies educators have a responsibility to respond. After all, the National Council for the Social Studies (NCSS) states that students should be educated for "informed civic action" and, to that end, a primary purpose of social studies is to help "students examine vast human experiences through the . . . collection and analysis of evidence from credible sources" (NCSS, 2023, n.p.). An informed person who can make reasoned decisions must be equipped to make sense of and critically evaluate information they will encounter in their everyday lives as citizens. They must be able to separate misleading from accurate information to make well-informed decisions that benefit their own individual interests as well as the common good.

Among social studies educators, one answer to the call to combat disinformation and misinformation has been in the form of research and scholarship on developing students' civic online reasoning—that is, their ability to effectively search for and evaluate social and political information on the internet (Breakstone et al., 2021; McGrew, 2020; McGrew et al., 2018). Such studies of civic online reasoning have found that students are easily duped by a website's top-level domain name, professional appearance, or About page content, and that they neglect to source and critically evaluate verbal and visual information they find on websites. Furthermore, students who are typically underserved by the American school system, including those from lower socioeconomic backgrounds and those who identify as

Black, perform significantly more poorly than other students in civic online reasoning tasks (Breakstone et al., 2021).

Data visualizations are among the information students struggle to evaluate online (Breakstone et al., 2018; McGrew et al., 2018). Like many adults, students tend to find data visualizations particularly persuasive, regardless of whether they can accurately interpret and analyze them (Breakstone et al., 2018; Cairo, 2019). Such credulity with respect to data visualizations is troubling. As this chapter will argue, data visualizations are designed to inform and persuade, and they regularly operate as evidence in contexts where people make important political and social decisions. Data visualizations profoundly affect our lives, not only because we see them more than ever before in the news we consume online, in print, and on television, but also because they influence policies with far-reaching consequences for society. But data and data visualizations can deceive just as easily as they can inform. If social studies education is to prepare students for their roles as citizens, it must prepare them to make sense of data visualizations that are used to persuade them, including helping them recognize when they are being misled.

## DATA AS EVIDENCE: A BRIEF HISTORY

Humans have been collecting and recording observations about the natural and human world for millennia. Ancient Egyptians, for example, recorded the times and heights of the Nile floods, and ephemeris tables recording the positions of moons, stars, and planets date back to early Indian and Babylonian civilizations (Friendly & Wainer, 2021). By the time of the Zhou dynasty in the first millennium BCE, the census, most likely used for taxes and conscription, had become an established institution of the Chinese government, revered later by the Confucius and in Confucian philosophy as a mechanism of good government (Whitby, 2020). However, the use of data and data visualizations as *evidence* for political and social arguments is a relatively new development.

The story of data and data visualizations as evidence often begins in the latter half of the 17th century with London haberdasher John Graunt. In 1662, Graunt published *Observations on the Bills of Mortality*, which gathered together London's weekly records of causes of death to make analytic observations about the city's population (Friendly & Wainer, 2021; Whitby, 2020). Several years later, around 1672, Graunt's friend, physician William Petty, invented the idea of "political arithmetic," a term to capture an early form of statistics in which people aggregated and used data to make comparisons over time, age, geographic region, or other categories for the benefit of government administration (Friendly & Wainer, 2021; Whitby, 2020).

However, it was not until the early 18th century that data and so-called political arithmetic were leveraged as evidence. This event seemingly first occurred in 1710 when Scottish minister and physician John Arbuthnot used the ratio of male to female births from Graunt's London christening records, which indicated that there were (unexpectedly) more male than female babies born in London, as evidence to argue that it must be Divine Providence that governs the human sex ratio. Although Arbuthnot's conclusions were wrong, largely because he did not account for higher female fetal mortality before birth, or for infant mortality between birth and christening, his public use of data as evidence for an argument was an important turning point (Friendly & Wainer, 2021).

Still, it would be decades before data visualizations entered the scene. The contributions of William Playfair, a Scottish engineer and political economist born in 1759, to the development of data visualizations cannot be overstated. Playfair invented the bar chart, line graph, area graph, and pie chart, in addition to contributing a host of other graphic features we now see as conventional, such as titles, axes, labels, grid lines, time period indicators, event markers to provide context, and color coding. While there were other important contributors to forms of data visualizations, including Jacques Barbeau-Dubourg, who is credited with the first timeline, and J. F. W. Herschel, who invented the scatterplot, Playfair was instrumental in creating visual displays that told stories with data, such as the graphic in Figure 2.1 (Friendly & Wainer, 2021). Playfair argued that graphics were superior to tables because they would make a "sufficiently distinct impression . . . to remain unimpaired for a considerable time," unlike tables that would leave a man "only a very faint and partial idea of what he has read" (Playfair, 1801a, p. xiv). However, during Playfair's lifetime, many people disagreed with his novel idea that graphs could "facilitate the attainment of information" (Playfair, 1801b, p. 14), viewing them as unserious and more imprecise than tables.

Around the time of Playfair's death, conditions arose that would propel data visualizations forward as a powerful form of evidence for arguments and decision-making. In France, England, and a handful of other western European countries, a multitude of social problems increased, creating a sense of urgency to find solutions. This need for solutions to social problems, coupled with recognition that widespread and systematic collection of social data could inform state policies for improving public welfare and economic growth, produced an avalanche of numbers—a wealth of data that were necessary ingredients for gaining new insight through data visualizations (Friendly & Wainer, 2021).

In France, the impetus for this shift was the high inflation, unemployment, food shortages, and perceived rise in crime in the period following the French Revolution. Starting around 1820, a deluge of data on births, deaths, marriages, literacy, and crime became available. Faced with competing theories on what was causing the problems and, therefore, what should be done to fix them, people began using these data to create different kinds of data visualizations to provide insight. One early and impactful example

**Figure 2.1. William Playfair, *Chart Showing at One View the Price of the Quarter of Wheat, and Wages of Labour by the Week, from 1565 to 1821***

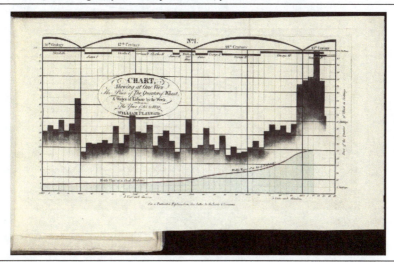

*Source:* Playfair, William, 1759–1823. (Undated)[Chart shewing at one view the price of the quarter of wheat, & wages of labour by the week, from the year 1565 to 1821]. https://collections.library.yale.edu/catalog/2066757

were thematic data maps, including what we now call *choropleth maps*, which use different shading or coloring within predefined areas (e.g., districts, counties, or states) to represent average values of a variable property or quantity within that area, and *dot maps*, which use dots corresponding to specific quantities to represent numbers and distribution of cases. These thematic maps revealed patterns otherwise invisible to the naked eye, especially when placed next to one another for purposes of comparison, allowing people to draw conclusions about the relationships between, for example, literacy and crime rates or poverty and suicide rates. Equally compelling data visualizations that emerged during this time were novel tables of data that allowed for simple cross tabulations between different variables (e.g., type of crime and age or sex) compared over time or spatial regions (Friendly & Wainer, 2021).

Two particularly famous cases of using data visualizations to support arguments and solve problems arose a few decades later in England. In 1854, a terrible wave of cholera struck what is now the Soho district of London. Physician John Snow, who had already formulated a theory that cholera was transmitted through water rather than through miasma, or bad air, which was the prevailing theory of the time, created a dot map of deaths in the district (see Figure 2.2). He observed on the map that there was a cluster of cases on Broad Street near a public water pump where

**Figure 2.2. John Snow's 1854 map of the London cholera epidemic**

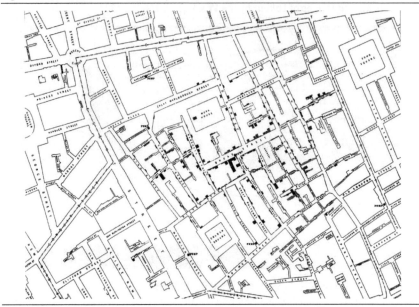

*Source:* Snow, 1854. (Wikimedia Commons, https://en.wikipedia.org/wiki/File:Snow-cholera-map-1.jpg)

surrounding residents drew their water (Friendly & Wainer, 2021). The map also led him to investigate and explain anomalies. For cases that were more distant from the pump, for example, Snow used interviews to uncover that the afflicted people went to school or work near the pump. And for locations near the pump that seemed to be spared, including a workhouse and a brewery, Snow found out that people were drinking from other sources—respectively, an onsite water pump and the stock of beer. Snow used his findings to convince authorities in charge of the community water supply, the Board of Guardians of St. James Parish, to shut down the Broad Street pump by removing its handle. With that, the high incidence of cholera cases in the area came to an end (Johnson, 2007; Snow, 1854; Tufte, 1997).

In another notable case, Florence Nightingale used data visualizations to persuade the British government to implement better sanitation measures in military hospitals. Nightingale led a team of nurses into the field hospitals in Crimea during the Crimean War, which was fought between Russia and France, Britain, and what remained of the Ottoman Empire, between 1853 and 1856. Nightingale was appalled by what she witnessed there, observing that far more soldiers died of preventable diseases due to poor sanitary conditions than from battlefield injuries. In 1855, the government sent its own sanitary commission to investigate the high number of soldiers' deaths in the hospitals. They discovered and subsequently fixed several structural and sanitation issues, which eventually led to a precipitous drop in the number of deaths from preventable diseases. Upon returning home, Nightingale dug into data she and others had gathered on causes of death in the war. She consulted with statistician and physician William Farr, a data visualization innovator in his own right who was also connected to John Snow and the London cholera epidemic, to help her analyze the data. Farr had invented a radial diagram visualization that Nightingale used and improved upon for her own reports, which she produced for Queen Victoria and strategically released to the public (Andrews, 2022; Friendly & Wainer, 2021). Though her reports contained many data visualizations, the most well-known and possibly the most impactful (see Figure 2.3) consisted of two rose diagrams to represent causes of death before (on the right) and after (on the left) the sanitary reforms in Crimea. Each wedge represents the number of deaths in a month, using color to distinguish between deaths from disease (blue), wounds (red), and all other causes (black). Moving from right to left, one can clearly see the drop in overall deaths and especially from those caused by preventable disease. Due in large part to Nightingale's efforts, including her shrewd methods for gaining publicity for her cause, the British government instituted a series of lifesaving reforms for military hospitals (Andrews, 2022).

Such stories illustrate the evidentiary and persuasive power that data visualizations can have in matters with far-reaching implications for the public. Indeed, the use of data visualizations as evidence only grew in the latter

**Figure 2.3. Florence Nightingale,** *Diagram of the Causes of Mortality in the Army in the East,* **1858**

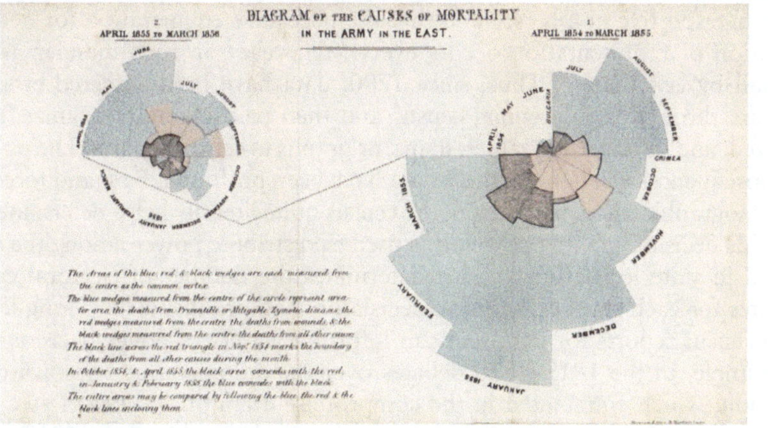

*Source:* Wikimedia Commons, https://commons.wikimedia.org/wiki/File:Nightingale-mortality.jpg

half of the 19th century, during the "golden age of graphics," when statisticians and government officials increasingly used data visualizations to make sense of the large amounts of data that had become available (Friendly & Wainer, 2021). While interest in data visualizations waned during the first half of the 20th century, innovations and interest rose once again beginning in the 1950s, due in part to advancements in technology, but also because of the emergence of either new or newly answerable questions for which data visualizations could serve as useful evidence (Friendly & Wainer, 2021). And now, in the 21st century, it is not a stretch to assume that people are affected by the interplay between data visualizations and decision-making every day of their lives.

## DATA AS EVIDENCE FOR DECISION-MAKING

Data visualizations have come to play a critically important role in people's decision-making and knowledge about the world (Kennedy et al., 2016). Information that affects our health, wealth, and well-being are increasingly visualized in maps, graphs, and charts. In democratic societies, where the ultimate power rests with citizens, this means that data visualizations hold a great deal of political significance. As Nærland (2020) has argued, data visualizations may have either "direct significance as part of the decision-making process in political institutions" or "less direct yet critical significance as a resource for citizenship and participation" (p. 64).

In the United States, census reports offer clear examples of data visualizations having direct political significance in decision-making processes. Article I, Section 2 of the U.S. Constitution mandates that Congress determine the number of representatives apportioned to each state "according to their respective numbers," and that the necessary enumeration for determination of representation occurs every "ten years, in such manner as they shall by law direct." Thus, since 1790, data have been gathered every ten years through the decennial census and then painstakingly organized, analyzed, and visualized as tables, maps, or graphs in census reports. The political consequences wrought by these data have been profound. First and foremost, demographic information from the census quite literally helps determine who holds decision-making power. It is used to distribute power among the states and in state legislatures, and it determines the number of electoral college votes for each state. In addition, legislators and presidents have long looked to census reports for data that can inform a variety of policy decisions. For example, in the 1819–1820 debates over the admission of Missouri to the union, which culminated in the compromise admitting Missouri as a slave state and Maine as a free state, legislators on both sides used 1810 census data showing population trends and shifts to support their arguments about the demographic impact of a new slave state. As another example, during the Civil War, President Lincoln's War Department used 1860 census data to measure the relative military strength of the Union and Confederacy and employed Census Office clerks to prepare annotated maps with county-level data on the number of "whites," "free colored," and "slaves," as well as amounts of livestock and crops. General William Tecumseh Sherman used this information to gauge the Confederacy's military strength and available resources on his fateful march through Georgia to the sea. In the 20th century, census data were used during World War I to identify men who had failed to register for the draft, during the Great Depression to measure the extent of unemployment and the need for relief measures, and during World War II to tabulate the number of Japanese Americans living on the West Coast who might be deemed a threat to security (Anderson, 2015). Policies and actions that were supported by these data affected countless lives at the time of their collection and for generations to come.

Data visualizations from other sources have affected the legislative process in the United States as well. For example, although there is currently a dearth of formal research on the role that data visualizations play as sources of information in legislative committee hearings or congressional debates, a simple search for the term "graph" in congressional records and hearings yields hundreds of results, dating back to 1960. Looking specifically at records from 2022, there were 33 separate meetings where at least one graph was referenced and shown as evidence for an argument, addressing topics such as the economy, the opioid crisis, COVID-19, climate change, and wildfires. In addition, thousands of scientists and social scientists have provided testimony at U.S. congressional hearings or served as advisors to committees, using data visualizations to provide information related to their area of expertise and shaping ideas and evidence that are brought to the floor (Liu et al., 2015; Maher et al., 2020).

Like the citizens they serve, policymakers use data visualizations featured in media to inform their decisions. Data visualizations are increasingly used by journalists to help readers understand and make decisions about complex issues (De Haan et al., 2018; Kennedy et al., 2021). Since the 1930s, the use of data visualizations in newspapers has steadily increased, with numbers growing at an higher rate from the early 1980s onward (Kopf, 2016). Now, newspapers like *The New York Times*, *Washington Post*, and *Wall Street Journal* are brimming with data visualizations, and news outlets from across the globe have prioritized increasing their emphasis on data storytelling formats (Kopf, 2016; Newman, 2021, 2023). Some journalists even report that data visualizations can drive a news story, serving as the evidentiary centerpieces of their articles (Kennedy et al., 2021). These data visualizations have political significance as well, influencing readers' beliefs, emotions, and, ultimately, decisions about a variety of social and political topics, from reproductive rights to immigration, to presidential elections (Allen, 2021; Amit-Danhi & Shifman, 2022; Kennedy & Hill, 2018).

Of course, the ways that data and data visualizations can influence people can differ wildly. Consider the use of data visualizations during the COVID-19 pandemic. Interactive and dynamic data visualizations surfaced on news, government, university, state, and local websites. On social media platforms like Twitter, people shared a dizzying array of data visualizations, including line graphs, area graphs, bar charts, pie charts, tables, maps, and multimodal dashboards. Many of these data visualizations were used not only to inform people about the rates of infection but to convince citizens to mask in public, and once vaccines became available, to get vaccinated. A recent study shows that antimaskers, too, were often quite adept at reading and creating data visualizations, using them as prolifically as pro-mask advocates, and in some cases using publicly available data to make sophisticated "counter-visualizations." They chose to emphasize death rates over infection rates, essentially arguing that the relatively few deaths as compared with infections did not justify taking away people's freedoms, and they focused on relatively low rates within individual communities outside of hot spots, which were usually big urban centers (Lee et al., 2021). They were not stating untruths about information in existing data visualizations per se, nor were they creating data visualizations that were factually inaccurate. They were simply emphasizing different information to provide evidence for a different argument. Their actions demonstrate the extent to which extracting information and conclusions from data and data visualizations is subjective and socially constructed, and how, in situations where data are interpreted in service of risk analysis and decision-making, the social objectives and values of producers and consumers play a part (Jasanoff, 1990; Lee et al., 2021).

And then there are undeniably misleading data visualizations, to which both policymakers and citizens are vulnerable. For example, at a 2015 hearing before the U.S. House of Representatives' Committee on Oversight and Government Reform (https://www.congress.gov/event/114th-congress/house-event/104009/text), which was convened to address Planned Parenthood's taxpayer funding, Committee Chairman Jason Chaffetz (R-Utah) showed a slide with the graphic displayed in Figure 2.4. Addressing Cecile Richards, President of Planned Parenthood, who stated she had never seen the graphic, Rep. Chaffetz said, "Here's the problem . . . in pink, that's the reduction in breast exams. And the red is the increase in abortions" (p. 20). Luckily, Richards's lawyer was there to point out the origin of the graphic, enabling her to retort, "My lawyer is informing me that the source of this is actually Americans United for Life, which is an anti-abortion group. So I would check your source." To that, representative Chaffetz responded, "Then we will get to the bottom of the truth of that" (p. 20).

Regardless of one's views on abortion, the graphic is deceitful. Although the left and right axes are not shown, it is a dual-axis chart with one axis indicating the number of cancer screenings and other preventative services

The Importance of a Data-Literate Citizenry 31

**Figure 2.4. Americans United for Life, misleading chart of services provided by Planned Parenthood Federation of America**

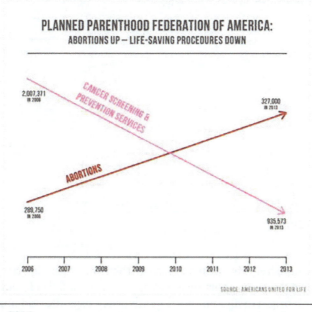

*Source:* Qiu, 2015.

provided, and the other axis indicating the number of abortions provided. The choice to use two vertical axes is in itself unnecessary, since both variables are the number of services provided. Even more egregious though, is they used two different scales for the invisible axes, with number of preventative services in the millions and the number of abortions in the thousands. Labeled in small print on the left side of the chart are the number of abortions and screening and prevention services provided in 2008, and on the right side, the same types of services provided in 2013. However, the number on the top right is far smaller than the number on the bottom right, even though the lines on the chart make it appear the number of abortions far exceeded other services. They also used the slope of the intersecting lines to make it appear that abortions increased at the same rate that other services decreased (Lee, 2015). Their removal of the left- and right-side axes suggests that they hoped viewers would notice the number of abortions went up and the number of other services went down without noticing that the number of non-abortion services is still much greater, and that the rates of change are far from equal (Cairo, 2019). A graph that uses acceptable conventions and more complete data about services provided by Planned Parenthood (see Figure 2.5) shows that non-abortion services

**Figure 2.5. PolitiFact, Graph showing changes in services provided by Planned Parenthood, 2006–2013**

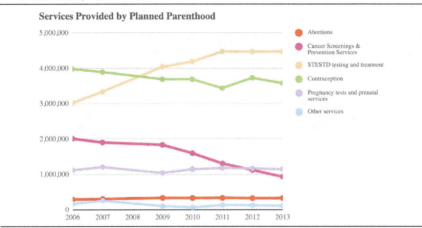

*Source:* Qiu, 2015.

vastly outnumbered abortion services at the time of the hearing, and that the rate of increase in abortion services was very small. However, neither the graphic's origin in an antiabortion advocacy organization nor its deceptive design stopped a U.S. congressperson from presenting it as evidence at a congressional hearing.

People like to share data visualizations. They seem objective and authoritative and are therefore convincing. Data visualizations are particularly useful tools for persuasion on social media because they can serve as efficient and effective means to communicate information. But data visualizations are also simple to manipulate, and can spread misinformation by distorting, obfuscating, or misrepresenting data.

## COMMON WAYS DATA VISUALIZATIONS CAN MISLEAD

Sometimes misleading data visualizations are the result of good intentions—they simply have been created by people who are bad or inexperienced at visualizing data or who have been careless. Other times, the creator may have lacked relevant information because of the limitations of the time or place in which they were creating the data visualization, or because of poor research methods. Misleading data visualizations can also be the result of purposeful manipulation, created or disseminated as propaganda by people who want to sway people's beliefs or opinions. The following sections address some common ways data visualizations can mislead us, providing examples of misleading data visualizations from politics and the media.

# The Importance of a Data-Literate Citizenry

**Omitting or Hiding Data**

Omitting or hiding data from a data visualization—or to borrow phrasing from the courtroom, not telling the "whole truth"—is one way to mislead readers. For example, in 2015, the pie chart on federal spending pictured on the top in Figure 2.6 circulated as a meme on social media. The problem with the chart, as Louis Jacobson of PolitiFact pointed out, is that it shows only the government's discretionary spending, and omits mandatory

**Figure 2.6. Comparison of a pie chart that misleads (top) by omitting data on federal spending with a bar chart that includes both discretionary and mandatory federal spending (bottom)**

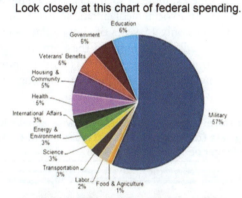

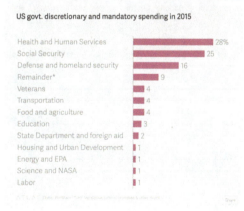

*Source:* Collins, 2015.

spending on programs like Medicare, Medicaid, and Social Security. These mandatory programs, of which food stamps are a part, account for 60% of all government spending, making military spending a smaller portion of all federal spending than the pie chart would lead one to believe (Jacobson, 2015). The graph on the bottom in Figure 2.6 shows what the chart would look like if mandatory spending were included. It is difficult to say if the person who created the pie chart-turned-meme purposely left out relevant data on government spending, or if they had a fundamental misunderstanding of the concept. Either way, readers with an incomplete understanding of government spending would be misinformed because of the incomplete picture the pie chart presented.

Another way that data visualization creators can manipulate information is to hide data from the dataset so that only trends or patterns that suit their point of view are included. One example of such "cherry-picking" of data is the climate graph that is part of the social media meme shown at the top in Figure 2.7. The pictured graph shows only 15 years of climate data—not enough to represent global climate trends. The graph on the bottom in Figure 2.7, which shows over 100 years of global temperatures, is a much more accurate representation of climate change, and clearly shows a warming trend.

**Figure 2.7.** Comparison of a graph that misleads viewers about climate change by cherry-picking data (top) with a graph that more accurately shows climate change over a longer period of time (bottom).

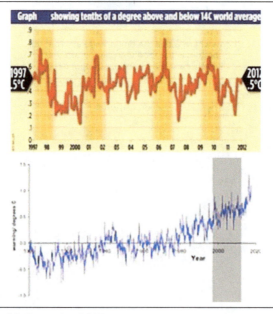

*Source:* Moreland & Rogowitz, 2017.

## Distorting the Presentation of Data

Sometimes data visualization creators can present all the relevant data but distort its presentation so viewers might draw inaccurate conclusions. For example, by manipulating the scale, designers can exaggerate, downplay, or otherwise distort changes in or relationships among values. With standard bar or area graphs, a relatively easy way to manipulate information is by omitting the baseline, usually by starting with a number other than zero on the vertical or *y*-axis. Bar graphs and area graphs encode messages about values through height and area, and we can understand value changes or degrees of difference based on these encodings. When people create a bar graph or area graph that does not start at zero, changes or differences can become exaggerated (Bergstrom & West, 2021; Cairo, 2019). For example, in March of 2014, Fox News broadcast a bar graph on enrollment in the healthcare exchanges that were a result of the Affordable Healthcare Act, shown on the top in Figure 2.8. The graph's baseline starts at 5,400,000, which exaggerates the difference between the goal for enrollment and those enrolled just days before the deadline. They also removed the labels on the *y*-axis, making it easier for viewers to miss the manipulation. Later, Fox News corrected the graph to the version shown on the bottom in Figure 2.8.

**Figure 2.8. Comparison of a graph that misleads by omitting the baseline (top) with a corrected version with a *y*-axis starting at zero (bottom)**

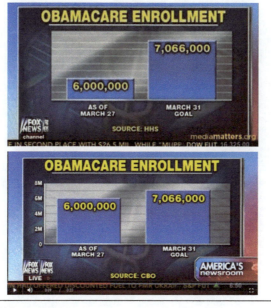

*Source:* Gold, 2014.

Contrary to popular belief, though, graphs need not always start at zero (Cairo, 2019). In line graphs, information is encoded by the slope of the line, and not starting the y-axis at zero does not necessarily affect the message. In fact, when small changes matter, it may be more honest to truncate the y-axis. Think about how seemingly small changes in body temperature, sodium levels, or white blood cell count can lead doctors to evaluate you as healthy or unhealthy. Small changes are also important with respect to climate, where every degree of difference in average temperatures over time can have a devastating impact on ecosystems. In this case, starting at zero on a graph could downplay the problem, as the graphs on global climate change in Figure 2.9 illustrate. Notice how the graph on the top, shared by *National Review*, barely shows any change at all, while the graph on the bottom shows the changes that matter in climate science. Rather than thinking only, "The y-axis should always start at zero," which is a common maxim, it might be better to think, "What difference would this make in the overall message if the baseline were different?"

**Figure 2.9. Comparison of a graph that misleads with an unnecessarily extended y-axis (top) and one that more accurately visualizes climate changes that have a significant impact (bottom)**

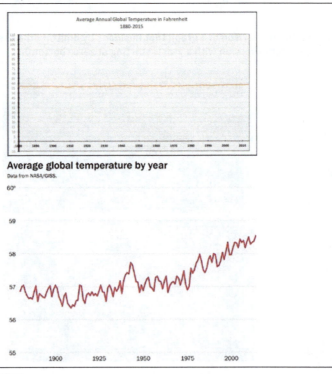

*Source:* Correll, 2023.

The Importance of a Data-Literate Citizenry

Another way to manipulate a data visualization is by using a scale with irregularities or inconsistencies. The Americans United for Life graph about Planned Parenthood discussed above distorted the information by unnecessarily using different scales on a dual-axis graph (along with other manipulations). Data visualization creators can also put dates out of order on an axis or vary the intervals between dates or values. For example, the COVID-19 graph on the top in Figure 2.10, released by the Georgia Department of Public Health, circulated quickly on social media after people noticed that the dates on the $x$-axis were out of order (April 28, 27, 29, May 1, April 30, May 4, 6, 5, 2, 7, April 26, May 3, 8, 9). It is hard to imagine that this was not done purposely since the reordering made it appear as though cases across counties were consistently declining, versus the reality that is shown more accurately in the graph on the bottom in Figure 2.10.

Readers expect that data visualizations will follow certain conventions, so they make assumptions about what colors, lines, shapes, or symbols represent. Therefore, going against conventions qualifies as another way to mislead readers. In graphs, for example, it is conventional to order numbers on the $y$-axis from smallest to greatest going up, and on the $x$-axis from left

**Figure 2.10. Comparison of a graph that misleads by disordering dates on the $x$-axis (top) with a corrected graph with dates in chronological order (bottom)**

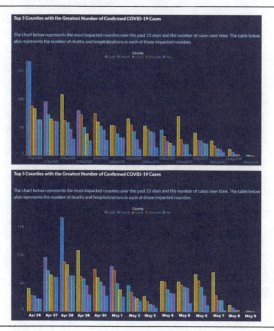

*Source:* deVilla, 2020.

**Figure 2.11. Comparison of a graph that misleads by going against the convention of numbering from bottom to top of the vertical axis (top) with a graph that uses the conventions (bottom)**

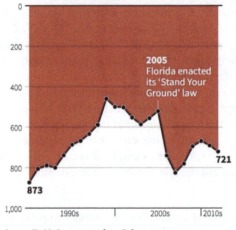

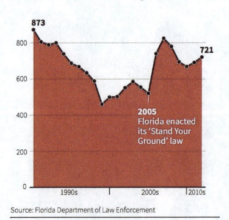

*Source:* Engel, 2014.

to right. The graph in Figure 2.11, which shows the number of murders in Florida before and after implementation of the "Stand Your Ground" law, goes against this convention. The graph gives the immediate impression to readers that after the law was implemented in 2005, allowing individuals to use deadly force if they believe that such force is necessary to prevent death or harm to themself or others, the number of murders decreased. When the conventions are implemented, as is shown on the bottom, you see that the opposite was true. This is to say nothing of the conflation of murders with gun deaths (which would also include suicides and accidental shootings)—an issue with the graph title or descriptions that will be discussed in the next section.

**Writing Inaccurate or Slanted Titles or Descriptions**

The title of a data visualization is often the first thing people read and can help activate a pathway for understanding what the graph is about. Kong, Liu, and Karahalios (2019) found that people interpret the title as the main message of a data visualization, regardless of whether the title aligns with what is shown in the data visualization. Therefore, a title or other descriptive text in or around a data visualization can be misleading. For example, the graph in Figure 2.12 was displayed online in *The New York Times* in 2019. The print version headline read "Record Numbers of Migrants are Coming into U.S., Deluging Agents." Both the online title and the print title are misleading, the former because it ignores data from previous years shown in the graph, and the latter because they are not record numbers based on what you can see in previous years (Kong, 2019).

There are ways that data visualizations can mislead beyond the examples I have provided here, including but not limited to pie charts that do not add up to 100, showing the wrong data or too much data, using the wrong type of data visualizations, and using disproportionate shapes or images to represent quantities. The possibilities seem endless. But what if more people had the skills to recognize misleading data visualizations? What if the civic online reasoning skills that social studies education scholars (e.g., Breakstone et al., 2018; Breakstone et al., 2021; McGrew, 2020; McGrew et al., 2018) already hope to achieve included the ability to spot untrustworthy graphs, maps, or other data visualizations? After all, the most powerful defense against misinformation is an educated population who can collectively make creating and spreading misinformation an exercise in futility. Social studies teachers, who are in the business of preparing students for their civic roles, have the power to help achieve such ends. If students learn about how to make sense of data visualizations, including how to spot misleading data visualizations, in their social studies coursework throughout their school careers, we will have a body politic better

**Figure 2.12. Example of a graph that misleads by ignoring data from previous years in its title**

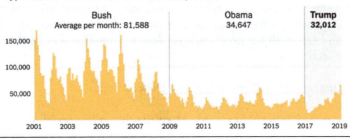

*Source:* Kong, 2019.

equipped to manage the various modes of information they encounter in their everyday lives. And, as I will argue in the next chapter, there are ample opportunities to teach about data visualizations while working within the content and skills social studies teachers are already expected to teach.

CHAPTER 3

# Data and Data Visualizations Across the Social Studies Disciplines

School teacher Emma Willard (1787–1870) lived and taught at a time when the United States and the rest of the world were undergoing sweeping political, social, and intellectual changes. Born in 1787, the year the U.S. Constitution was adopted by the Constitutional Convention in Philadelphia, Willard was among the first generation of U.S. women educated outside of the home and quickly advanced in her studies to become a teacher in the school she had attended. By the time she opened the Troy Female Seminary in New York in 1821, with the goal of providing a more advanced and intellectual education to women than was available at the time, the United States had purchased the Louisiana Territory and Florida, and with that, had begun the rapid expansion of its transportation and communication networks. From early in her teaching career, Willard turned to graphics to capture the momentous changes and expansion that surrounded her, often asking her students to create maps as more than just an exercise in memorization and artistry—a common practice in women's education at the time—but to help them learn and understand geographic concepts such as projection and scale (Schulten, 2022). She believed that students learned best through the visual explanations that graphics could provide and that, as part of the learning process, "well-designed graphics could do the heavy lifting, especially if students helped to create them" (Schulten, 2022, p. 26).

Willard was disappointed by the dry and narrative-heavy geography textbooks popular during her time, and so, beginning in the 1820s, began publishing her own textbooks that were filled with maps of space and time, innovative and engaging forms of data visualizations that she herself created. In *A Series of Maps to Willard's History of the United States, or Republic of America* (1828), for example, she included a map on the migrations of Native Americans—notably, as a prelude to, not a part of, formal U.S. history—that used color, proportional sizing, and connecting lines to illustrate the "locations and wanderings of the aboriginal tribes" (see Figure 3.1).

Later in her career, Willard also experimented in her books with "maps of time," bucking against traditional practices in history teaching like the memorization of dates. Her most ambitious graphic, *The Temple of Time* (see Figure 3.2), was meant as an interactive tool for students, on which they could plot significant events and people chronologically (from back to front) and thematically (shown on the temple ceiling), while also comparing U.S. history (represented on the pillars and floor to the left) to the histories

**Figure 3.1. Emma Willard's map *Locations and Wanderings of the Aboriginal Tribes***

*Source:* Willard, 1828.

**Figure 3.2. Emma Willard's temporal graphic *The Temple of Time***

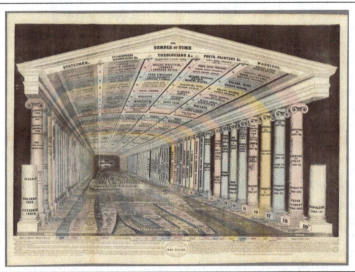

*Source:* Willard, 1846.

of other civilizations (represented in the right-hand pillars and the "stream of time" on bulk of the floor). Importantly, throughout her books, Willard provided instruction on how to make sense of and use the spatial and temporal graphics she included, demonstrating her conviction that they were tools for learning and understanding, not just decorations or a means for rote memorization (Schulten, 2022).

Emma Willard's intentional and systematic use of data visualizations in the classroom made her unique as an educator during her time. What is more remarkable is that she might continue to stand out as rare today. Recent research suggests that most teachers of social studies do not regularly teach data literacy, and many of them do not think it is important (Shreiner & Dykes, 2012). This lack of attention to data literacy persists despite the fact that data visualizations play an important role in the core disciplines of social studies, and that leaders in education have long recommended their use in social studies instruction. To be sure, as this chapter will argue, social studies standards documents across the United States recommend that students analyze, create, and use data visualizations. Furthermore, data visualizations are prevalent in textbooks and other curricular resources teachers use in social studies, so students need to be able to make sense of them. Perhaps more importantly, data visualizations are integral parts of the disciplines that make up the subject of social studies, helping to define the way disciplinary knowledge is produced and disseminated. Therefore, neglecting to teach data literacy in social studies risks leaving students with an incomplete understanding of the subjects they study in school, and an inability to fully engage with the forms of knowledge that help us make sense of the physical, social, and political world.

## STANDARDS, ASSESSMENTS, AND RESOURCES

Although Willard was a pioneer in her time, by the late 19th century graphics in textbooks had become commonplace and education leaders encouraged the use of maps and charts as standard practice in teaching history and geography (Schulten, 2022). The National Education Association's seminal *Report of the Committee of Ten on Secondary School Studies*, published in 1894, echoed many of Willard's recommendations for including graphics in history and geography instruction. The Committee of Ten's report was the culmination of the first large-scale effort to address curricular uniformity in a nation where education was a matter left to the states, and it summarized reports from multiple discipline-specific conferences, including ones for the core disciplines of social studies (Hertzberg, 1981). Summarizing the report of the History, Civil Government, and Political Economy Conference, the NEA Committee of Ten (1894) reported that the study of history should be accompanied by "topography and political geography" as well as "historical and commercial geography," and that teachers would need maps and other visual aids in their classrooms to properly teach about the past (pp. 29–31). They further noted, echoing the then decades-old sentiments of Willard, that students should engage in the "drawing of historical maps" to learn history (pp. 29–31).

In relaying the report of the Geography Conference, the Committee of Ten expressed surprise at geography experts' strong recommendations for the use of maps, charts, and other visual aids—still novel pedagogical methods in a subject that had long been a regular part of the school curriculum. The Committee of Ten wrote, "The methods which [participants in the Geography Conference] advocate require not only better equipped teachers, but better means of illustrating geographical facts in the schoolroom, such as charts, maps, [and] globes" (NEA, 1894, p. 32).

The degree to which the recommendations of the Committee of Ten gained a foothold in classrooms in subsequent decades is unclear. The Committee's calls for curricular uniformity and equal education for all students aroused considerable controversy among advocates of local control of education, and even the Committee recognized that their recommendations would take time, effort, and improved teacher preparation to implement (Hertzberg, 1981). Despite continuing concerns over local control, however, curriculum standardization had become the norm by the end of the 20th century. Recommendations for content and skills became enshrined in national and state curricular frameworks and standards documents—veritable policy tools intended to influence teachers' curricular choices and, in some cases, bring about instructional reforms (Porter & Smithson, 2001).

The standards movement in the United States took off in the 1990s, after President George H.W. Bush and the nation's governors introduced an initiative in 1989 to develop national standards for schools' core academic subjects, which they believed would make the United States more internationally competitive (Nash et al., 2000). Throughout the decade, professional organizations associated with social studies subjects, including the Center for Civic Education, the National Council for Economic Education, the National Council for Geographic Education, and the National Center for History in the Schools, brought together leaders in their respective disciplines to create consensus national standards documents. In some cases, particularly in the case of the National Standards for United States History, this process was fraught with controversy, but these organizations nonetheless produced national standards documents to guide curricular design (Nash et al., 2000). As states then revised their own standards to align with the national frameworks, curriculum standards and the standardized tests used to measure students' achievement became driving forces for curricular changes in social studies classrooms (Council for Economic Education, 2010).

Recommendations for using data and data visualizations in the disciplines of social studies can be found throughout the various national standards documents. For example, *The Voluntary National Content Standards in Economics*, developed by the Council for Economic Education, first published in 1997 and revised in 2010, suggest that students at all school levels should collect and analyze data about topics such as the value of goods, national revenues and expenditures, and inflation and interest rates. The *Standards in Economics* also recommend that secondary students should construct data visualizations such as timelines and pie charts (Council for Economic Education, 2010).

*The National Geography Standards*, first published in 1994 and revised in 2012, are full of recommendations for working with data and data visualizations. Beginning in elementary school and continuing throughout secondary school, the *Geography Standards* recommend students analyze, interpret, evaluate, construct, and use printed and digital geographic representations, including various types of maps (e.g., isopleth, choropleth, flow maps, and cartograms), tables, and graphs. As early as middle school, the *Geography Standards* also suggest that students observe, analyze, and evaluate different kinds of geographic data, including self-collected data and data they gather from online sources (Heffron & Downs, 2012).

*The National History Standards* are also explicit about the use of data and data visualizations, with recommendations that students think historically by interpreting and creating timelines, and analyzing and using historical maps, tables, charts, and graphs. They also recommend students gather quantitative historical data such as tax records, statistical compilations, and economic indicators; interrogate historical data for bias and distortion; and analyze quantitative data on topics like migration, wealth distribution, and economic changes (National Governors Association Center for Best Practices & Council of Chief State School Officers, 2010a).

The *National Standards for Civics and Government*, in contrast, are vague about the use of data and data visualizations. They contain only implicit references, like asking middle school students to explain the importance of geographic factors in shaping American society or the effects of political and demographic trends in the world, or asking high school students to evaluate current issues concerning representation like legislative redistricting, which would necessarily involve the use of maps.

The National Council for the Social Studies' (2013) *College, Career, and Civic Life (C3) Framework for Social Studies State Standards* has displaced the 1990s national standards documents as the primary influence on the development of social studies curricula. The NCSS released the *C3 Framework* with the intention of incorporating and extending the recent *Common Core State Standards for Literacy* in history and social studies, and giving social studies a more prominent role in literacy education across grade levels (Lee & Swan, 2013; Swan, 2013). The document is also intended to "frame the ways students learn social studies content" and help states upgrade their standards "to include the application of knowledge within the disciplines of civics, economics, geography, and history" (National Council for the Social Studies, 2013a, p. 6). Since its publication, the *C3 Framework* has prompted or influenced state standards revision efforts throughout the United States (Hansen et al., 2018; New et al., 2021).

Authors of the *C3 Framework* highlight the importance of data and data visualizations throughout the document, emphasizing the use of data to build arguments and explanations, and to communicate conclusions in social studies. As for visualizations of data, maps are most prominently featured in the framework, particularly in the geography section, where it is recommended that students construct and use maps and other geographic representations to provide explanations, descriptions, and adaptations of arguments and explanations. Graphs play a lesser role in the *C3 Framework* but are also explicitly referenced under geography, where it is recommended that students construct graphs and use them to describe places. And timelines are referenced in a glossary, where the framework authors define a multi-tiered timeline, as well as implied by references to constructing chronological sequences in the section on history.

Although the national standards' and the *C3 Framework*'s inclusion of data and data visualization offers a glimpse of data literacy's role in contemporary U.S. social studies instruction, it is ultimately *state* standards to which teachers are held accountable. A 2020 analysis of curriculum standards from all 50 states and the District of Columbia revealed that all standards documents contain explicit references to maps, timelines, graphs, or charts, typically beginning in early elementary school (Shreiner, 2020). In addition, there are numerous implicit references to data and data visualizations throughout standards documents—that is, places where standards, while not explicitly referring to data visualizations, invite the use of data visualizations by requiring that students learn about chronologies, movement, patterns, distributions, or growth. State-level expectations for teaching about data and data visualizations are indicated in standardized tests as well, with released test items (here, from California, Michigan, New York, and Texas) providing a glimpse of the data visualizations students might see on their state subject-area or end-of-course assessments (see Figures 3.3, 3.4, 3.5, and 3.6).

Undoubtedly, such attention to data and data visualizations in state standards and standardized assessments reflects widespread acknowledgement that they are important sources of information in social studies. However, the degree to which state standards documents address data and data visualizations comprehensively and consistently varies widely from state to state, and most standards documents provide little guidance for teachers about how to help students make sense of data visualizations (Shreiner, 2020). Maps are the only type of data visualization that standards commonly

**Figure 3.3. Released test item from the California Standards Test for History and Social Science**

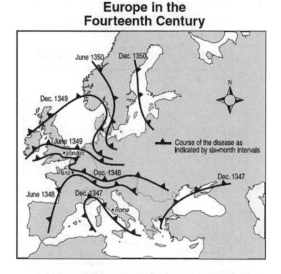

The map above illustrates the spread of what disease?

A yellow fever

B cholera

C bubonic plague

D malaria

*Source:* California Department of Education, 2009.

address across grade levels from elementary through secondary school, while timelines, graphs, and charts have only spotty references throughout standards documents, sometimes mentioned seemingly randomly in one grade level and never mentioned again. Moreover, several states' standards documents contain no mention of working with maps, graphs, or charts in the discipline of history, and students from over half the states in the United States are not required in civics classes to learn about seemingly important sources of information like data maps or surveys, nor are they required to examine the variety of economic indicator graphs that should be prevalent in economics. Finally, throughout the states, strikingly meager attention is given to critical data literacy skills like evaluating data and data visualizations for manipulation and bias (Shreiner, 2020).

The inconsistent ways state standards address data and data visualizations may help explain why some teachers, particularly relatively new and

**Figure 3.4. Released test item from the Michigan Student Test of Educational Progress**

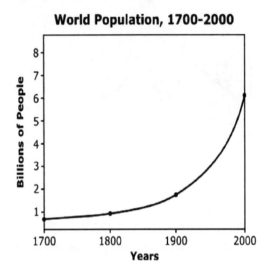

*Source:* Michigan Department of Education, 2023.

inexperienced teachers, believe it is unimportant to teach data literacy in social studies (Shreiner & Dykes, 2021). The fact remains that students will encounter a wide variety of data visualizations in their social studies education, to a far greater extent, indeed, than standards documents would lead one to believe.

For example, social studies textbooks are filled with data visualizations. A 2018 analysis of 42 social studies textbooks revealed that students reading a typical textbook in their social studies class would encounter a different data visualization, on average, every 13 or 14 pages in elementary

# Figure 3.5. Released test item from the New York Regents Exam in Global History and Geography II

Base your answers to questions 26 through 28 on the map below and on your knowledge of social studies.

**Where Your Clothes Were Made**

In 2016, the United States imported almost 27 billion articles of clothing. Here are the top 10 countries those clothes came from.

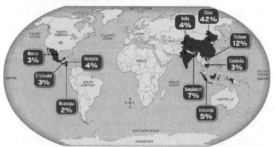

Source: *New York Times Upfront Magazine*

26 Which type of social scientist is most likely to use the information shown on this map?
 (1) economist (3) historian
 (2) anthropologist (4) sociologist

27 Which statement is best supported by the information shown on this map?
 (1) Many African nations manufacture large quantities of clothing for export.
 (2) Many Asian nations lack the technology necessary for industrialization.
 (3) United States clothing imports come primarily from Asia.
 (4) Central America imports the majority of its clothing from India.

28 Based on the information shown on this map, what can be inferred from the fact that 42% of imported clothing is made in China?
 (1) Chinese governmental policies support manufacturing for export.
 (2) The Chinese government enforces strict regulations protecting factory workers.
 (3) China has strong legal measures in place to protect the environment near factories.
 (4) The Chinese government encourages exportation to Central America.

*Source:* The University of the State of New York, 2023.

# Figure 3.6. Released test item from the Texas Assessment of Academic Readiness for Social Studies

3 This table shows the population of enslaved people in two regions of the United States in 1840.

**U.S. Enslaved Population by Select Region, 1840**

| Region | Enslaved Population |
|---|---|
| Northeast | 765 |
| South | 2,427,986 |

Source: U.S. Census Bureau

Which statement describes a factor that MOST contributed to the population difference shown in the table?

A The South had a society that relied on wage labor.

B The South had an economy that relied on cotton.

C The South had a variety of natural resources.

D The South had an abundance of large cities.

*Source:* Texas Education Agency, 2022.

49

school, every 7 or 8 pages in middle school, and every 4 or 5 pages in high school (Shreiner, 2018). And the variety of data visualizations students might encounter in their texts is stunning. The same study uncovered 388 unique types of data visualizations, including 38 unique types at the elementary level, 113 at the middle school level, and 237 at the high school level. These data visualizations also become more complex at each level of school.

To put this in perspective, imagine a student who regularly uses textbooks as part of their social studies education, say beginning in the 4th grade. The student will encounter various kinds of maps, tables, pie charts, bar graphs, timelines, and line graphs as they turn the pages, perhaps one for each excerpt they are assigned. By the time they enter middle school, the student will see nearly twice the number of data visualizations in their assigned readings, including multi-set, stacked, and layered forms of the data visualizations they first studied in elementary, along with additional visualization types like population pyramids, time series, and bubble charts. By high school, the frequency and variety of data visualizations in the average textbook will further increase. Such variety, frequency, and increasing complexity of data visualizations are not recognized in any state standards document for social studies (Shreiner, 2018).

But what about teachers who do not use textbooks in social studies? Will their students also be exposed to data visualizations? Most likely, they will. A recent national survey indicates that teachers in 86% of public schools turn to instructional resources they find online to a moderate or large extent (Gray & Lewis, 2021). Data visualizations are common in such online resources designed for social studies classrooms. In fact, nearly one-third of the history lesson plans found on popular curricular websites—including those from C3 Teachers, EDSITEment, Facing History and Ourselves, Learning for Justice, Library of Congress, National Archives, Stanford History Education Group, and World History for Us All—contain one or more data visualizations, or ask students to work with data. Teachers who turn to these websites for readings, slides, or other resources are likely to put a data visualization of some kind in front of their students. As is the case in textbooks, data visualizations on such websites are wide-ranging, including relatively simple, static data visualizations as well as complex or interactive data visualizations (Finholm & Shreiner, 2022).

Data visualizations are prevalent sources of information in the school subject of social studies because they are important within the academic disciplines that make up the social studies. They are used within the communities of practice that specialize in the structured forms of knowledge and ways of knowing that we refer to as civics (a branch of political science), economics, geography, and history (Bruner, 1960; Moje, 2015). As the next section will argue, scholars across these disciplines rely on data visualizations to communicate and provide evidence for their arguments, and this reliance will likely only increase at pace with the availability of data and visualization software. This places an onus on social studies teachers to help prepare students for the data literacy demands that will be placed on them beyond K–12 and in a world where disciplinary knowledge influences economic, social, and political decision-making.

## DATA LITERACY FOR DISCIPLINARY LITERACY

*The C3 Framework* emphasizes imparting to students the "disciplinary concepts and practices" that will give them the "capacity to know, analyze, explain, and argue about interdisciplinary challenges in our social world" (NCSS, 2013, p. 6). That is, the *C3 Framework* stresses the importance of "disciplinary literacy," or teaching the social studies disciplines' specific ways of reading, writing, speaking, thinking, and reasoning in order to help individuals understand, construct, apply, critique, and communicate knowledge (Fang & Coatoam, 2013; Lee & Swan, 2013; Moje, 2015; Shanahan & Shanahan, 2008). Arguments for disciplinary literacy rest on the premise that disciplines are discourse communities with specialized knowledge and specialized ways of knowing, and that to truly understand a discipline students must engage in the discourse community's specialized inquiry and literacy practices, using "a variety of representational forms . . . to communicate their learning, to synthesize ideas across texts and across groups of people, to express new ideas, and to question and challenge ideas held dear in the discipline and in broader spheres" (Moje, 2008, p. 99). Engaging in disciplinary inquiry and literacy practices, , scholars argue, can provide students with requisite knowledge for today's globalized, technologically advanced, information-saturated world (Goldman et al., 2016; Shanahan & Shanahan, 2008; Wineburg & Reisman, 2015). Indeed, there has been ample evidence in the social studies and other subject areas that disciplinary literacy instruction results in positive learning gains for students (e.g., De La Paz, 2005; De La Paz et al., 2014; De La Paz & Felton, 2010; Dobbs et al., 2016; Hynd-Shanahan, 2013; Monte-Sano & De La Paz, 2012; Reisman, 2012).

Although each of the social studies disciplines has unique elements, all of them have common or overlapping features as well. They all involve framing problems, evaluating how others have addressed the problems, and communicating findings and conclusions about problems (Moje, 2015). Moreover, as was reflected in the national standards documents discussed earlier, the social studies disciplines all value and use data and visual representations of data. Political scientists, whose discipline helps define civics courses in schools, use survey and polling data, voter registration data, election results, and graphs of political trends and relationships to reason about political phenomena (Barbour & Wright, 2015). Economists work with visual representations of economic data, including time series or line graphs that show how economic variables change over time, or scatterplots that show relationships between economic variables (Council for Economic Education, 2010; Goodwin et al., 2017). And geographers use maps, globes, satellite data, and census data to reason about past and contemporary problems, and technologies to collect, analyze, and display data, including geographic information systems (GIS), remote sensing, and global positioning systems (De Blij, 2012; Johnson et al., 2011; Morin, 2012; National Geographic Society, 2016; National Research Council, 1997).

Historians work with data and data visualizations as well (Gibbs, 2016; Nokes, 2022), and it is worth zooming in to take a closer look at how historians use them, not least because history is the social studies discipline that students spend the most time studying in school, yet it remains widely misunderstood as a discipline. Most of the American public believes that the discipline of history is nothing more than an assemblage of names, dates, and other facts about what happened in the past, while historians view it as an effort to explain the past through inquiry and examination of evidence (Burkholder & Schaffer, 2021). Historians ask questions about the past and attempt to accurately reconstruct and explain events and processes that are available to us only through the remnants of the past (Gaddis, 2002). They question what was important in the past, what has changed and continued over the course of time, whether things have changed for better or worse, what motivated actors in the past, what caused particular events and processes, what arose as the result of particular events and processes, and how the chaos and complexity of the past can be organized to help us make sense of it (Gaddis, 2002; Lévesque, 2008). Factual knowledge as a basis for making sense of the past is important—after all, you must know dates and the chronological sequence of events to reason about cause and consequence in relation to those events—but names, dates, and other such facts are certainly not the whole of history.

The public's inaccurate perceptions of history may come from the fact that so many people have experienced school history as an exercise in memorization from textbooks and lectures, not as inquiry involving investigation and analysis of artifacts from the past (Burkholder & Schaffer, 2021; Wineburg, 2018). Several scholars of history education (e.g., Bain, 2000; De La Paz et al., 2014; Lévesque, 2008; Reisman, 2012; Seixas & Morton, 2013; Wineburg, 2001) have been working for decades to change the way history is taught in schools by promoting historical thinking and literacy, uncovering the realities of disciplinary practices in history and inviting students into a more authentic historical inquiry process. However, few scholars elevate the use of data and data visualizations as part of historical inquiry, or position making sense of data and data visualizations as an aspect of historical literacy worthy of focused attention.

Yet data and data visualizations are an important part of the discipline of history. To answer their questions about the past, historians analyze, interpret, and use a variety of primary and secondary source evidence, both verbal and visual (Nokes, 2012). They work with books, manuscripts, personal correspondence, journals, newspapers, political cartoons, oral histories, sound recordings, photographs, prints, and paintings, but they also work with maps, charts, graphs, and statistical records. And while much of their work with evidence is done in libraries and archives, historians also work with digitized datasets and technologies such as GIS or text mining and data visualization software. In recent decades especially, harnessing the sorting and analytical powers of computers and the digitization of primary sources have led to a proliferation of available data, large quantitative datasets, and new methods for processing and visualizing quantitative data. Historians have always used quantitative data to some extent, but as Gibbs and Owens (2012) have argued:

> Having access to vastly greater quantities of data, markedly different kinds of datasets, and a variety of complex tools and methodologies for exploring it means that the term *using* signifies a much broader range of data-related activities than it had previously. (n.p.)

More historians are working in the domain of digital history and with big data, while leaders in flagship historical organizations (e.g., Gibbs, 2016; Grossman, 2012) have acknowledged that the use and interpretation of data are increasingly important aspects of the historical discipline and disciplinary training.

The increasing importance of data visualizations to the historian's craft is evident in their written arguments and explanations. Consider, for example, articles published in the *American Historical Review*, which is the official journal of the American Historical Association and publishes articles from every major field of historical study across the world. Data visualizations have been part of historians' evidence-based contributions to the journal since its first issue in 1895, but the percentage of articles with data visualizations has been trending upward over the journal's existence, with a noticeable uptick in the late 1960s (see Figure 3.7). We can see a similar trend in the *Journal of American History*, the official journal of the Organization of American Historians, published since 1914 (see Figure 3.8). Again, data visualizations have always been a part of the journal, but the percentage of articles with data visualizations has been increasing over time.

It is now common to find articles with data visualizations in history journals. Since 2006, when all four journals were in publication at the same time, about one quarter of the research articles in the *Journal of Global History*, *Journal of World History*, *Journal of American History*, and the

**Figure 3.7. Percentage of articles with data visualizations in the *American Historical Review*, 1895–2022**

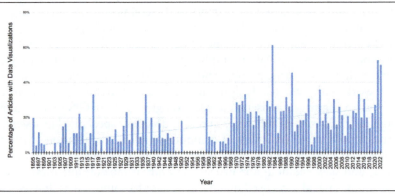

**Figure 3.8. Percentage of articles with data visualizations in the *Journal of American History*, 1914–2022**

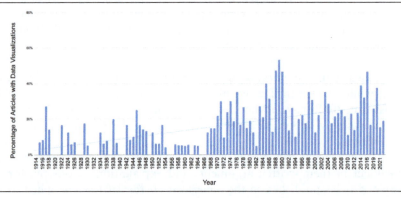

*American Historical Review* have contained at least one data visualization (see Table 3.1). Put another way, many of the historians who write about U.S. history and world history, the two areas of history students study in school the most, use data visualizations in their practice.

Though such studies of historical writing are revealing about historians' use of data and data visualizations to communicate arguments and explanations, published writing does not necessarily show us the multitude of *primary source* data visualizations historians use in the process of historical inquiry. Though in some cases historians will include a primary source data visualization in their writing for readers to examine (Shreiner, 2023), the data visualizations in their articles are more often secondary data visualizations—ones they have produced from analysis of primary source statistics. The primary source data and data visualizations they have used in their original research might only make their way into footnoted citations, which downplays their

**Table 3.1. Number and percentage of historical research articles with data visualizations from four top-tier history journals, 2006-2022**

| Journal title | Total # of articles | # of articles with data visualizations | % of articles with data visualizations |
| --- | --- | --- | --- |
| *Journal of Global History* | 371 | 108 | 29% |
| *Journal of World History* | 334 | 59 | 18% |
| *Journal of American History* | 311 | 76 | 24% |
| *American Historical Review* | 439 | 106 | 24% |
| Totals | 1455 | 349 | 24% |

importance in historical inquiry. For students to engage deeply with the past, they should work with primary source data and data visualizations, not just the secondary source data visualizations that others have created. The next chapter takes up the topic of primary source data visualizations, demonstrating not just the variety of primary source materials that support data literacy, but also the roles that data and data visualizations have played in the human past.

CHAPTER 4

# Primary Source Data and Data Visualizations

German-born Herman Moll (1654?–1732) was the most famous cartographer of 18th-century Britain. His collection of maps, *The World Described*, was the most popular and important atlas of its day, and his maps were well known throughout Europe for their aesthetic quality and integration of visual, graphic, and verbal elements (British Library, n.d.; Zukas, 2021). From a present-day perspective, Moll's maps were also unabashed representations of British imperialistic and economic interests (Crowley, 2016). They told stories of Anglo-British imperial expansion and capital accumulation and organized the world into competing sovereign nation-states (Zukas, 2021).

Moll's well-known "Beaver Map," for example, highlighted European territorial disputes in North America, while underscoring the economic opportunity in the region as exemplified by the industrious and valuable fur-bearing beavers in the map inset (see Figure 4.1). Another example of Moll's British Empire–centered work, a 1710 map of Africa, shows large political entities on the continent where there were none, most likely because Moll presumed nation-states to be the norm and therefore projected them upon Africa—despite the experience of traders and explorers who reported on hundreds of smaller ethnic enclaves and political fiefdoms in Africa (see Figure 4.2). The map also demonstrates Moll's unsubstantiated insistence, written on the map, that there were White Christians living in the territory called Guinea (Delaney, 2007).

Moll's maps, like other maps stretching back thousands of years, are as much representations of the mapmaker's knowledge and beliefs, and the historical, geographic, and cultural context for these beliefs, as they are of the spaces they were intended to represent. This chapter focuses on such data visualizations, which can serve as primary sources for the study of the past. Primary sources are the raw materials of history. They are the remains of the past, the relics and records originating from a time and place under investigation. Historians use them to uncover the truth about the past, piecing together how people lived, what their environment was like, what and when events happened, how events came to happen, who was involved in events, and what people knew and believed. As important as primary sources are,

**Figure 4.1. Herman Moll's *A New and Exact Map of the Dominions of the King of Great Britain on ye Continent of North America*, commonly known as the "Beaver Map"**

*Source:* Moll, 1715.

they do not speak for themselves; historians must carefully analyze them, accounting for the knowledge, viewpoints, and biases of the people who created them while considering what they both reveal and conceal. To truly understand the discipline of history, and to evaluate the historical arguments of others, students must learn to work with primary sources, analyzing,

Primary Source Data and Data Visualizations 59

**Figure 4.2. Herman Moll's 1710 map of Africa**

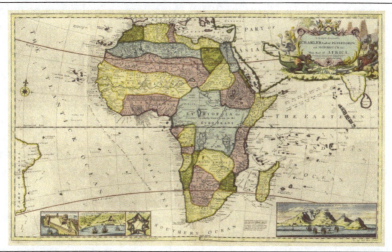

*Source:* https://commons.wikimedia.org/wiki/File:1710_moll.jpg#/media/File:1710_moll.jpg

interpreting, and using them regularly in their history education. Students must be exposed to the wide variety of primary sources that help us understand the past (Lévesque, 2008; Nokes, 2022). This includes primary source data and data visualizations. Studying primary source data visualizations can expose students to important relics and records of the past, sharpen their understanding of data visualizations as human constructions, and help them see how data have been used toward both just and unjust ends. In what follows, I highlight only a small fraction of the primary source data visualizations available for study, organizing them thematically by topics relevant to world and U.S. history in schools.

## MAPS AS WORLDVIEWS

Maps, which visualize geospatial and spatiotemporal data, are probably the most studied type of data visualization in social studies classrooms. Nonetheless, too few students will spend time learning about maps as primary sources, or examining how maps, including those on their classroom walls, are culturally mediated products of the time and place from which they came. Only in rare cases will a graduating senior have learned that the division of the world into the continents, nations, and states they were expected to memorize is itself a peculiarity of the historical and cultural context in which we reside (Lewis et al., 1997; Yearwood, 2014).

Maps have played an important role throughout human history. Locating ourselves spatially is an instinct common among animals, but only humans have been able to graphically represent their views of space for others to see and use (Brotton, 2013). Maps are embodiments of uniquely human capabilities, providing evidence for one of the most fundamental questions we ask when trying to make sense of the past: What makes humans different? The earliest versions of what we might call a map are in prehistoric artworks that show a landscape, and date back to 30,000 BCE (Brotton, 2013). Maps to help people find their way from one point to another, or wayfinding maps, appear much later in the historical record, including an Egyptian map on papyrus from about around 1160 BCE that may have been used to help Pharoah Ramses IV obtain blocks of sandstone for use in statuary, and a Chinese map drawn on wooden boards, dated from about 300 BCE during the Qin dynasty, showing routes to trees used for timber (Akerman & Karrow, 2007).

But maps are more than just wayfinding devices. They have also been used to chronicle important journeys or migrations, to help people visualize the world, its regions, people, and natural resources, and, as discussed in Chapter 2, to display data as evidence for social, political, and economic arguments. Maps reveal the activities, thoughts, and perspectives of the people who created them, helping us understand how people of the past saw the world, where they had gone, where they thought they could go, who they thought they could conquer, what they feared, and what problems they hoped to solve.

In short, maps are visual representations of people's worldviews. While it is a fact that the Earth is a life-sustaining planet that exists in the universe among other planets, the "world" is a social concept—a person's interpretation of space based on their experiences, observations, and culturally mediated understanding. Hence, we use phrases like "They are my whole world," "They live in their own world," or "Their world came crashing down around them." Maps, whether of a city, state, nation, hemisphere, or the entire planet, express people's understanding of the physical space of the planet, but they also capture people's ideas and beliefs about the world and its people (Akerman & Karrow, 2007; Brotton, 2013). Therefore, maps can serve as valuable primary source evidence in the study of history, providing insight into people's worldviews and how they were shaped by the geographical and other observed information at their disposal, as well as by their conceptions of space within and beyond what they could see and experience.

For example, the Babylonian Map of the World (see Figure 4.3), now held by the British Museum, can provide a window into the worldviews of people living in ancient Mesopotamia. It is the first known map of the world, dating to approximately the 6th century BCE. Carved on a tablet discovered near Sippar in southern Iraq in 1881, the map itself consists of two concentric circles around a central compass hole with everything emanating from this sacred core (Brotton, 2014). The center circle has a band down

Primary Source Data and Data Visualizations 61

**Figure 4.3. The Babylonian Map of the World and a drawing of the map**

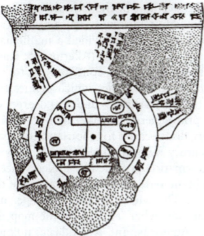

*Sources:* Map: https://commons.wikimedia.org/wiki/File:Babylonian_Map_of_the _World,_700-500_BC.jpg; drawing: https://commons.wikimedia.org/wiki/File:Meissner _Babylonien_und_Assyrien_clay_map_1925.jpg#/

the middle to represent the Euphrates River, which runs from a semicircle representing mountains at the top to a perpendicular band labeled "swamp" toward the bottom. Babylon is labeled in the rectangle cutting across the river, and there are small circles around it labeled with some neighboring cities and regions. The outer circle is labeled as "bitter water" or "bitter river," which is often translated as "ocean." Outside of the ring of water are eight triangles, only five of which have been preserved, which represent the dangerous outer limits of the Babylonian world. Four triangles are labeled as "islands" or "regions," and the fifth is identified as "great wall." The cuneiform inscriptions alongside and on the reverse side of the map describe distances between the eight regions, as well as various sea monsters, wild animals, and literary and mythological figures (Brotton, 2013; Delnero, 2018; Horowitz, 1988). Though we may never know the map's true meaning and purpose, it is nonetheless evidence of an early attempt to impose order and structure on the world, and it is as much an encapsulation of Babylonian mythology as geographic understanding (Brotton, 2013, 2014).

A more familiar view of the world appears in the world map of the "inhabited earth" credited to Claudius Ptolemy (90–168 CE). Although there is no evidence that Ptolemy himself created a map, the extensive geographic knowledge of the Greek and Roman empires that he summarized and synthesized around 150 CE in the treatise known as *Geography* changed mapmaking forever (Akerman & Karrow, 2007). *Geography* evaluated previous measurements of the earth, suggested methods for projecting what he and other scholars of his time knew to be a spherical earth onto a plane, provided a topographical account of the latitude and longitude of more than 8,000 locations throughout Europe, Asia, and Africa, explained the role of astronomy in geography, and provided a mathematical guide for making maps of the Earth and its regions (Akerman & Karrow, 2007; Brotton, 2013). Ptolemy's most significant contribution to mapmaking was the *graticule*, a grid or network of lines which defines the now-familiar 180 degrees of latitude between the poles and 360 degrees of longitude from an arbitrarily defined prime meridian (Akerman & Karrow, 2007). After its creation, *Geography* disappeared for thousands of years, only to reappear as copies in 13th-century Byzantium along with maps created by Byzantine scribes using the information provided by Ptolemy (see Figure 4.4).

Ptolemy's world centered on the Mediterranean at the heart of the Greek and Roman empires. The Mediterranean, Europe, northern Africa, and parts of Asia appear somewhat familiar on the map, but far eastern Asia, southern Africa, the Americas, and Australasia, unknown to Ptolemy, are missing. In addition, Ptolemy overestimated the size of the Mediterranean and underestimated the circumference of the Earth (Brotton, 2013, 2014). He believed that Africa and the Far East were linked by land enclosing the Indian Ocean, which consequently appears as a huge lake on the map, and that the inhabited world ended south of the Equator along a parallel running through Egypt and Libya. Also an astrologer, Ptolemy included astrological figures like Sagittarius on the map, reflecting his belief that celestial events influenced human affairs (Brotton, 2014).

Most maps inspired by Ptolemy are oriented with north at the top, as is now familiar to most people in the West, but as Brotton (2013) has argued, "[T]here is no purely geographical reason why . . . Western maps have naturalized the assumption that north should be at the top of all world maps" (p. 10). In fact, most early Islamic world maps, even those that were influenced by Ptolemy, were oriented with south at the top because many of

**Figure 4.4. Ptolemy's World Map as drawn in a 15th-century Italian manuscript, British Library (Harleian MS 7182, ff 58-59) https://commons.wikimedia.org/wiki/File:PtolemyWorldMap.jpg#/media/File:PtolemyWorldMap.jpg**

*Source:* https://commons.wikimedia.org/wiki/File:PtolemyWorldMap.jpg#/media/File:PtolemyWorldMap.jpg

the communities that converted to Islam in the seventh and eighth centuries lived north of Mecca and therefore had to face south during their prayers. Orienting the maps with south at the top made Mecca the focal point. The 1154 CE world map created by Muslim Arab scholar Al-Sharif al-Idrisi (see Figure 4.5) is one such south-oriented map, and like other world maps, it reflects both the geographic knowledge and belief system of its creator (Brotton, 2014). It is a hybrid of Islamic, Greek, Norman, and Latin cartographic traditions, reflecting the cultural exchanges and intensifying hemispheric interactions of the period in which it was created (Akerman & Karrow, 2007; Brotton, 2013).

Al-Idrisi's map is centered on Mecca, the center of the Islamic world, and shows the earth encircled by the sea and surrounded by fire, which was an idea taken from the Quran (Akerman & Karrow, 2007; Brotton, 2014). Sicily, which is the large island in the cluster of four islands in the Mediterranean, is drawn to look much larger than it really is relative to other Mediterranean islands. Al-Idrisi's homeland of Africa is also vast, with the Nile River and the mountains that were assumed to be the source of the Nile featured prominently (Akerman & Karrow, 2007; Brotton, 2014). The depiction of the mountains is notable because it is an early attempt to develop a cartographic symbol system, now likely familiar to modern readers (Brotton, 2014). Like Ptolemy's, al-Idrisi's knowledge was limited, as is evidenced by the expanse of southern Africa occupied only by mountain ranges, and by

**Figure 4.5. Al-Idrisi's south-oriented world map as drawn in a 15th-century Cairene manuscript, Bodleian Library (MS. Pococke 375 fol. 3v-4)**

https://commons.wikimedia.org/wiki/File:Al-Idrisi%27s_world_map.JPG#/media/File:Al-Idrisi's_world_map.JPG

the misrepresentation of lands east of the Arabian peninsula, including the absence of the Indian peninsula and the unlabeled assortment of islands drawn only from vague knowledge of a distant archipelago (Brotton, 2014). And, as with the Ptolemaic map, the Western hemisphere is missing entirely.

With his 1500 map, Juan de la Cosa of Spain was the first cartographer to show the Americas as a distinct landmass (see Figure 4.6). The map was originally intended to show newly discovered western territories to the Spanish monarchy, and thus shows the west on a much different scale than the east. Like other maps, de la Cosa's map reflects his worldview, shaped by both his geographical understanding and his political and religious belief system. For example, as a ship pilot and navigator, de la Cosa was able to depict the Caribbean islands of Cuba, Hispaniola, and the Bahamas (drawn just to the left of the compass on the map) relatively accurately, probably because of the time he spent sailing through the area. The dark line of longitude running north and south on the map is the meridian politically determined by the 1494 Treaty of Tordesillas, giving everything west of the line

Primary Source Data and Data Visualizations 65

**Figure 4.6. Juan de la Cosa's world map showing the Americas as a distinct landmass, Naval Museum, Madrid**

https://commons.wikimedia.org/wiki/File:1500_map_by_Juan_de_la_Cosa_rotated.jpg#/media/File:1500_map_by_Juan_de_la_Cosa_rotated.jpg

to Spain and everything east of the line to Portugal. The West African coast is also mapped somewhat accurately, because the area had already been intensively explored and settled by the Portuguese. At the same time, while the map provides newly accurate depictions of lands discovered and explored by Europeans, it contains several notable inaccuracies, such as showing India without a peninsula. Moreover, the map carries on the ancient cartographical tradition of including religious iconography, such as the drawing of the three Magi bearing gifts as they ride toward Syria, a reference to the biblical story of the birth of Jesus (Brotton, 2014).

The maps in this section provide just a small sampling of the primary source maps students can use to study people's worldviews throughout time and space. In doing so, students will learn that maps, including contemporary maps, are always reflections of the knowledge and beliefs of the people that created them. Furthermore, studying a chronological sequence of maps can give students a sense of change and continuity over time—whether in people's understanding and beliefs, or in political boundaries and relationships. Indeed, using data and data visualizations to illuminate change and continuity over time is the focus of the next section.

## CENSUS DATA AND DATA VISUALIZATIONS

Change and continuity are central concepts in the discipline of history, providing meaning and coherence to the past. Because we cannot possibly study everything in the past, we select events based on their historical significance. However, ascribing historical significance to events would not be possible without the ability to perceive change and continuity—changes in a political or social order, changes in people's thinking or activities, or shifts that have relevance in the present because of the new political, social, or ideological continuities that arose from them (Lévesque, 2008). To perceive change and continuity, we must be able to see how events are related to one another chronologically as well as qualitatively or quantitatively. Data visualizations are a useful tool for such analyses, and knowing this, historians often use or construct them to communicate change and continuity over time (Shreiner, 2023). In addition, historians often turn to primary source data visualizations to study changes and continuities. In U.S. history, there is no better historical record of changes and continuities than the U.S. census.

Governments have been conducting censuses for hundreds of years. The Greek historian Herodotus claimed in *Histories* that a census was taken in Egypt as early as the mid-6th century BCE under the pharaoh Amasis II, and the Romans made the census a fundamental part of the social order within the republic, and then their expansive empire (Whitby, 2020). While many censuses in history were used primarily for taxes and conscription, the U.S. census was designed as a mechanism of representative government, providing data on the nation's population every ten years in order to determine how representation in Congress should be apportioned among the states (Whitby, 2020).

Though it is not without flaws and inaccuracies, the U.S. census has provided some of the most reliable information we have on the people and economic activities of the United States since it was first administered in 1790. Furthermore, as Anderson (2015) has argued, the U.S. census is "a crucial marker for American history" (p. 3), helping us date events like the end of the frontier in the West in 1890, and the creation of an urban nation in 1920. For students and scholars of history, the U.S. census offers a treasure trove of information about the nation's past, including a plethora of data and data visualizations that can provide insight into changes marking each passing decade.

Each decennial U.S. census on its own provides a snapshot of the historical period in which it was administered and can be used to address questions about the status of the nation during a particular timeframe. At the same time, it is also worthwhile to consider how government priorities change from decade to decade. Questions kept, added, or removed for each census reflect the concerns, debates, priorities, prejudices, and innovations of the respective period. For example, the 1850 census was heralded as the first "scientific" census due to the growing influence of statisticians, who were instrumental in convincing members of Congress to broaden the scope of the schedules to include individual-level rather than just family-level questions, and to break up the census into six separate schedules: free inhabitants, slaves, mortality, agriculture, manufactures, and social statistics (Schor, 2017). Notable on the slave schedule for the 1850 census is that enslaved people were listed by "owner," not individually, and recorded by numbers, not by their names, as free people were listed. These choices are not only indicative of the dehumanization that characterized the institution of slavery, but also reflect debates in Congress as to whether slaves should be considered as people or property. In addition, the slave schedule asked if an enslaved person was "Black," to be marked with a "B," or "Mulatto," to be marked with an "M" (Schor, 2017). Reflecting the White supremacist ideas of the time, this question was added to the schedule at the prodding of scientists who wanted to compare the lifespan of slaves who had White ancestry with those who did not (Nobles, 2000).

Census data was used by people in the past, as it is now, to inform policy decisions and strategies. Students can also use census data reports to consider how the information may have influenced significant events. For example, how might information from the 1860 census be used to address questions about the American Civil War (1861–1865)? Tables of demographic data like the one in Figure 4.7 can help students gauge the relative military strength of the Union and Confederacy, including the approximate number of White men aged 18 to 45 who could serve in the military from the free states, border states, and seceded states. Indeed, this was an exercise in data analysis undertaken by Abraham Lincoln himself (Anderson, 2015). Likewise, a map on the distribution of the slave population in the counties of the southern states (see Figure 4.8) was used during the war to infer the relative strength of Confederate sentiment through correlation with the density of the slave population (Anderson, 2015).

For analyzing changes and continuities from one census to the next, it is also useful to examine data compiled from different decennial census reports. Although students can do this on their own by finding similar data from other reports, many census reports include visualizations showing change and continuity. The data from the table in Figure 4.9 provides a case in point. In the decades prior to the Civil War, the population of the United States had grown rapidly, and was characterized by a rise in immigrant-filled cities, new family farms to the west, and a growing number of enslaved people. Such changes fueled sectional tensions leading up to the Civil War. Calculating rates of change in the data on the total population, or perhaps the slave population alone, can provide powerful insight into the profound changes taking place in the young republic.

Whether using tables, graphs, or maps created for the census reports, students should also evaluate the motivations for presenting the data in a certain way, or for using particular language in a data display. Consider the display in Figure 4.10, which uses data from the 1890 Census and was included in the 1898 publication *Statistical Atlas of the United States, Based on the Results of the Eleventh Census*. The atlas was created under the

**Figure 4.7. Table from the 1860 census, prior to the Civil War, showing the number of White males who are of military age**

*Number of White Males in the United States between the ages of 18 and 45 years—Census of 1860.*

| State. | White males, 18 to 45 years of age. | State. | White males, 18 to 45 years of age. |
|---|---|---|---|
| Alabama | 99,967 | New Hampshire | 63,610 |
| Arkansas | 65,231 | New Jersey | 132,219 |
| California | 109,975 | New York | 796,881 |
| Connecticut | 94,411 | North Carolina | 115,369 |
| Delaware | 18,273 | Ohio | 459,534 |
| Florida | 15,739 | Oregon | 15,781 |
| Georgia | 111,005 | Pennsylvania | 555,172 |
| Illinois | 375,026 | Rhode Island | 35,502 |
| Indiana | 265,295 | South Carolina | 55,046 |
| Iowa | 139,316 | Tennessee | 159,353 |
| Kansas | 27,076 | Texas | 92,145 |
| Kentucky | 180,589 | Vermont | 60,580 |
| Louisiana | 83,456 | Virginia | 196,587 |
| Maine | 122,238 | Wisconsin | 159,335 |
| Maryland | 102,715 | | |
| Massachusetts | 208,419 | Total States | 5,535,054 |
| Michigan | 164,007 | District of Columbia | 12,797 |
| Minnesota | 41,296 | Territories | 76,214 |
| Mississippi | 70,295 | | |
| Missouri | 232,781 | Total States and Territories | 5,624,065 |

*Source:* Kennedy, 1864.

**Figure 4.8. Map showing the distribution of the slave population of the Southern states of the United States compiled from the census of 1860**

*Source:* Hergesheimer, 1861.

direction of Henry Gannett (1846–1914), who served as geographer of the U.S. censuses of 1880, 1890, and 1900, and was the driving force behind the census bureau's series of statistical atlases, which are often regarded as representing a high point in early census cartography and data visualization (Friendly & Wainer, 2021). Data visualizations such as this provide

Primary Source Data and Data Visualizations                                  69

**Figure 4.9. Population of the United States decennially from 1790 to 1850**

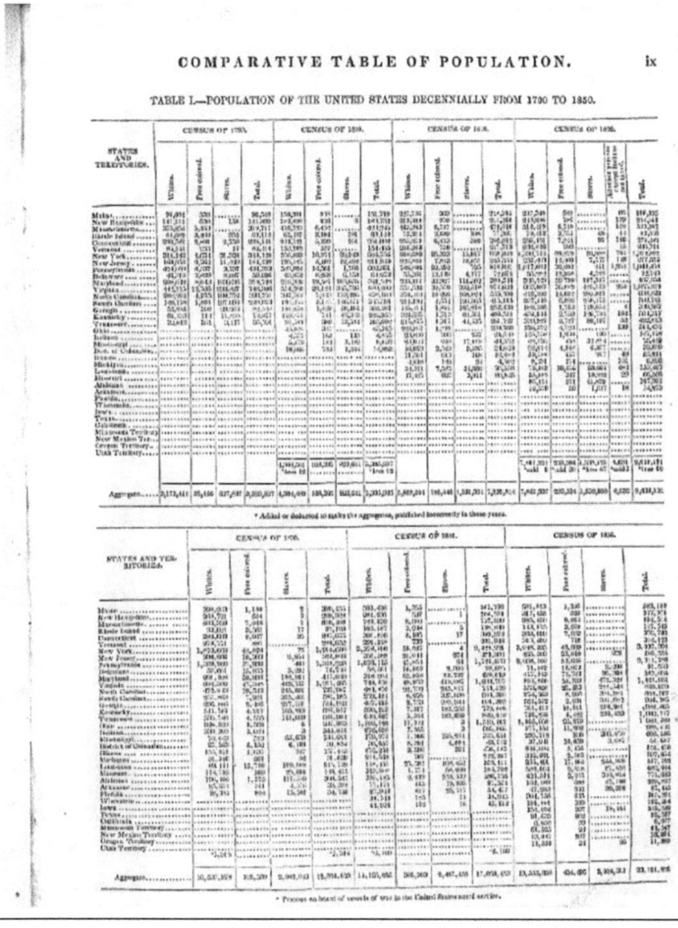

*Source:* DeBow, 1853.

evidence of changing demographics, to be sure, but equally interesting is the use of language as evidence of ideologies at the turn of the century. Indeed, one cannot really understand the demography without scrutinizing the categories used in the display.

First, "colored" was terminology adopted in census publications beginning with the 1880 census and referred to both Black and mixed-race (known as "Mulatto" at the time) people. Stemming from White supremacist and Social Darwinist ideas, the term was intended to separate anyone with a "drop of blood" of African origin from White people. In a similar vein, the sorting of anyone not considered "colored" into "Native Stock" or "Foreign Stock" was rooted in nativist ideologies and a heightened realization that

**Figure 4.10. Growth of the elements of the population, 1790 to 1890**

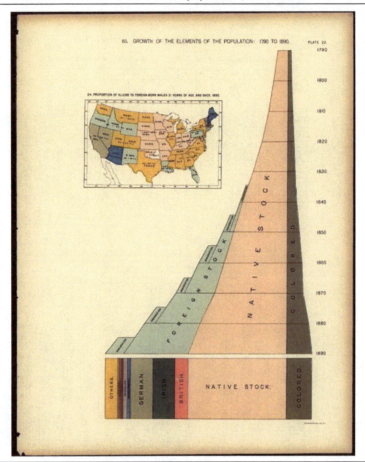

*Source:* United States Census Office & Gannett, 1898.

the United States was a nation of immigrants. "Native Stock" referred to anyone born in the United States with two parents who were both born in the United States, whereas "Foreign Stock" included anyone born abroad, as well as anyone born in the United States with either one or two foreign-born parents (Schor, 2017).

Data and data visualizations gathered through the U.S. census offer a fascinating look at not only demographic and economic changes throughout the nation's history, but also social and ideological changes, as evidenced by census questions, categorizations, and publications. However, when using the records produced by the U.S. Census Bureau we must recognize them as relics of power—shaped by those given authority in Congress and in the census offices, and by statisticians and scientists in privileged positions.

Indeed, throughout history, governments have collected data about the populace as a mechanism of power and control (D'Ignazio & Klein, 2020; Williams, 2020). On the one hand, collecting data has been an essential tool of statecraft, making large, complex societies more legible to those in power who are removed from the people but nonetheless must have a general understanding of people's activities and conditions to understand and try to solve social and economic problems (Scott, 1998). On the other hand, collected data have also served to essentialize groups of people or mask issues confronting individuals and subsets of people. At worst, they have been used in nefarious ways, aiding in government-sanctioned oppression and discrimination (Scott, 1998). It is to this latter use of data and data visualizations that we now turn.

## DATA AND DATA VISUALIZATIONS USED AS TOOLS OF OPPRESSION

The messages shared through data and data visualizations always represent the thoughts of the people who shared them, and while the intentions behind the collection and visualization of data can be genuine and ethical, they can also be tainted by greed, prejudice, or ill-will (Williams, 2020). In some ways, quantitative data pose a danger not found in other sources of information because they are so often perceived as factual and unbiased. The potential perniciousness embedded in data and data visualizations became clear in the latter half of the 19th century with the rise of scientific racism—that is, the pseudoscientific ideas that emerged in the context of colonial ideologies, oppression, and exploitation to categorize people by race, manufacture innate racial differences in character and intelligence, and justify the social hierarchy (Saini, 2019). Proponents of so-called race science could fashion data to fit their preexisting narrative, hiding pertinent contextual factors or faulty statistical methods from an unsuspecting, uninformed public, many of whom were all too willing to accept information that fit with their own racist views.

Consider, for example, the presentation of population data from the pre-Civil War 1860 U.S. census, which were released in 1864 with the prospect of the emancipation of the slaves at top of mind for many White Americans. In his introduction to the 1860 census report, Joseph C. G. Kennedy, Superintendent of Census, used data to address White fears about emancipation by arguing that Black people, owing to their supposed inferior status, were bound for extinction. He presented the tables shown in Figures 4.11 and 4.12 along with other tables to illustrate that the rate of growth among the Black population had declined and could be projected to continue declining. Kennedy wrote:

> With the lights before us, it seems, therefore, quite rational to conclude that we need not look forward to centuries to develop the fact that the white race is no

more favorable to the progress of the African race in its midst, than it has been to the perpetuity of the Indian on its borders, and that, as has been the case in all other countries on this continent where the blacks were once numerous, the colored population in America, wherever, either free or slave, it must in number and condition be greatly subordinate to the white race, is doomed to comparatively rapid absorption or extinction. (Kennedy, 1864, p. xii)

However, Kennedy's numbers and predictions were highly flawed. For example, when using Figure 4.11 as evidence for his argument, Kennedy did not account for the fact that the number of free Blacks was dependent on the number of emancipations, as well as the age ranges within the emancipated population, both of which were dependent on the political and economic context and the actions of enslavers, rather than natural factors alone (Schor, 2017). And in making projections based on the declining proportion of Blacks to Whites (see Figure 4.12), Kennedy did not account for the fact that the growth of the White population could be explained by immigration as well as natural factors, whereas the growth of the Black population, given that the slave trade had been abolished, was entirely dependent on natural factors (Schor, 2017).

**Figure 4.11. Census of slaves and free colored from the 1860 census**

*Census of slaves and free colored.*

| Census of— | Free colored. | Increase, per cent. | Slaves. | Increase, per cent. | Free colored and slaves. | Increase, per cent. |
|---|---|---|---|---|---|---|
| 1790 | 59,466 | .......... | 697,897 | .......... | 757,363 | .......... |
| 1800 | 108,395 | 82.28 | 893,041 | 27.97 | 1,001,436 | 32.23 |
| 1810 | 186,446 | 72.00 | 1,191,364 | 33.40 | 1,377,810 | 37.58 |
| 1820 | 233,524 | 25.23 | 1,538,038 | 28.79 | 1,771,562 | 28.58 |
| 1830 | 319,599 | 36.87 | 2,009,043 | 30.61 | 2,328,642 | 31.44 |
| 1840 | 386,303 | 20.87 | 2,487,455 | 23.81 | 2,873,758 | 23.41 |
| 1850 | 434,449 | 12.46 | 3,204,313 | 28.83 | 3,638,762 | 26.62 |
| 1860 | 487,970 | 12.32 | 3,953,760 | 23.39 | 4,441,730 | 22.07 |

*Source:* Kennedy, 1864.

**Figure 4.12. Probable future population of the United States**

*Probable future population of the United States.*

| Year. | Free colored and slaves. | Aggregate of whites and colored. | Percentage of colored. |
|---|---|---|---|
| 1870 | 5,421,900 | 42,328,432 | 12.81 |
| 1880 | 6,618,350 | 56,450,241 | 11.72 |
| 1890 | 7,942,020 | 77,266,989 | 10.28 |
| 1900 | 9,530,424 | 100,355,802 | 9.50 |

*Source:* Kennedy, 1864.

Uses of data to feed discriminatory ideas are also found in the papers of Harry H. Laughlin, a eugenicist who served as the superintendent of the Eugenics Records Office located in Cold Spring Harbor, New York, from its founding in 1910 to its closure in 1939. The eugenics movement in the United States was a legalized campaign to methodically terminate certain racial and ethnic groups, lower social classes, and other groups of people deemed genetically inferior. The goal was to make way for what eugenicists believed was a "super race" made up of people of purely Germanic and Nordic origins. Their tactics included segregation, marriage prohibition, deportation, and forced sterilization. In addition, eugenicists believed that most immigrants arriving after 1890, those of Eastern and Southern European descent, were genetically undesirable. It was therefore necessary to erect an international barrier to continuing waves of immigrants by targeting U.S. immigration policy (Black, 2012).

In 1920 Laughlin became the official eugenics authority for the House of Representatives' Committee on Immigration and Naturalization chaired by Albert Johnson. Gaining an audience with the committee chaired by Johnson, who himself was an avid eugenicist, was the perfect opportunity to influence immigration restriction. On November 21, 1922, Laughlin presented a report, "Analysis of America's Modern Melting Pot," which consisted of numerous "scientific" graphs and charts to prove to the committee that certain groups of immigrants were degenerate by nature and therefore a financial and social burden on American society. One such graph (see Figure 4.13) attempted to illustrate the relative "social inadequacy" of different ethnic and racial groups based on whether they fell below or above a quota for residence in state institutions. Social inadequacy was a concept Laughlin himself invented and included "feeblemindedness" (a term he never clearly defined), insanity, crime (with no distinction made among the types of crimes committed), epilepsy, tuberculosis, blindness, deafness, deformity, and dependency (defined as the "old and infirm") (Black, 2012).

Even setting aside the xenophobia, racism, and ablism underlying Laughlin's graph, the statistical reasoning represented in the graph is highly flawed. First, Laughlin came up with the "quota fulfillment" measure in the graph by sampling from about 50% of the custodial institutions in the United States. However, he pulled his sample from states with a higher than average foreign-born population, thereby making it more likely the institutions would have a higher percentage of foreign-born people admitted. In addition, he sampled only from public institutions, where the poorest people would have gone, not from private institutions where people from wealthier and more established families would have gone. The even graver error is the way he determined his "quota." He based his quota on the percentage of a race or ethnicity in the entire population, figuring that you would expect the same percentage represented in institutions. For example, in 1910 the population of the United States was about 1.5% Italian.

**Figure 4.13.** Harry H. Laughlin, *All Types of Social Inadequacy*, graph presented before Congress in 1922

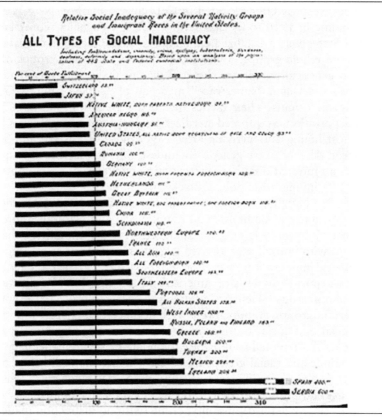

*Source:* Laughlin, 1923.

Laughlin reasoned that if Italians in the United States were equally susceptible as other ethnicities to conditions necessitating institutionalization, the quota for Italians in custodial institutions should be 1.5%. At face value this probably sounded reasonable to most people, but as Joseph M. Gillman, a contemporary of Laughlin's, pointed out, Laughlin committed serious statistical errors through this reasoning. Gillman (1924) wrote:

> In the first place, as numerators he uses the inmates in the custodial institutions as of 1921, but as denominators he uses the various races and nativities as of 1910. In the second place, he divides the number of specific inadequacies by the whole of the respective population groups, instead of first allowing for the respective age and sex proportions of the population which are variously represented in custodial institutions. He, so to speak, divides two bushels of

wheat by three bushels of rye, and gets a "quota" of two-thirds, or 66 per cent of potatoes. (p. 36)

In other words, Laughlin was not just using data and data visualizations to discriminate against different ethnic groups, he was using *misleading* data and data visualizations. With the help of Laughlin's flawed testimony, Congress passed the Immigration Act of 1924, also known also as the Johnson-Reed Act, which would radically restrict non-Nordic immigration in the United States.

Only after the Nazis' eugenicist methods of extermination were revealed to the world did the eugenics movement in the United States cease to hold favor among many of the U.S. elites who had previously embraced and funded it. By the end of the movement, at least 60,000 Americans had been coercively sterilized, and the immigration quotas that emerged out of the era were not amended until 1952 with the McCarran-Walter Immigration and Naturalization Act (Black, 2012). The eugenics movement, and the copious data and data visualizations that capture its methods, mark a dark chapter in American history. This entire period of scientific racism was one in which, as investigative journalist Black (2012) has argued, "influential and eloquent thinkers were able to slap numbers and a few primitive formulas on their class and race hatred, and in so doing create a passion that transcended simple bigotry" (p. 76).

## DATA VISUALIZATIONS IN SOCIAL MOVEMENTS

While it is an unfortunate truth that data have been gathered and used by those with power and authority to harm the people they are about, history has also shown us multiple ways in which people have used data to uplift their own or others' communities. The past has borne witness to several individual reformers and activists—people with little more at their disposal than the will to effect change—collecting and using data to benefit groups who have been marginalized, oppressed, or forgotten. Data visualizations used as part of social movements for civil rights and the public good not only help us better understand the social causes for which they were produced, but also provide insight into the ways that humans have attempted to use data and data visualizations to achieve social justice.

W. E. B. Du Bois was at the forefront of such work. At the end of the 19th century, Du Bois was asked to contribute a social study about African American life to an exhibit at the 1900 Paris Exposition. The fair was intended to highlight accomplishments throughout the world over the previous century and to encourage people to look forward to what was to come in the 20th century. One building at the fair was devoted to the "social economy," and the section reserved for the United States was to include an exhibit devoted to the history and "present conditions" of African Americans. The exhibit Du Bois designed for the site included 200 books written by African Americans, as well as 500 photographs highlighting business enterprises, social life, and education of African Americans. With the images, Du Bois intended to diminish racist caricatures of the day and demonstrate that there was no so-called "Negro type." Also within the display were 63 charts, graphs, and maps, divided into two parts. The first part was a case study of the Black population in Georgia, titled *The Georgia Negro: A Social Study*, and the second was a more national and global study titled *A Series of Statistical Charts Illustrating the Condition of the Descendants of Former African Slaves Now in Residence in the United States of America*. Du Bois and his team drew their data for the charts partially from Atlanta University reports, but also from official governmental reports, including the United States census (Battle-Baptiste & Rusert, 2018).

However, Du Bois's data visualizations differ markedly from those included in the census and other governmental reports. With the data visualizations in the exhibit, Du Bois sought to visually convey the "color line"—a term coined by Frederick Douglass in 1881 in reference to racial segregation—that existed in Georgia and the rest of the country, while also telling a compelling data narrative about progress made by Black people since the Civil War (Battle-Baptiste & Rusert, 2018). His work directly refuted ideas stemming from the scientific racism of the time, which held that the Black population would naturally decrease, and that Black people were intellectually inferior and incapable of learning (Morris, 2018). By comparing African Americans with White people from the United States and other parts of the world (see Figures 4.14 and 4.15), Du Bois sought to establish the Black South as an integral part of modernity, a nation within a nation made up of people who had more in common with the people of the "thinking world" abroad than with those in the segregated United States (Battle-Baptiste & Rusert, 2018).

Du Bois's data narrative is powerful on its own but was made even more powerful by virtue of the fact that, unlike data visualizations from official U.S. Census Bureau reports that used some of the same data, his were representations of Black people from a Black perspective—a response to what he called "double consciousness," or the experience of always seeing oneself through the eyes of another (Battle-Baptiste & Rusert, 2018). Moreover, Du Bois contextualized the data visualizations within his display with material artifacts like a wooden frame made by a former slave and a three-volume, handwritten compilation of the Black Codes of Georgia, including the slave codes and current segregationist policies. As scholars Whitney Battle-Baptiste and Britt Rusert (2018) argued, such choices told a story not of "black progress in a forward-looking, modern nation" but created "a sense of the gains that had been made by African Americans *in*

Primary Source Data and Data Visualizations 77

**Figure 4.14. W. E. B. Du Bois, *Occupations of Negroes and Whites in Georgia***

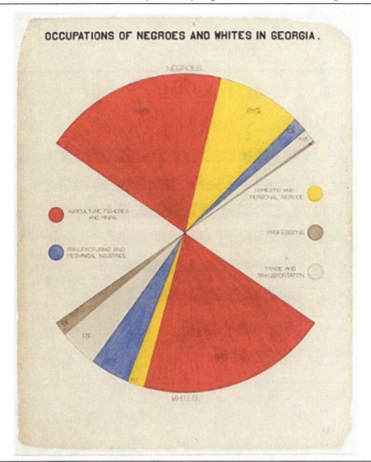

*Source:* Du Bois, 1900a.

*spite* of the machinery of the white supremacist culture, policy, and law that surrounded them" (p. 22).

The elements of dissent baked into Du Bois's work might best be captured from a comparative perspective. Consider, for example, the data visualizations included in a report authored by Henry Gannett, geographer of the 1880, 1890, and 1900 U.S. censuses (see Figure 4.16). The data visualizations appear objective enough. They were part of a report entitled *Statistics of the Negroes in the United States*, an "occasional paper" funded by the Slater Fund, a financial endowment established in 1882 by John Fox Slater, a Connecticut textiles manufacturer, to support the industrial and

**Figure 4.15. W. E. B. Du Bois,** *Illiteracy of the American Negroes compared with that of other nations*

*Source:* Du Bois, 1900b, 1900c.

vocational higher education of newly freed African Americans in the South, with an early emphasis on training teachers. The preface to the document states that the Fund would "publish from time to time papers that relate to the education of the colored race" (Gannett, 1894, p. 4).

Despite the seemingly benevolent purposes of the Slater fund and Gannett's report, it is laden with language reflecting the scientific racism of the time. For example, when writing about the different growth rates in the White and Black populations shown in Figure 4.16, Gannett makes clear reference to the White fears that Kennedy wrote of in his 1860 census report. Gannett states:

Primary Source Data and Data Visualizations 79

**Figure 4.16. H. Gannett, two charts, "Total Population of White and Negro Elements" and "Proportion of the Negro Element to the Total Population"**

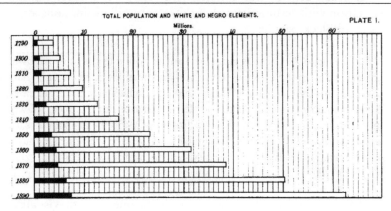

*Source:* Gannett, 1894.

These figures, and the conclusions necessarily derived from them, should set at rest forever all fears regarding any possible conflict between the two races. We have before us the testimony of a century to show us that the negroes, while in no danger of extinction, while increasing at a rate probably more rapid than in any other part of the earth, are yet increasing less rapidly than the white people of the country, and to demonstrate that the latter will become more and more numerically the dominant race in America. (Gannett, 1894, pp. 6–7)

In another section of the paper, Gannett comments on how the rate of increase in urban centers was slower for Blacks than whites, coloring his interpretation with assumptions about the "natural" inclinations and capabilities of all Black people:

> While the negro is extremely gregarious and is by that instinct drawn toward the great centers of population, on the other hand he is not fitted either by nature or education for those vocations for the pursuit of which men collect in cities, that is, for manufactures and commerce. The inclinations of this race, drawn from its inheritance, tend to keep it wedded to the soil, and the probabilities are that as cities increase in these states in number and size, and with them manufactures and commerce develop, the great body of the negroes will continue to remain aloof from them and cultivate the soil as heretofore. (Gannett, 1894, p. 12)

While there is nothing obviously racist in Gannett's data visualizations themselves, they were nonetheless used as evidence for racist conjectures and assertions.

Du Bois presents the same data on changes in the White and Black population quite differently, perhaps most notably adding date labels to his graph to provide context for the observed population changes (see Figure 4.17). First, Du Bois labels the date of the "suppression of the slave trade," which influenced population growth by ending the addition of enslaved people brought directly from Africa to the population, but which also serves as a reminder of the oppression and hardship that Black people had to overcome. In the middle of the graph, the label "European immigration" helps to explain growth in the white population, reminding viewers that it is not by some superior ability to successfully reproduce that there is a steady growth rate among White people. At the same time, the label "Emancipation" serves as another reminder that Black people were enslaved for most of the time depicted on the graph, while it also frames an increase in the rate of Black population growth in the 1870s and 1880s. Du Bois's graph is thus a source of information as well as a counter-interpretation of census data, seemingly aimed directly at those who would diminish the significance of Black population growth and the progress that African Americans had accomplished, even in the face of great adversity. And these are but a few of the data visualizations Du Bois and his team created, which can now be used in the study of history.

Another historical figure who used data and data visualization to effectively counter racist arguments and seek justice was journalist and activist Ida B. Wells-Barnett. A contemporary of Du Bois, Wells-Barnett used information she gathered from newspapers, including the *Chicago Tribune* of her hometown, to present data on the number, location, and reported causes of lynching throughout the United States. In 1895, she published *The Red Record: Tabulated Statistics and Alleged Causes of Lynching in the United*

Primary Source Data and Data Visualizations 81

**Figure 4.17. W. E. B. Du Bois, *Comparative rate of increase of the White and Negro elements of the population of the United States***

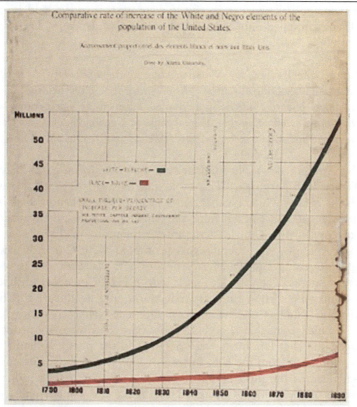

*Source:* Du Bois, 1900b.

*States* with information on lynching from 1893 and 1894. As preface to the organized data in her book, Wells-Barnett stated that the purpose of her report was to "reproduce a record which shows that a large portion of the American people avow anarchy, condone murder and defy the contempt of civilization" (p. 17), clarifying too that the numbers were gathered and recorded in newspapers by white men, not Black, and thus, "Out of their own mouths shall the murderers be condemned" (p. 17).

A few years later, Wells-Barnett (1901) published another compilation of such statistics in an article entitled "Lynching and the Excuse for It" for the newspaper *The Independent*. Her article was in response to comments made by social reformer Jane Addams in an earlier issue of the newspaper. Although she meant to condemn lynching, Addams had written, "Let us assume that the Southern citizens who take part in and abet the lynching of negroes honestly believe that that is the only successful method of dealing with a certain class of crimes." Recognizing that the "class of crimes" Addams was referring to consisted of alleged assaults against Southern White women, Wells-Barnett set out to disprove this widely held misconception. Using compiled data from newspapers as evidence for her argument, she wrote:

> Negroes are lynched for 'violating contracts,' 'unpopularity,' 'testifying in court" and 'shooting at rabbits." As only negroes are lynched for 'no offense,' 'unknown offenses,' offenses not criminal, misdemeanors and crimes not capital, it must be admitted that the real cause of lynching in all such cases is race prejudice, and should so be classified. (Wells-Barnett, 1901, p. 1135)

She then presented a table summarizing and visualizing cases of lynching (see Figure 4.18), arguing, "This table tells its own story, and shows how false is the excuse which lynchers offer to justify their fiendishness. Instead of being the sole cause of lynching, the crime upon which the lynchers build their defense furnishes the least victims for the mob" (p. 1136).

Jane Addams, whose comments prompted Wells-Garnett's argument, was also no stranger to the effectiveness of data visualizations in social reform movements. The founder and leader of Hull House, which opened in 1889 to provide shelter, childcare, education, and healthcare to Chicago's urban poor, Addams and her partner Florence Kelley created a series of maps of Chicago neighborhoods to show that rents were not proportional to wages and that landlords were preying on the poor (Williams, 2020). Kelley, four men from the U.S. Bureau of Labor, and the residents of Hull House collected the information in the maps as part of a national study of poverty in Baltimore, Chicago, New York, and Philadelphia commissioned by the U.S. Congress in 1892. Recording information with questionnaires, they went from door to door and into homes and sweatshops, asking

**Figure 4.18. I. Wells-Barnett, table summarizing and visualizing cases of lynching Source: Wells-Barnett, 1901**

| Year | Race prejudice | Murder | Rape | Total lynchings |
|---|---|---|---|---|
| 1896 | 31 | 24 | 31 | 86 |
| 1897 | 46 | 55 | 22 | 123 |
| 1898 | 39 | 47 | 16 | 102 |
| 1899 | 56 | 23 | 11 | 90 |
| 1900 | 57 | 30 | 16 | 103 |
| Total | 229 | 179 | 96 | 504 |

*Source:* Wells-Barnett, 1901.

**Figure 4.19. Maps from *Hull-House Maps and Papers***

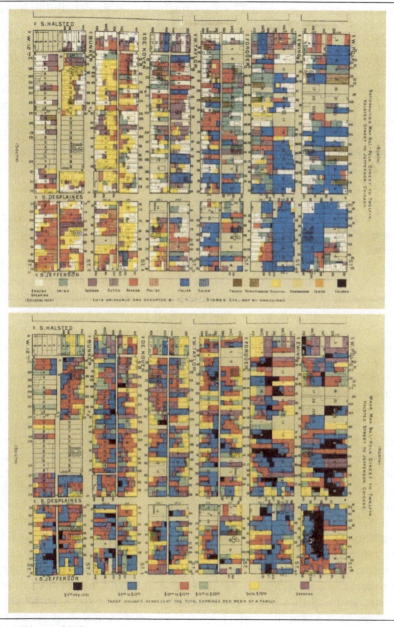

Source: Bienen, 2012.

residents questions about their ethnic origins, the number of people in the household, the wages earned by the principal wage earner, and how many weeks the principal wage earner had been employed.

The colorful maps that resulted and were published in *Hull-House Maps and Papers* (Residents of Hull House, 1895) allowed viewers to easily see the clustering of nationalities and the distributions of weekly wages among the neighborhood residents. By comparing the maps, viewers could also see a correlation between nationalities and wages (see Figure 4.19). The maps' impact on social research and informed policymaking was profound. For example, Du Bois was inspired by the Hull House maps for his social study of African Americans in Philadelphia, *The Philadelphia Negro*. Together, these projects raised awareness about structural issues surrounding poverty, helping people understand that it was impossible to rise out of poverty when wages were lower than the most basic living expenses.

Data and data visualizations have played an important role in numerous episodes of history. Those presented in this chapter barely scratch the surface of maps, graphs, tables, and other data visualizations that are available for inquiry. Even those data and data visualizations from the past that are included in the previous and subsequent chapters of this book provide only a small glimpse of what is available. My purpose in this chapter was not to provide an exhaustive compilation of primary source data and data visualizations, but to showcase how important they are as a category of primary sources. Not only are numerous data and data visualizations directly related to historical events students are typically required to study in school, but they also provide opportunities for students to engage with important historical concepts, including historical perspective, change and continuity over time, and human agency.

As students study such data visualizations, they might find themselves having to reconcile the good that people like Du Bois, Wells-Garnett, Addams, and Kelley could do with data visualizations, with the harm done with them by the likes of Kennedy and Laughlin. Yet this is just another reason that data literacy should be taught in social studies classrooms. Studying data visualizations from the past can help students develop habits of mind necessary for *critical and humanistic* data literacy. They can see data visualizations as authored sources of information carrying messages that reflect the motivations and biases of its authors and, at the same time, they can see data visualizations as sources of power—sources of power that may be used to oppress and discriminate, but that can and should also be used to work toward social justice. Indeed, as the next chapter will argue, social studies teachers have a crucial role to play in teaching a critical, humanistic form of data literacy. And their role is one that cannot be adequately fulfilled by other subject-area teachers.

CHAPTER 5

# A Special Role for Social Studies Teachers
## Teaching Critical, Humanistic Data Literacy

Lillian Gilbreth (1878–1972) was one of the first female engineers in the United States, an expert in industrial psychology, the first woman to become full professor in the engineering school at Purdue University, and the first woman elected to the National Academy of Engineering. She was also a mother of 12 children, two of whom would grow up to write the book *Cheaper by the Dozen* based on their life in the Gilbreth household. Gilbreth and her husband Frank were pioneers in the efficiency movement of the early 20th century, most often associated with Frederick Winslow Taylor, whose 1909 book, *The Principles of Scientific Management*, helped define an era in which people sought to apply scientific insight to eliminate waste in all areas of the economy and society. As part of their efficiency research, the Gilbreths conducted time and motion studies on repetitive household labor, hoping to increase efficiency and reduce fatigue. They used photographs such as the one in Figure 5.1 to conduct "micromotion studies." By affixing lights to workers and filming their activities against a gridded background while a chronometer kept time, they created a data visualization they could use to track and time the worker's motions and determine the optimal movements for achieving the work with the least time and effort (Witzel, 2022).

After her husband's death, Gilbreth continued this work as an independent consultant and, in 1928, published *The Home-Maker and Her Job* with advice on how to do housework more efficiently and thereby obtain more "happiness minutes" (Witzel, 2022). Gilbreth intended efficiency to give women more time to themselves. However, research on housework time studies indicate that the processes she recommended provided no overall timesaving to women working in the home. Even as time spent on some household chores decreased, women's overall volume of work stayed the same, probably because their time was filled with additional expectations for cleanliness or childcare (Witzel, 2022). According to Witzel (2022), the failure of such studies to save time was partly because they made workers mere data sources, aggregating and abstracting their individual labor in the name of efficiency, without considering their lives, experiences, and societal pressures. In essence, as is captured by the haunting image of the spectral woman behind the data visualization in Figure 5.1, they erased the women behind women's work (Witzel, 2022).

The erasure of the complex human beings that serve as the data points in data visualizations is an imminent concern in our datafied world. Amid increasing calls to teach data literacy in K–12 schools, several scholars (e.g., D'Ignazio & Klein, 2020; Irgens et al., 2020; Lee et al., 2021) have called attention to the importance of teaching a critical and humanistic stance toward data and data visualizations. They stress that overemphasis on basic data literacies, absent opportunities to discuss inequities in data practices and the ideological, historical, and political dimensions of data production and usage, risks oversimplifying the historical, social, political, and economic dimensions of complex problems in an imperfect democracy (Philip & Rubel, 2019).

Three key propositions lie at the core of critical and humanistic data literacy work. First, data and data visualizations tell stories that are both interpretation and interpretable. They are narrative structures in which ideological meanings are intentionally and unintentionally encoded by creators through verbal and visual elements, and then decoded by end users. However, as is the case with any story, the readers' interpretations can differ from each other and from that of the creator (Philip et al., 2016; Philip & Rubel, 2019). Data visualizations can become ideological sites where meanings of race, gender, and other forms of identity are contested (Philip & Rubel, 2019). Consequently, teachers should consider a data display's intended message and help students unpack the intended message, but they

**Figure 5.1. An image from the Gilbreths' motion efficiency studies**

*Source:* Poynar, 2023. National Museum of American History, Archives Center. (n.d.). Cyclegraph of female at gridded table and gridded background. Table height is adjustable and her feet are on a box. Frank and Lillian Gilbreth Collection. https://sova.si.edu/record/nmah.ac.0803/ref74?t=W&q=woman

should also consider students' understanding of the concepts encoded in data displays and how students' personal knowledge and experiences will influence their interpretations (Johnson et al., 2021; Lee et al., 2021).

Second, the generation, collection, representation, visualization, analysis, interpretation, and communication of data are never neutral or objective. They are always premised on a set of assumptions, which are rooted in worldviews shaped by personal, cultural, and sociopolitical factors and work to reproduce and challenge forms of power in society (D'Ignazio & Klein, 2020; Gillborn et al., 2018; Hullman & Diakopoulos, 2011; Irgens et al., 2020; Philip et al., 2016). Data can obscure or exclude some perspectives and histories while highlighting or emphasizing others (Perez, 2019). Students should therefore have opportunities to engage in open discourses and critiques around data's origin, representation, and usage and the ways in which data can produce and reproduce injustice (Philip et al., 2013; Shreiner & Martell, 2022).

Finally, data are powerful. The ability to understand, create, and argue with data and data visualizations is increasingly important for democratic participation (e.g., Irgens et al., 2020; Philip et al., 2016; Philip & Rubel, 2019). Students should not only know this; they should also practice it. They should learn that data provide an avenue through which they can understand and address societal issues as well as issues that affect their lives and the lives of people in their communities. And they should learn that they, too, can work with data. They can comprehend and critique data; generate, organize, and visualize data; and use data to build arguments and to communicate with others (boyd & Crawford, 2012; Hullman & Diakopoulos, 2011; Irgens et al., 2020; Philip et al., 2016; Philip & Rubel, 2019; Philip et al., 2013; Shreiner, 2020).

Unfortunately, attention to critical, humanistic data literacy skills is mostly absent from recommendations for data-based instruction in schools (Drozda et al., 2022). This is certainly true of social studies curriculum frameworks. Neither the *C3 Framework* nor state standards documents sufficiently address critical data literacy (Shreiner, 2020). Indeed, although all state social studies standards documents in the United States recommend students work with data visualizations at some point in their schooling, only a handful mention critical data literacy skills such as identifying the source of data visualizations or evaluating them for biases and manipulations (Shreiner, 2020).

As I will argue in this chapter, teaching critical, humanistic data literacy in social studies is vital and social studies teachers have a central role to play in helping students acquire such data literacy skills. Many proponents of data literacy in schools focus primarily on infusing it more deliberately into mathematics (e.g., LaMar & Boaler, 2021; Levitt, 2022) or computer science education (e.g., Yongpradit et al., 2016). While I agree that teaching data literacy in such STEM courses is important, it is not enough. Building justice-oriented data literacy is an interdisciplinary task (Louie, 2022), and, as I will argue in the following sections, the specialized knowledge and skills of social studies teachers, along with their curricular requirements, make social studies classes an ideal setting for developing critical, humanistic data literacy.

## THE IMPORTANCE OF SOCIAL STUDIES TEACHER CONTENT KNOWLEDGE

Data and data visualizations are full of symbols, lines and shapes, numbers, and words that work together to convey a particular message that must be decoded by viewers (Philipet al., 2016; Philip & Rubel, 2019). Because data and data visualizations abound with domain-specific concepts, researchers who study data literacy argue that students should work with data visualizations within a specific disciplinary context, rather than as abstractions disconnected from content (Shah & Hoeffner, 2002). Correct interpretation of data and data visualizations is highly dependent upon a reader's background knowledge. It follows, then, that if students' content knowledge matters when they are trying to make sense of representations of data, their teachers' content knowledge matters too.

Decades of research tell us that teacher content knowledge plays a critical role in instructional decision-making and quality of instruction (Ball et al., 2008; Charalambous & Hill, 2012; Hill & Charalambous, 2012). Teacher content knowledge is complex and multifaceted. It is made up of knowledge of the curriculum, but also knowledge of their subject area, including its key concepts and theories, and a construct known as *pedagogical content knowledge* (PCK), which involves knowing which concepts students will find easy or difficult and how to address difficulties with appropriately sequenced and relevant explanations, illustrations, and examples (Ball et al., 2008; Shulman, 1986).

Social studies teachers have subject matter content knowledge and PCK that are crucial for building the critical, humanistic data literacy skills fundamental to democratic citizenship. The data and data visualizations that affect us most and that influence people's decisions are those that we encounter in our everyday lives. They are data and data visualizations pertaining to social, political, and economic topics. The concepts associated with these topics are the domain of social studies teachers. It is social studies teachers who are most likely to have the subject area content knowledge to understand the meaning and nuances of the concepts represented through everyday data, and it is they who have the PCK to help students understand the concepts.

Consider the multiline graph from the U.S. Census Bureau in Figure 5.2. A math teacher might use this graph to teach about median versus mean or about calculating differences between groups. These concepts are certainly important for students to grasp, and a math teacher likely has the subject matter content knowledge and PCK to help students understand them. A social studies teacher would be more apt to discuss the concept of income inequality along racial and ethnic lines and provide a historical context for such inequalities. A social studies teacher would also be more likely to ensure students know what a recession is and how it affects individuals, and help students understand what a $20,000 difference in annual family income means for access to home ownership, education, and healthcare. The social studies teacher also might be more inclined to unpack the racial representations in the graph and consider how key demographic features are masked. For example, students reading the Figure 5.2 graph might think that the U.S. "Asian" population—a category that includes a huge array of ethnic groups with vastly different experiences—must be doing quite well financially. But the graph hides Asian Americans living in poverty and tells readers nothing about groups that fall below the median. Furthermore, it masks gender- and age-related inequalities across racial and ethnic categories. Social studies teachers could raise such questions with students, all while working within the civic goals and curricular standards of their subject area.

**Figure 5.2. U. S. Census Bureau, *Real Median Household Income by Race and Hispanic Origin: 1967 to 2022***

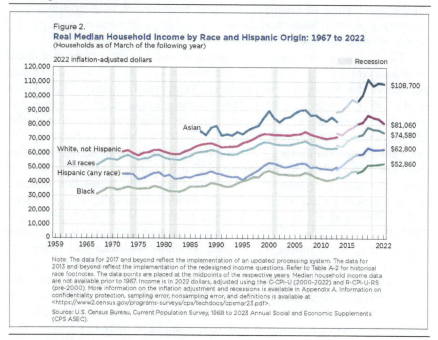

*Source:* Semega & Kollar, 2022. https://www.census.gov/content/dam/Census/library/visualizations/2022/demo/p60-276/figure2.pdf

## THE RELEVANCE OF HISTORICAL THINKING SKILLS

It is not just social studies teachers' conceptual understanding that positions them to teach critical, humanistic data literacy skills; it is also the discipline-based critical analysis skills they are already inclined to have students practice. Most social studies teachers throughout the United States have at least some training in teaching the discipline of history, and since at least the first decade of the 21st century, "historical thinking" has become a standard in history teaching (Keirn & Martin, 2012). The idea of teaching historical thinking is premised on the rejection of history classrooms as sites of information transmission and memorization, promoting them instead as sites of analysis, interpretation, and questioning (Keirn & Martin, 2012; Lévesque & Clark, 2018). In the United States, the concept of historical thinking is grounded in the work of Wineburg (1991, 2001), who identified historical thinking heuristics—sourcing, contextualizing, and corroborating—used by professional historians as they read and make sense of historical documents (Lévesque & Clark, 2018). The identification of these heuristics inspired an explosion of classroom resources (Keirn & Martin, 2012; Lévesque & Clark, 2018), and it has framed research on students' ideas about historical evidence and their historical reading and writing strategies (e.g., Monte-Sano et al., 2014; Reisman, 2012; Wineburg et al., 2011), along with studies on the application of historical thinking heuristics in reading about contemporary political issues and online sources (e.g., Breakstone et al., 2018; McGrew et al., 2018; Shreiner, 2014).

The first heuristic, *sourcing*, involves identifying the author of a document and considering their biases and motivations, as well as noting when and where the document was produced (Leinhardt & Young, 1996; Rouet et al., 1997; Wineburg, 1991). This heuristic has as much relevance and importance with respect to data and data visualizations as to other modes of information (D'Ignazio & Klein, 2020; McGrew et al., 2022). For critical, humanistic data literacy, sourcing is essential. It shows recognition that there are humans behind the data, and that it is important to consider the personal, cultural, and sociopolitical motivations and biases that underlie the generation, collection, and visualization of data (D'Ignazio & Klein, 2020; Gillborn et al., 2018; Hullman & Diakopoulos, 2011; Irgens et al., 2020; Philip et al., 2016). Sourcing, properly understood, must be more than just ensuring that a source is provided, which by itself can lead viewers to believe that a data visualization is objective and does not need to be further scrutinized. It includes questioning the situated knowledge and intentions of the person or organization that produced the information (D'Ignazio & Klein, 2020; Kennedy et al., 2016). Social studies teachers who already hold the practice of sourcing in high regard might be more likely than other teachers to call students' attention to the source of a data visualization and evaluate its reliability, or to caution students should they encounter a data visualization that does not provide a source.

Another historical thinking heuristic, *contextualization*, is also relevant to critical, humanistic data literacy. Contextualization involves considering the immediate context of the document, and zooming out to consider surrounding events that occurred at the time, as well as what preceded and followed the event represented by the document (Leinhardt & Young, 1996; van Drie & van Boxtel, 2008; Wineburg, 1991). It requires imagining the physical and social setting of a document's creation, considering how the setting may have played a role in the document's creation and inherent biases, and making sense of the document with the setting in mind (Nokes, 2022). Context matters when making sense of data and data visualizations too. As D'Ignazio and Klein (2020) argue, "When approaching any new source of knowledge, whether it be a dataset or dinner menu (or a dataset of dinner menus), it's essential to ask questions about the social, cultural, historical, institutional, and material conditions under which that knowledge was produced" (p. 152). Failing to consider context risks ignoring potential power differentials underlying the collection of data, and the socially and culturally mediated assumptions made about the people from whom the data was collected. It further risks not accounting for how people's experiences tied to gender, race, ethnicity, socioeconomic status, or other identity traits may be lost in the aggregate (D'Ignazio & Klein, 2020; Perez, 2019). For social studies teachers already committed to teaching contextualization as part of historical thinking, considering the context surrounding data and data visualizations is a natural fit.

*Corroboration* is the third heuristic central to historical thinking. It involves cross-checking claims or evidence against one another, paying attention to any similarities or differences, and attempting to explain the differences (Nokes, 2022). Again, this is also an important aspect of critical, humanistic data literacy. People may get their data from different sources, use different methods for collecting data, aggregate or disaggregate data differently, visualize data in ways that tell different stories, or may simply interpret data differently. Accounting for these differences and recognizing that data can be represented and interpreted differently by different people also make up a core principle of critical, humanistic data literacy.

Additionally, the act of corroboration can go far in raising questions about the extent to which data represent the actual experiences of the people they purportedly represent. For example, in the United States, poverty is measured as falling below an absolute income level, adjusted for inflation. At this writing, the poverty line for a family of four is a $30,000 annual income. Many experts argue that an absolute poverty measure fails to capture the relative experiences of people, and that poverty should be measured instead according to what the consensus view of poverty is, rather than by an absolute income standard. In other words, you might talk with someone from a family of four whose income is $40,000 per year and they would share that they feel like they are living in poverty based on the hardships they endure in their particular setting (Maier & Imazeki, 2013). Acknowledging such discrepancies is part of a critical, humanistic approach to data, and one that social studies teachers might naturally fold into their teaching of disciplined thinking.

## TAKING DATA-INFORMED ACTION

While taking a critical, humanistic stance toward data and data visualizations produced by others is important, it does not go far enough on its own. Proponents of critical, humanistic data literacy also stress the importance of helping students understand that they have the power to work with and use data around topics that are interesting and relevant to them and their communities. Past data collection was largely the activity of governments, corporations, and institutions—those who held the most power in society and who could choose to collect or not collect data based on their own interests. Now there are previously unattainable, large, open public datasets that anyone can access and explore, and many people have access to data collection devices, including their mobile phones, that allow them to collect, process, and display data (Williams, 2020).

Social studies teachers can support working with data in service of justice-oriented civic action projects. The NCSS argued in 2016 that social studies teachers should "develop a commitment to social responsibility, justice and action" (pp. 180–182). Furthermore, NCSS's (2013) *C3 Framework* describes social studies as "the ideal staging ground for taking informed action because of its unique role in preparing students for civic life" (p. 62). The document recommends students study "characteristics and causes of local, regional, and global problems; instances of such problems in multiple contexts; and challenges and opportunities faced by those trying to address these problems over time and place" (p. 62). They also recommend that students "apply a range of deliberative and democratic strategies and procedures to take action in their classrooms, school, and out-of-school civic contexts" (p. 62).

Most, though not all, states have used the *C3 Framework* and its recommendations for action-oriented instruction to revise their own standards, with some states purposefully incorporating standards that provide substantive opportunities for students to engage in social action projects (Bond et al., 2021; New et al., 2021). Admittedly, the educational system as a whole has not prioritized teaching students to take action for social and political change, and many social studies teachers wrestle with "covering" all the content required by standards while also incorporating civic action projects (Bond et al., 2021; Martell & Stevens, 2020). A recent review of precollegiate data science education projects reveals some projects that educators have designed and implemented aimed at either understanding or acting upon local problems while addressing topics like migration, elections, and segregation that fall fully within the domain of social studies (Lee et al., 2022). Below is a summary of three such projects, all of which were taught or could be taught in a social studies classroom:

- Students in a racially diverse, urban 5th-grade classroom investigated and shared their experiences with a recent rodent issue in their local community. Students then generated questions to guide their investigation of the problem and identified and explored datasets available through their city government. In trying to repurpose the data for their investigation, students actively interrogated the data and data collection methods, noting unusual pattern fluctuations over time and identifying weaknesses or biases in the data. Moreover, students made decisions about how data from their investigations should be visualized to tell compelling stories to others about their findings and the impact on their community (Wilkerson & Laina, 2018).
- Seventh-graders in a majority African American urban social studies classroom used online, interactive, historical census data GIS webmaps to investigate population changes over time in predominantly African American neighborhoods in their city. Students were required to describe patterns in African American movement and "White flight," show how the African American population changed in different parts of the city, and use prior knowledge to explain reasons people may have moved, including by making connections to segregation and the Great Migration. The process afforded students opportunities to narrate to an audience how they worked with data, animate the data representations by telling stories about the movement of the people represented by the data, incorporate data into extant U.S. and local narratives, and connect their own personal stories to the stories in the data (Radinsky, 2020; Radinsky et al., 2014).
- Racially diverse middle and high school youth participating in a free 3-week, 2-days-per-week summer workshop at an urban public library were asked to model their family "geobiographies," or personal family migration stories, with open large-scale datasets of socioeconomic data and data visualization tools available on the sites Social Explorer and Gapminder. The goal of the workshop was for each participant to explore the relationship between national and global migration trends and their family's migration story. They presented their stories on PowerPoint slides, using

the maps they constructed on the data websites to visualize their findings. In the process, students learned about numerous push-pull factors in past migrations, the complexity of family decisions to move, the relationship of their family to the larger society, and how to contribute their individual narratives to local public history (Kahn, 2020).

The subject of social studies provides the right context for teaching critical, humanistic data literacy. It provides an avenue for building the kind of data-literate population we so desperately need. As I have addressed throughout the book so far, teaching data literacy fits the mission of social studies, and so, not surprisingly, most state standards require some degree of data literacy instruction in social studies. Moreover, social studies resources are full of data and data visualizations, so students are encountering them on a regular basis anyway. Teaching data literacy can also support disciplinary literacy in social studies, including in history, where students can engage with primary source data and data visualizations related to content and themes that are common in the social studies curriculum. Fortunately, as I have argued in this chapter, social studies teachers already have specialized knowledge and skills that prepare them for teaching critical, humanistic data literacy. This knowledge includes having a deep understanding of the social and political concepts often addressed in the types of data and data visualizations we encounter in our everyday lives.

I recognize that many social studies teachers will still see teaching data literacy as a daunting task. Regardless of their knowledge of the content represented in data and data visualizations, social studies teachers often feel unprepared and ill equipped to teach about the data and data visualizations themselves, even if they know data literacy is important and want to teach it (Shreiner & Dykes, 2021). The next section of this book seeks to provide a remedy to this problem by addressing the ways that students can learn from data and specific kinds of data visualizations in social studies, and some common challenges they may face when working with data and data visualizations. The hope is to help teachers build their professional knowledge and equip them with some strategies to use in the classroom.

Part III

# HOW CAN DATA LITERACY SUPPORT STUDENT LEARNING IN SOCIAL STUDIES?

CHAPTER 6

# Timelines as Tools for Historical Thinking

Time is a mysterious and elusive concept. Time moves quickly and slowly. It passes and is gone. Time gets away from us, and it sneaks up on us. Time is not the same as change or movement, but it is nearly impossible to imagine it without change or movement. We measure time by the movement of the Earth, the passing of sands through an hourglass, the steady shifting of gears, the frequency of microwaves, and the decay of elements. We "keep track of time" with tools like clocks to mark the passing of the day, and calendars to mark the passing of the year; we just as readily keep time through our basic human needs and functions, such as "lunchtime" and "bedtime," or by shared experiences, such as "before COVID-19" and "after COVID-19." That is, while we try to objectively measure and keep time to function in our everyday lives, we also ascribe meaning to time and its passage through our subjective experiences, or our "sense of time" (Wilschut, 2012).

In social studies, we deal with the concept of *historical time*. Historical time is also both objective and subjective. It involves knowing when and in what order events happened, but it is also about developing a sense of the duration, intensity, and significance of events. When we study history, it is not enough to just know that something happened in the past. There are few great lessons or insights to be drawn from a simple chronicling of events. To make the past more concrete, accessible, and relatable, to give it meaning, an element of subjectivity must come into play. We subjectively select some events as being more worthy of our attention (and, yes, our time) than others, categorize them into segments of time such as the "Modern Era" or the "Middle Ages," and connect them into coherent narratives with explanatory power. These narratives help shape our understanding of the past and our sense of historical time (Wilschut, 2012). And through our sense of historical time, we can develop historical consciousness, recognizing links between past, present, and future, and seeing ourselves within the long reach of time (De Groot-Reuvekamp et al., 2014; Popa, 2022).

Timelines carry the potential to capture both the objective and subjective elements of historical time. They are temporal data visualizations that use labeled points, tick marks, or similar visual elements on a straight line or bar to locate people, events, or processes in time. Some timelines are scaled, with the distance between each tick mark representing a specific span of time, while others are not (Wills, 2012). In any case, timelines provide information about when and over what span of time an event occurred, as well as information about the sequence in which multiple events occurred. But timelines are limited in the people, events, and processes they can reflect. For each timeline we see, the timeline creator has chosen an idea or theme on which to focus and selected data points that they deem historically significant. They are essentially presenting their own interpretation of history, even if the temporal locations of the data points they have chosen are all factually and objectively correct.

Timelines have become such a common way of depicting events and the order in which they occurred that it is easy to lose sight of the fact that they too have a history. Like other data visualizations, the timelines we are accustomed to seeing today, and indeed the concept they manifest of history as a continuous, linear sequence, are the products of trial and error, and of intellectual, cultural, and social influences (Friendly & Wainer, 2021; Kracauer, 1966; Rüsen, 2007). Timelines are also relatively new. The first modern timeline is typically credited to English scientist and theologian Joseph Priestley, who, in 1765, published the *Chart of Biography* (see Figure 6.1), which shows dates along the top and bottom of the chart and uses lines within the main field to indicate when famous historical figures were born and died (Rosenberg & Grafton, 2013). Shortly thereafter, in 1769, Priestley published *A New Chart of History* (see Figure 6.2) showing complex societies and empires throughout time and using the same temporal scale as the *Chart of Biography* for easy comparisons across the timeline. His visualizations, which were innovative in assuming an analogy between time and measured space on a horizontal line, proved to be a turning point, usurping the multi-column table or matrix as the normative temporal visualization. Not only were Priestley's temporal visualizations effective at displaying dates and chronological relationships within one view, they also captured historical ideas, most notably the theory of historical progress and acceleration into the modern era (Rosenberg & Grafton, 2013).

Today, timelines are downright ordinary. Indeed, they are one of the most prevalent data visualizations in elementary, middle, and high school social studies textbooks, and they are regularly included in online social studies curricular materials (Finholm & Shreiner, 2022; Shreiner, 2018). Most U.S. state standards require students to learn about timelines in elementary social studies, often as early as kindergarten or first grade. However, these state requirements often do not extend beyond the early elementary grades (Shreiner, 2020). This lack of consistency in state standards is unfortunate. Many researchers (e.g., Blow et al., 2012; De Groot-Reuvekamp et al., 2018; Hodkinson & Smith, 2018; Stow & Haydn, 2012) agree that students should learn about historical time and timelines throughout school,

Timelines as Tools for Historical Thinking 99

**Figure 6.1. Joseph Priestley, *Specimen of a Chart of Biography*, 1765**

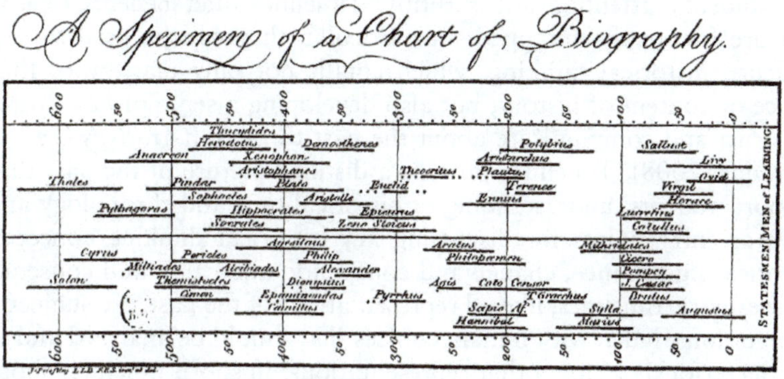

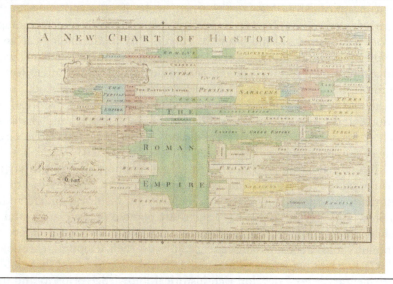

Source: https://commons.wikimedia.org/wiki/File:PriestleyChart.gif#/media/File:PriestleyChart.gif

**Figure 6.2. Joseph Priestley, *A New Chart of History*, 1769**

Source: https://commons.wikimedia.org/wiki/File:A_New_Chart_of_History_color.jpg#/media/File:A_New_Chart_of_History_color.jpg

largely because teachers cannot assume that students entering their classrooms have already developed understanding of historical time, even by the middle and high school grades. Too often, though, timelines are simply treated as embellishments or unquestioned facts to be shown but not analyzed or evaluated (Finholm & Shreiner, 2022; Shreiner, 2018).

Timelines should be viewed as pedagogical tools worthy of teachers' and students' attention and scrutiny. Timelines offer benefits to learning that are frequently untapped. In particular, they can be used to support students' historical thinking, which entails not only mastery of the substance or content of history, but also developing a sense of how historians construct and communicate about the past through narratives (Lee, 2005; Lévesque, 2008). Timelines provide a distilled picture of the past that can support students' understanding of historical time and chronology and can serve as entry points for discussing key historical thinking concepts like historical significance, change and continuity, and cause and consequence. Furthermore, timelines, like all representations of the past, are subjective interpretations, laden with human choices that should be analyzed and evaluated as seriously as any other representations. In short, timelines should be taught, and the sections that follow outline why and how.

## SUPPORTING CHRONOLOGICAL UNDERSTANDING

The concept of *chronology*, or the arrangement of dates and events in their order of occurrence, plays an important role in people's understanding of history and historical time (Stow & Haydn, 2012). Chronological understanding is multifaceted. It involves recognizing and operationalizing words and symbols used to measure and denote time (e.g., before, after, decades, centuries, BC, AD, BCE, and CE); developing a "sense of period," or being able to sequence and understand the characteristics of historical time periods; and being able to place individual events, people, and changes in their corresponding historical time periods (Blow et al., 2012; De Groot-Reuvekamp et al., 2014; Popa, 2022; Stow & Haydn, 2012).

To say that chronological understanding is important is not to say that it is the whole of historical understanding. And it is certainly not to suggest that memorization of dates is prerequisite for historical understanding. As Stow and Haydn (2012) have rightfully pointed out, we want students to understand complex relationships between events, including change and continuity and cause and consequence, not just their temporal, chronological relationships. Moreover, Barton and Levstik (1996) found that children in elementary school develop rich historical knowledge prior to and independently of their use of the chronological vocabulary and conventional historical periods associated with chronological understanding. A student's ability to sequence events may be solely because of his or her numerical understanding, not because of his or her historical knowledge. Chronological understanding is nonetheless helpful for reasoning about change and continuity over time, as well as about causal relationships, and thus plays a central role in historical thinking.

Timelines can serve as useful tools to support students' chronological understanding (De Groot-Reuvekamp et al., 2018; Hodkinson & Smith, 2018). A primary function of timelines is to visually display *sequence*, or the order in which people, events, or other phenomena existed or occurred. Sequence is encoded on timelines through *chronological conventions*—that is, generally accepted ways of communicating information such as ordering events and their corresponding dates from left to right or top to bottom to signify the temporal relationship of events, and using common chronological terminology to indicate quantities of time or the passage of time (Blow et al., 2012). Chronological terminology includes vocabulary like *decade* and *century*, as well as notations such as BCE for Before Common Era and CE for Common Era, or BC for Before Christ and AD for *Anno Domini*, which is Latin for "In the Year of the Lord." When dealing with time on a very large or universal scale, common terminology includes BP for Before Present or YA for Years Ago.

Using timelines as visual aids that can be pointed to or written on can be helpful for teaching chronological conventions and the proper sequencing of events. For example, teachers can point out on a timeline in which events are sequenced left to right that BCE or BC on the left come before CE or AD on the right, or that 20,000 years BP is counting years backward (right to left) from the current time and thus comes before 10,000 BP. Enhancing timelines with images can provide additional supports for learning, especially for young children who may be able to use their preexisting sense of historical time to sequence images but need help applying corresponding chronological vocabulary and notations (Barton & Levstik, 1996; Dawson, 2004; De Groot-Reuvekamp et al., 2018; Stow & Haydn, 2012). Students in elementary school and beyond can also learn about sequencing events based on chronological terminology through movement, creating a "human timeline" by taking assigned cards or posterboard with events labeled by chronological terminology and positioning themselves and their cards in the correct order (Dawson, 2004).

I note here that understanding sequence is not entirely dependent on knowing adult chronological terminology. Indeed, students can develop basic temporal distinctions such as "long ago" and "close to now" as early as kindergarten, and students tend to add more nuanced temporal categories, such as the "Era of the World Wars" or the "Middle Ages," as their knowledge increases (Barton & Levstik, 1996; De Groot-Reuvekamp et al., 2018; De Groot-Reuvekamp et al., 2017). However, as students move through school, they will have increasing demands placed on them to make sense of discipline-specific chronological terminology, whether reading it in textbooks or articles, or hearing it in lectures and videos. If they do not understand what the terms mean and how they denote the sequence in which events occurred, and if they do not have commonly defined terminology with which to communicate, their ability to reason chronologically will be hindered (Blow et al., 2012; Hodkinson & Smith, 2018).

At the same time, it is crucial to be aware that the ability to correctly sequence events or periods can mask students' confusions about important temporal concepts like *duration,* or how long a historical event or phenomenon lasted, and *concurrence,* or the overlapping of events in time. Students may be able to sequence the beginning of events, while remaining unaware that the duration of one event means that it overlapped with another. If students do not understand that events happened concurrently, they may have trouble reasoning about causal chains of events or determining how one event influenced another (Blow et al., 2012). Indeed, both duration and concurrence are integral to the understanding of historical time, and developing the historical consciousness to envision where one fits within the scope of time (De Groot-Reuvekamp et al., 2014; Popa, 2022).

Timelines can be helpful tools for teaching about duration and concurrence. Timelines can provide a quick reference point for the duration of events or developments by using "year X–year Y" as a label for temporal data on a line or by using color-coded bars that stretch across labeled years. Timelines can also communicate both duration and concurrence by using bars or other shapes in multiple layers, as displayed in Figure 6.2. Furthermore, timelines can help us grasp spans of time that are nearly impossible to imagine on our own. For example, you can probably easily imagine a minute, a day, or even a year, but not necessarily a century or millennium. For children and adolescents who have a less concrete frame of reference for time periods than adults, this can be particularly challenging. Timelines can help us visualize long spans of time or durations by equating them to visual measurements that are easier to grasp or by comparing spans of time that we can experience firsthand with those we cannot. For example, it is easier to imagine how long a century is when we equate one year with a millimeter and juxtapose one millimeter (equaling one year) with 100 millimeters (equaling one century). And it is easier to imagine how (relatively) briefly modern humans have primarily used farming instead of foraging for food if we equate 200,000 years of modern *Homo sapiens* to a 7-hour school day and illustrate to students that modern humans have been dependent on agriculture for only the last 25 minutes of that day.

Unfortunately, many published timelines do little to help students recognize duration and concurrence. In fact, they might promote misconceptions for students. For example, some timelines display only points indicating when events begin or end, even though historical phenomena can vary in duration from hours to hundreds or thousands of years and may therefore partially overlap with other events on the timeline. This can be confusing or misleading for students (Blow et al., 2012). Even when timelines try to show duration, they can do so poorly. Consider a timeline that uses bars to represent duration—are they using the same scale for all the bars? Say,

1 cm = 1 year? Are they helping students conceptualize the difference between a 1-year event and a 100-year event? Have they clearly represented an event that lasted as long as 200,000 years, like the time that *Homo sapiens* survived as foragers? Attending to ways that timescales are represented on timelines and discussing a timeline's particular representation of time with students may foster their understanding of duration, and thus their sense of historical time.

Understanding duration is important on its own, but it is also important because it is linked to the development of a *sense of period*, another aspect of chronological understanding (Dawson, 2004; De Groot-Reuvekamp et al., 2014). Historians use a device called *periodization* to divide the past into different periods, eras, or epochs based on patterns of change or trends that they have identified as significant. Periodization schemes are also reflected in national and state standards documents that divide content expectations according to historical periods or eras, and in textbooks or on social studies websites where such schemes often frame the organizational structure. Developing a sense of period entails learning about the years that demarcate historical periods and being able to name and sequence historical periods. More importantly, a sense of period means understanding features that characterize historical periods and why historians have demarcated them as they have (Blow et al., 2012; De Groot-Reuvekamp et al., 2014; Stow & Haydn, 2012).

Through words and, better yet, images, timelines can assist students in temporally locating defining social, cultural, economic, and political events or features of historical periods (Blow et al., 2012; De Groot-Reuvekamp et al., 2014). Consider the timeline Stearns (2011), a prominent world historian, included in his book *World History: The Basics*. He lists developments that characterize what he calls the "main periods in world history" (p. 19) and juxtaposes them against a larger framework for history that includes the Hunting and Gathering Age, Agricultural Age, and Industrial Age (see Figure 6.3). In the Early Modern Period (1450–1750), Stearns highlights the Columbian exchange, global trade, and the gunpowder empires, indicating their role as defining phenomena of the period. Moreover, he shows that the beginning of the period coincides with the "rise of science," which exists at the cusp of the Agricultural Age and Industrial Age. Because timelines like this offer a snapshot of multiple historical periods, students might use them to examine the events that have been included in a historical period and infer the period's characteristic patterns, trends, or changes, and compare them with other historical periods.

Many timelines that students see in school textbooks, usually at the beginning of units or chapters, show the periodization scheme used to frame the narrative within that section (Shreiner, 2018). It is useful to have students examine such timelines, not only when they begin studying the period, but also after studying the period when they have more knowledge

**Figure 6.3. P. N. Stearns, timeline of the three major historical ages and associated periods or events at other scales**

| | | | |
|---|---|---|---|
| **Hunting and Gathering Age** | | | Early Developments: 2.5 million BCE ff; emergence of the species, tool use, global migrations |
| | | | 1,500,000–790,000 BCE: use of fire |
| | | | 500,000 BCE: Hunting with spears |
| | | | 200,000 BCE: *Homo sapiens sapiens* |
| **Agricultural Age** | | | Neolithic Revolution (agriculture): 8000 BCE ff; rise of patriarchy |
| | **Bronze Age** | | 4000–1500 BCE |
| | | | Early Civilizations (river valley) – 3500 BCE–1000 BCE: organized states, more cities, writing |
| | **Iron Age** | | 1500 BCE ff |
| | **Spread of major religions** | | Classical period (1000 BCE–500 CE): expansion of key civilizations, integration of regional territory, more regular interregional trade |
| | | | Postclassical period (600–1450 CE): spread of civilizations, spread of world religions, rise of wider trans-regional trade networks, expansion of regional influences and imitations |
| | **Rise of Science** | | Early Modern Period (1450–1750): Columbian exchange, global trade, gunpowder empires |
| **Industrial age** | | | Long 19th Century (1750–1914): industrial revolution, rise of Western Power and imperialism, greater global economic inequality, emancipations |
| | | | Contemporary (1914 ff): rebalancing of world power/decolonization; population explosion; globalization and new global technologies; replacement of agricultural institutions like monarchy, aristocracy, patriarchy; new levels of collective violence |

*Source:* Copyright ©2011. From P. N. Stearns, *World History: The Basics*. Reproduced by permission of Taylor and Francis Group, LLC, a division of Informa PLC.

to draw upon. At that point, students might benefit from critically evaluating the choices on the timeline. Are there important events missing? Are events included that you would not have included? Students could even create their own timeline to outline the historical period and compare with the historian's or textbook writer's timeline. Moreover, several educators (e.g., Barton & Levstik, 1996; Dawson, 2004; Stow & Haydn, 2012; Wood, 1995) advocate the use of visual images in helping students develop a sense of period, as, for instance, having students sort images of clothing, transportation, technologies, and other cultural trappings into their respective periods. Indeed, timelines by themselves may be useless without instruction alongside images and relevant stories (Wilschut, 2012).

The concept of the historical period can be puzzling when students are confronted with slightly different frameworks that reflect historians' disagreements over periodization. Bentley (2000) called periodization "among the more elusive tasks of historical scholarship" (p. 376), so it is no surprise that different interpretations of historical periods emerge. For example, in the

*National Standards for History* (National Center for History in the Schools, 1996), the content standards for modern world history are periodized as Intensified Hemispheric Interactions, 1000–1500 CE; The Emergence of the First Global Age, 1450–1770; An Age of Revolutions, 1750–1914; A Half-Century of Crisis and Achievement, 1900–1945; and the 20th Century Since 1945. This periodization scheme is also reflected in state standards documents across the country. However, the College Board's (2020) Advanced Placement (AP) *World History: Modern* course uses slightly different periods, dated 1200–c.1450; 1450–c.1750; 1750–c.1900; and c.1900–present. Timelines could be used to alleviate rather than create confusion if teachers juxtapose displays of different periodization schemes to help students more readily see similarities and differences, and then discuss reasons for the discrepancies.

## UNDERSTANDING HISTORICAL NARRATIVE

Chronology and periodization have important roles in shaping history, but, as Tawney (2011) has argued, "Time, and the order of occurrences in time, is a clue, but no more" (p. 54). He continues, "[P]art of the historian's business is to substitute more significant connections for those of chronology." Put another way, the task of the historian is to take temporal phenomena occurring in sequence and "grasp them together" into a coherent whole—into historical narratives, stories, or accounts with a beginning, middle, and an end, and with some sort of theme that gives the past meaning (Carr, 1986; Lévesque, 2008). Timelines can be thought of as distillations of historical narratives into the key events that play a part in the story. Timelines often accompany fleshed-out historical narratives, highlighting the narrative's events and their chronological sequence. Timelines are extremely simplified because they represent stories about the past that are actually complex and meandering as linear and unidirectional (Rosenberg & Grafton, 2013). Yet they nonetheless offer ways to teach students about historical thinking concepts that play an important role in historical narratives.

*Historical significance* is one such concept of historical thinking. It is at the root of understanding what the discipline of history is, how it is constructed into narrative, and why some narratives differ in their emphases. For example, how often have you felt that you did not learn about something in history class that you should have learned? Some topics are not addressed in school history classes because the teacher, the writers of the curriculum the teacher is using, or the historians whose work is influencing the curriculum had different ideas than students, or, indeed, than other scholars do, about what is historically significant (Harris & Girard, 2014). As Lévesque (2008) has argued:

> Because they cannot study everything that happened in the past, historians are necessarily selective in their own investigations. Certain historical events, personages, dates, or phenomena are more important to their studies than others... History, to be meaningful, depends on selection and this, in turn, depends on establishing criteria of significance to select the more relevant and to dismiss the less relevant. (p. 42)

Historians make choices about historical significance based on at least five criteria: importance, profundity, quantity, durability, and relevance (Lévesque, 2008). First, historians might consider an event historically significant if it had *importance* to the people who lived at the time, regardless of whether their judgments about its importance were subsequently shown to be justified. An event's *profundity*, or how deeply it affected people, as well as the *quantity* of people it affected, are other criteria for historical significance. In addition, historians make arguments about historical significance based on the *durability* of an event, or how long it lasted. And finally, historians make judgments about historical significance based on an event's *relevance*, or relationship to current interests, arguing that people and events in the present are affected by the past, or that we can make sense of present developments by looking to the past.

However, nonhistorians, including students, may have their own reasons for ascribing significance to past events, and these reasons may differ from their teachers' reasons, or from textbook writers', curriculum writers' or historians' reasons. Their judgments about historical significance will no doubt affect their interest in and engagement with historical content (Seixas, 1994, 1997). For example, students may make judgments about historical significance based on their *intimate interests*—that is, whether an event or development is important to them personally or to their loved ones. They may also deem events historically significant if they have *symbolic significance*, providing some justification for a people's existence, importance, or power, or appealing to patriotic sentiments. Or events may hold significance if they provide lessons that can be applied to the present (Lévesque, 2008).

Creating and analyzing timelines offers opportunities for students to grapple with and operationalize the concept of historical significance. As with historical narratives, as soon as a person begins making a timeline, they make choices about what to include or to leave out. These choices can be influenced by background knowledge, identity, historical positionality, ideology, or many other factors (Peck, 2010; Salinas et al., 2012). Students could first explore the concept of historical significance and its dependence on individual choices by making timelines of their lives, limited to perhaps 8–10 events, and then discussing what guided their choices. Were their chosen events important turning points in their lives, events that shaped their identity, or events that help explain their lives today? Discussion of their choices can provide an entry point to discuss why historians make choices in historical narratives as well. In addition, students can make timelines of events they deem most important in local, national, or world history and compare their criteria for determining historical significance to historians' criteria.

Students might also critically analyze timelines in textbooks or other curriculum materials, considering the criteria used to determine which events should be included on the timeline, and addressing absences. For example, in their work with pre-service teachers, Salinas et al. (2012) show that allowing students to expand the classic narrative of the Civil Rights Movement that starts with Rosa Parks's protest—taking it back, for instance, to the anti-lynching work of Ida B. Wells-Barnett (see Chapter 4)—helps them see the enduring history of African Americans working together for freedom and justice. Such activities may help students better understand how history is constructed, provide teachers insight into how students' ideas about historical significance will or are affecting their engagement with historical content, and provide students with opportunities to counter dominant historical narratives (Salinas et al., 2012; Seixas, 1994).

Timelines also offer opportunities to help students understand the concept of *change and continuity over time*. As also discussed in Chapter 4, change and continuity are about seeing history as not merely a list of events, but a series of related developments that show transformations or shifts over time, or that signal stability over time. Recognition of such relationships is what has allowed historians to colligate, or group together, separate events into outwardly simple terms that actually denote complex or long-lasting processes—terms like *industrialization, urbanization,* or *revolution* (Lévesque, 2008). Teachers can use timelines to help students analyze relationships among events, and to think about how and why events on a timeline are related, what large-scale processes they might represent, or to what degree a sequence of events represents change or continuity.

Timelines can also serve as visual aids to help students connect change and continuity across multiple temporal frames, particularly in world history where questions about the proper chronological architecture have been a persistent preoccupation of scholars and educators (Bain, 2012; Bain & Harris, 2009; Dunn, 2000). Skillfully navigating and managing multiple levels in world history requires teachers and students to be, according to Bain (2012), both "parachutists" and "truffle-hunters" who can view the past at different levels, using "'big' pictures or frameworks to situate and connect a wide range of macro- and micro-historical details . . . located across multiple temporal and spatial scales" (p. 114).

In a similar vein, other scholars of history education (e.g., Howson, 2007; Shemilt, 2009) have emphasized the importance of students having "usable big pictures" of the past in which to situate the details of history, and some historians (e.g., Austen, 2010; Beezley, 2011; Bender, 2006; Gilbert & Reynolds, 2012; Ropp, 2010) have used a nested approach in the study

**Figure 6.4. The Big History Timeline**

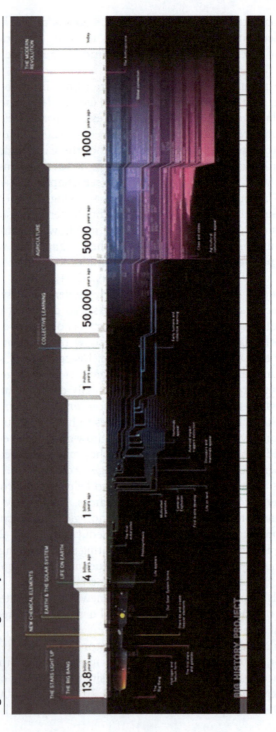

*Source:* OER Project, 2023.

of history, situating regional or national histories within the bigger picture of world history. Stearns (2000) has argued, for example, that fundamental transitions from hunting and gathering to agricultural society and from agricultural to industrial society led to shifts in economic organizations, political structures, human populations, family life, gender roles, and belief systems (see Figure 6.3). He writes, "This chronological typology must continue to shine through as the least controvertible chronological organization of the global human experience" (p. 369). Similarly, Bender (2006) has argued that using a nested approach is a way to help people better understand changes in national history, which "is connected with and partially shaped by what is beyond it" (p. 3). Timelines, or rather a timeline holding a nested series of smaller timelines (like the one used for the Big History curriculum, which examines history from the Big Bang to the present), can help students navigate different temporal scales of history, and make connections between the changes observed at each level, including within different spatial regions across time (see Figure 6.4).

Finally, teachers can also use timelines to teach about historical *causes and consequences* in history. For historians, causation is multifaceted, involving a combination of short-term factors like human motivation, actions, and proximal events, as well as long-term contextual factors like ideologies, institutions, cultures, and conditions (Chapman, 2003; Lee & Shemilt, 2009). Students' explanations for why things happened, on the other hand, are often monocausal—that is, they tend to think one event led to another, which led to another, and so on, in a monocausal chain (Lee & Shemilt, 2009). Uncritically viewing timelines, which are often represented as a simple line of events, might exacerbate such misconceptions. However, students can more closely analyze the relationships among events on timelines by using connecting lines and arrows to trace relationships, or categorizing causal relationships by labeling, color coding, or annotating events according to the type of cause: political, social, or economic; proximal or distal; short-term or long-term; trigger or catalyst; or more or less important (Chapman, 2003). Students can also build their own complex timelines that visually capture some of the nuances of cause and consequence in history, showing causal categories by using different symbols, colors, or timeline layers. These analytical exercises can then serve as scaffolding for students to build narratives or arguments about events or phenomena of the past.

In sum, timelines need not be static, boring representations of events in history meant only as factual references, or worse, mere embellishments. They can and should be seen as tools to support students' historical understanding. But time is only one dimension that plays a role in students' understanding of social studies topics. For students to truly grasp the nuances of past, present, and possible futures, they must also think about *space*. And so it is to maps, those most crucial tools for spatial reasoning, that we turn next.

CHAPTER 7

# Maps for Spatial Thinking and Problem Solving

To own your own home has been a quintessential part of the "American Dream" throughout much of modern U.S. history. It can be traced back to Thomas Jefferson's 18th-century idealization of the yeoman farmer as the foundation of the new republic, and it drove hundreds of thousands of 19th-century settlers to journey westward and stake a claim to land. Then, beginning in the early 20th century, the idea was shaped into U.S. government policy (Cannato, 2010). In the wake of the 1917 Bolshevik Revolution and the rise of the Communist party, the U.S. Department of Labor invested in a campaign dubbed "Own Your Own Home," which was designed to encourage people to buy single-family homes, thereby literally and figuratively investing in America and its ideals. In 1921, the campaign moved to the Commerce Department, where Secretary Herbert Hoover became the nation's leading promoter of homeownership throughout the decade. Even as the country sank into the Great Depression in the early 1930s, the Hoover administration continued to encourage homeownership, reasoning that home construction and sales would help boost the economy (Cannato, 2010; Rothstein, 2017). Yet by the time Franklin D. Roosevelt took office in 1933, the campaign for increased homeownership had gained little traction. Most mortgages required 50 percent down payments, interest-only payments, and 5- to 7-year repayment plans, and owning a house was prohibitively expensive for working- and middle-class families. Moreover, the Great Depression had left more people unable to afford homes and put current homeowners at risk of foreclosure (Rothstein, 2017).

To rescue property-owning families on the brink of default, the Roosevelt administration created the Home Owners' Loan Corporation (HOLC), which provided mortgages with low interest rates to middle-class families needing to refinance their homes (Rothstein, 2017). To help middle-class renters afford to buy a house for the first time, the administration created the Federal Housing Administration (FHA), which insured bank mortgages that covered 80 percent of purchase prices, had loan terms of 20 years, and were fully amortized, meaning that when borrowers made payments, they were paying part of the principal, or the original amount borrowed, as well as accrued interest (Mitchell & Franco, 2018; Rothstein, 2017). FHA-insured loans meant people could build equity over time and eventually fully own the home they had borrowed money to purchase. Together, the HOLC and FHA promised to relieve the housing crisis and boost the construction of houses, bring American families out of existing or potential financial ruin, and allow people to invest in property and build assets for themselves and their families over time.

Before refinancing a mortgage, though, HOLC wanted to ensure that a loan to the homeowners was low-risk—that borrowers could pay their loans back in full and that the home, which served as collateral, would maintain its value. They deployed examiners, often local real estate agents, to classify neighborhoods in major metropolitan areas according to their perceived level of lending risk. The HOLC then created "Residential Security" maps of cities with neighborhoods color-coded green for the "Best," blue for "Still Desirable," yellow for "Definitely Declining," and red for "Hazardous." Among the factors determining a neighborhood's grade were the age and condition of houses, transportation access, closeness to parks, proximity to polluting industries, and the economic class and employment status of residents (Mitchell & Franco, 2018; Rothstein, 2017). Another factor, though, was racial composition. Regardless of other factors, if Black people lived in a neighborhood, it was color-coded red, or "redlined," reducing the likelihood that homeowners living in the neighborhood would receive low-interest HOLC mortgages (Mitchell & Franco, 2018).

The HOLC maps most likely impacted FHA lending decisions as well (Mitchell & Franco, 2018). The FHA's *Underwriting Manual* advised that loans for properties in segregated, Whites-only neighborhoods were the lowest risk, and they consequently subsidized builders who were constructing Whites-only subdivisions with stipulations that no homes be sold to African Americans. Moreover, many of the appraisers who assessed the value of potential FHA-insured properties had also done so for the HOLC (Rothstein, 2017). As Rothstein has argued, regardless of the degree to which redlining affected lending practices, the HOLC maps "put the federal government on record as judging that African Americans, simply because of their race, were poor risks" (2017, p. 64).

The consequences of redlining continue to reverberate today. Such practices limited African Americans' access to capital and credit, thereby creating long-lasting effects on neighborhoods' economic health and household accumulation of wealth (Jan, 2018). Redlining also established segregation patterns that we continue to see in metropolitan areas. A recent study by researchers at the National Community Reinvestment Coalition (NCRC) used digitized maps to investigate the association between HOLC map classifications from the 1930s and the current economic and demographic status of neighborhoods at the city level. They found a significant statistical correlation between HOLC high-risk grading, majority-minority presence, and economic disadvantage in neighborhoods across the country (Mitchell & Franco, 2018).

Accompanying the report on the NCRC website are a series of interactive maps (https://dsl.richmond.edu/socialvulnerability), created in collaboration with the Digital Scholarship Lab. They allow viewers to compare the HOLC maps and maps divided into census tracts (small statistical subdivisions of a county or statistically equivalent entity) populated with the 2018 Social Vulnerability Index (SVI) scores issued by the U.S. Centers for Disease Control and Prevention. The SVI is used to assess a community's capacity to prepare for, respond to, and recover from human and natural disasters (Mitchell & Franco, 2018).

The insight these maps provide is disturbing. In Grand Rapids, Michigan, for example (see https://dsl.richmond.edu/socialvulnerability/map/#loc=11/42.952/-85.661&city=grand-rapids-mi, also pictured in Figure 7.1 ), the tract labeled D2 was labeled on the HOLC map as "Hazardous" and noted as having an "Infiltration of Italians & Negroes." Furthermore, "Type of Inhabitants" was listed as one of the "Detrimental Influences." In 2018, the tract had a 72.1% minority population, one of the highest in the city, and an abysmally high SVI score of .996.

Only with maps are we afforded such insight. Maps help us visualize a multitude of data. These include spatial data, or where an object is located or an event has occurred (e.g., the HOLC zones and census tracts in Figure 7.1); attributes or characteristics of an object, people, or events (e.g., HOLC

**Figure 7.1. "Not Even Past: Social Vulnerability and the Legacy of Redlining" map**

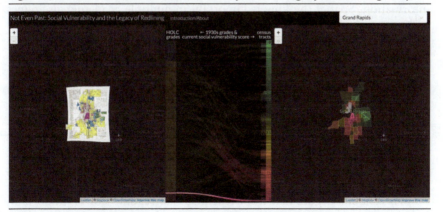

*Source:* The Digital Scholarship Lab and the National Community Reinvestment Coalition, 2023 (https://dsl.richmond.edu/socialvulnerability/map/#loc=11/42.952/-85.661&city=grand-rapids-mi)

ratings and demographic and economic data); and temporal data, or when events happened or attributes existed (e.g., the 1930s and 2018).

While maps often represent existing worldviews, as discussed in Chapter 4, they also shape our worldviews. They are external representations of space that influence our internal, or cognitive, representations of spaces, including those we can directly experience, such as our neighborhoods and towns, and those we will not or cannot directly experience, such as the entire Earth. Maps allow us to discover, visualize, and explore the ways that history has shaped the spaces we inhabit or experience in the present. They allow us to see large-scale movements, connections, relationships, or patterns normally outside of human perception. Maps can show both the world and parts of the world at the same time, making it possible for us to make comparisons or see how events in one part of the globe relate to the whole. Much more than just wayfinding devices or static records of where places are located, maps are powerful tools that enable us to make sense of and reason about the world around us, explore the spatial ramifications of political and social decision-making, and see ourselves as participants in the production of the spaces and places surrounding us (Mitchell & Elwood, 2012). In short, maps help us to think spatially.

*Spatial thinking* consists of the knowledge, skills, and habits of mind to use spatial concepts, visual representations of space, and processes of reasoning to solve problems and make decisions (National Research Council, 2005). The researchers behind NRDC maps on redlining (see Figure 7.1), for example, employed spatial thinking by recognizing that fair housing issues require a spatial perspective, drawing upon knowledge of census tract units to compare the redlined zones to current economic and demographic data, and utilizing computing tools to generate and visualize meaningful information. Spatial thinking is important in multiple academic disciplines and careers, and critical for democratic citizens charged with thinking about space-based policy issues ranging from border disputes and refugee crises, to zoning laws and urban development, to voter demographics and representation (Mitchell & Elwood, 2012; National Research Council, 2005).

But spatial thinking is also undertaught in school (National Research Council, 2005). This is certainly true in social studies, where maps are at once common and underutilized (Bednarz et al., 2006; Shreiner, 2018). Social studies textbooks are filled with maps, but they typically provide little support for teaching spatial thinking, and teachers sometimes do little more with maps than teach students map-reading skills (Bednarz et al., 2006; Jo & Bednarz, 2009).

This chapter argues that while teaching map-reading skills is important, it is insufficient. Social studies education should equip students to think *about* maps, think *with* maps, and think *through* maps. That is, students should learn about the visual elements of maps and the key spatial concepts embodied in them; use maps to support their understanding of social studies concepts and processes; and manipulate or create maps to think spatially and critically about real-world contexts and problems (Bednarz et al., 2006; Liben, 2001; National Research Council, 2005). In the sections that follow, I expound on the benefits and challenges of each one of these aspects of working with maps.

## THINKING ABOUT MAPS

Students will encounter maps on a regular basis in their social studies education. They are the most common type of data visualization included in both elementary and secondary social studies textbooks and in online lesson plans (Finholm & Shreiner, 2022; Shreiner, 2018). In textbooks, the maps students encounter become more complex and multilayered in higher grade levels (Shreiner, 2018). Students need opportunities to think about maps and how they work, including the spatial concepts that underpin them (Bednarz et al., 2006; Liben, 2001).

Although some adults are skeptical about young children's abilities to think and learn about maps, there is evidence that children as young as 3 years can already understand that maps help us navigate, indicating a readiness to learn that targeted instruction can build upon (Bednarz et al., 2006; Liben, 2001). As they begin thinking further about maps in school, elementary students should learn that all maps are partial representations of space that were created with intention, which, in turn, influences what details are included or left out of a map (Gregg & Leinhardt, 1994; Roberts & Brugar, 2014). They should recognize that maps are representations *of* something, but they are also representations *for* something (Liben, 2001). Some maps were created as wayfinding or navigational devices, while other maps were created to summarize and visualize vast amounts of data either to provide information or to serve as evidence or illustration. Exposing students to simple maps at an early age and talking about the visual elements of a map, including titles, keys, legends, and surrounding text, is one way to teach about a map's purpose (Bausmith & Leinhardt, 1998; Roberts & Brugar, 2014). Additionally, students should discuss what different maps show or how they might be used for different purposes (Wiegand, 2006).

Thinking about the purpose of a map also requires students to think about its source. This is crucial for understanding that all maps were created by individuals with specific intentions, which in turn, influenced how they represented space within a particular framework, what they included on the map, and what they left out. As illustrated by the primary source maps in Chapter 4, a cartographer's interpretations of space were influenced by information available at the time the map was made, as well as by their motivations and biases, and these influences should be identified and taken into account when using a map to visualize the spaces they represent (Gregg

& Leinhardt, 1994; Monmonier, 1996; National Research Council, 2005). The habit of identifying and evaluating a map's source will be particularly important when, in middle or high school, students engage more frequently with online political maps, and analyze historical maps that have been used as tools of colonization or discrimination, as propaganda or advertisement, or for military operations or defense (Monmonier, 1996).

Helping students think about maps also involves developing students' understanding of spatial concepts, including primitive spatial concepts that represent basic factual information about the world, such as *identity, location,* and *magnitude,* and simple spatial concepts that are derived from and represent relationships between primitives, such as *distance* and *direction* (Jo & Bednarz, 2009; Mohan et al., 2015). Students' understanding of primitive and simple spatial concepts can be supported with activities that encourage them to describe where objects are in the classroom or in their home, or to identify familiar places on large, simple tabletop or floor maps (Gersmehl, 2014; Mohan & Mohan, 2013; Wiegand, 2006). Young students can also talk about how some objects represented on a map are bigger than others, and may be quite interested in learning about extremes like the biggest or smallest country (Mohan & Mohan, 2013). They can engage with the concept of relative distance using terms such as *near, far,* or *next to,* and they can use a map to direct themselves through relatively small, familiar places like their school or to find hidden prizes or other specific objects (Wiegand, 2006). As early as 2nd grade, students can also measure distances on a map with guidance from a teacher or other adult, and some are ready to learn cardinal directions (Mohan et al., 2015).

Students' grasp of primitive and simple spatial concepts generally improves with age and instruction, such that by the end of elementary school, students are capable of and should be encouraged to locate both familiar and foreign places on a map (Mohan et al., 2015). By the time they reach the end of 4th grade, students can typically understand *coordinate systems* on a map and are therefore capable of using absolute location (i.e., coordinates of latitude and longitude). By 5th or 6th grade, students are often capable of determining distances and directions on a map, though they still need encouragement and prompting from their teachers to do so (Mohan et al., 2015).

Complex spatial concepts, including *scale, projection,* and *symbolization,* are also important for thinking about maps but are more difficult for students to understand. It is important for students to recognize that maps are objects themselves, while they also represent objects in real space (Liben, 2001). Because they are limited by the space that they inhabit as objects— that is, they are typically smaller than the spaces they represent—they cannot possibly show us everything about those spaces. This is where *scale,* or the distance on the map relative to the real distance, comes into play. The scale at which a map is drawn is usually indicated by a ratio, text, or a graphic—another visual element that students need to look for when reading maps (Monmonier, 1996). However, scale is highly abstract, making it conceptually difficult, even for students in middle school and beyond (Mohan & Mohan, 2013). Understanding scale requires proportional reasoning, measuring abilities, and recognition of the relationship between a map's scale and the amount of detail that can be shown (Gregg & Leinhardt, 1994; Roberts & Brugar, 2014).

Even the language associated with scale can be confusing. *Large-scale* maps are maps that represent a relatively small space, and *small-scale* maps represent a relatively large space. It can become doubly confusing for students when they look at the numbers telling viewers the scale at which the map is drawn. For example, if you had two maps, the first with a scale of 1:63,360, where 1 inch equals 1 mile, and the second with the scale of 1:12,672,000, where 1 inch equals 200 miles, which would be the larger-scale map? The first is the larger-scale map, but if you were using this scale to create a map on a standard sheet of paper, you could not possibly show more than 93.5 square miles—not quite big enough to draw a map of Milwaukee, Wisconsin. Using the second scale, however, you could draw the contiguous United States. It is easiest to see the reason behind this when you think of the ratios as fractions: 1 divided by 1 has a larger value (hence, a larger scale) than 1 divided by 200. Mathematically demonstrating this for students can help them better understand the language associated with scale and how scale affects what you can and cannot show on a map (Monmonier, 1996).

*Projection* is another complex, and thus challenging, spatial concept. Map projections, of which there are many (see Figure 7.2, which shows only a small fraction of projections), transform the curved three-dimensional surface of the Earth into a flat two-dimensional plane, and, in doing so, inevitably create some distortion. This distortion affects the shape of landmasses, distances, and directions (Monmonier, 1996; Wiegand, 2006). It is important to understand projection because it establishes the geometric correspondence between a map and reality (Anderson & Leinhardt, 2002). For example, the Mercator projection, devised by Gerard Mercator in 1569 for navigational purposes, famously makes Africa look much smaller and Greenland look much bigger than they are (see Figure 7.3). As Tim Marshall (2016) pointed out in his book *Prisoners of Geography*, "You could fit the United States, Greenland, India, China, Spain, France, German, and the UK into Africa and still have room for most of Eastern Europe" (p. 117). Mercator projections also distort distances between points. Because the distance to the poles has been exaggerated by stretching of the lines of latitude and longitude on a Mercator projection, a line of shortest distance between two points would also be stretched. Therefore, unless two locations are directly on a single line of longitude or on the equator, the shortest distance between them on the Mercator projection is a curved line.

**Figure 7.2. T. Jung, An image comparing map projections (detail from Map-Projections.net)**

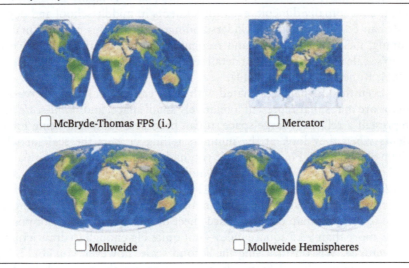

*Source:* Jung, n.d. https://map-projections.net/imglist.php

**Figure 7.3. N. R. Kaye, *Mercator projection versus the true size of countries***

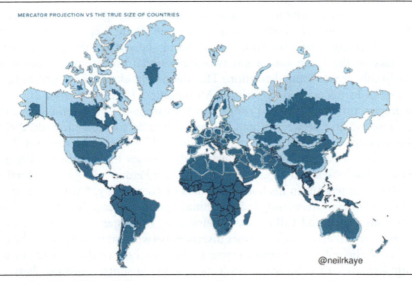

*Source:* Routley, 2021.

If students do not learn about projections and their distortions in schools, there is no reason to think that they will ever understand the concept, and they may walk away from school with misconceptions about the world. The consequences of such misconceptions became clear for President Gerald R. Ford in 1975, when his plane stopped in Fairbanks, Alaska, on a taxpayer-funded diplomatic trip to Japan. While there, President Ford gave a re-election campaign speech while his plane was refueled to continue the journey. Critics blasted him for taking a "detour" to Alaska and using taxpayer money to benefit his campaign. But it was not really a detour. Ford's critics wrongly used a straight line on a Mercator projection to determine the shortest distance for his trip. If they had used a curved line as they should have, they would have seen the stop was on the shortest route and was a necessary refueling stop (Liben, 2001).

Such misconceptions are common. People tend to reason within a map, instead of using a map as a tool to reason about the Earth's surface, and with little to no understanding of map projection, this reasoning is more likely to be misguided (Anderson & Leinhardt, 2002).

Symbolization is yet another important spatial concept that requires instruction. When considering maps as data visualizations this concept is particularly important because everything on a map is a symbol, whether it is qualitative data (related to differences in kind or existence of real world phenomena; e.g. the existence of abundant natural resources like lumber or fish in an area) or quantitative data (related to measurements or amounts of real-life phenomena; e.g., the number of people or the literacy rates in an area). To represent such data, map symbols can employ different geometries (i.e., points, lines, or area) and different visual variables (i.e., shape, size, hue, value) (Manson, 2017), and they can display varying degrees of visual correspondence to the real-world objects they represent.

For young elementary school students, abstract, unrelated symbolization can be difficult to understand (Mohan et al., 2015). In kindergarten and 1st grade, for example, students may expect the color, quantity, or size of an object on a map to match their attributes in the real world (e.g., a blue road on a map should be blue in real life, or one cow representing the cattle industry means there is one giant cow) (Bednarz et al., 2006; Mohan et al., 2015). Their thinking will likely transition sometime between 2nd and 4th grades, but they still need help in understanding that symbols are merely imperfect representations of reality. By the end of elementary school and beginning of middle school, however, students should be able to understand that symbols do not always look like their referents (Mohan et al., 2015). Students' transition to use of such abstract symbolization will be helpful as they begin to work with more complex maps, including choropleth maps, connection maps, and dot maps. However, misconceptions related to symbolization can continue through middle and high school, and beyond. For example, even adults mistakenly believe that uniform point symbols such as those used to indicate the location of cities cover the entire area of a city, or that graduated point symbols that differ in size according to variables like population indicate the size of the city (Bednarz et al., 2006).

Even as students learn about map elements and become practiced in using legends to make sense of the symbolization in a map, the symbol system in the legend should still be reviewed with students before any independent work—not least because definitions of the symbols may contain conceptual terminology that is challenging for students (Mohan & Mohan, 2013). Consider the map in Figure 7.4. It depicts the process of ratification of the U.S. Constitution and is one version of a thematic map commonly found in U.S. history textbooks. When teaching this map, a teacher would want to ensure that students are clear about all terminology it uses, including *ratification, majority support,* and *federal system,* and that they can appropriately use the legend to make sense of the information provided by the map, including knowing that smaller political units within each state have been shaded. Helping students think about this map and what it represents should also raise questions about the information provided and its accuracy.

**Figure 7.4. M. Gilbert, Map,** *The ratification of the Federal Constitution,* **1985**

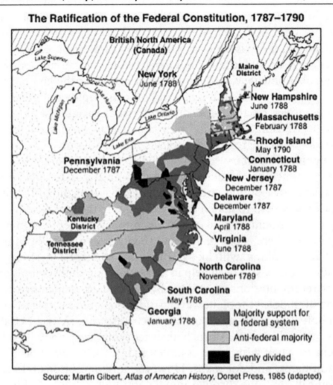

*Source:* http://apushcanvas.pbworks.com/f/1574395825/Ratify%20Map.jpg

Maps for Spatial Thinking and Problem Solving 121

**Figure 7.5. CSAC, Map of North Carolina's final vote for ratification, November 21, 1789**

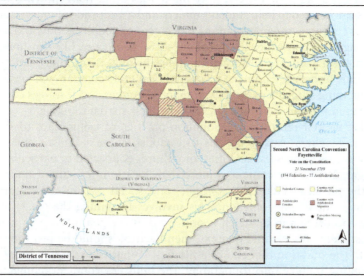

*Source:* Center for the Study of the American Constitution, 2023. https://csac.history.wisc.edu/wp-content/uploads/sites/281/2019/09/NC-Maps.pdf

For example, looking closely at North Carolina on the map, the color coding shows that anti-federalist votes, or those opposed to the ratification of the Constitution, dominated. How is it possible that ratification was supported? In fact, the map displays results of North Carolina's *first* vote on ratification, held in August 1789, in which the majority voted against ratification. A map that correctly represents North Carolina's part in the ratification process (see Figure 7.5) should show the results of the *second* vote, held in November, which would then correspond to the date on the label in Figure 7.4.

Like other data visualizations, maps can mislead just as easily as they can inform. Therefore, helping students think *about* maps and what they represent is important. Such instruction across grade levels can help ensure that students are equipped to fully comprehend and evaluate the information presented in maps. And by thinking about maps, students will be better prepared to think *with* maps.

## THINKING WITH MAPS

Most social studies teachers would agree that maps are useful (Brugar, 2017). Research suggests that many teachers use maps in social studies instruction primarily to show the location of places they are studying (Brugar, 2017).

Location is no doubt important when studying places in the past or present, but maps, in all their variety, have many uses other than showing location. Maps can be used to help students understand a multitude of important social studies concepts, ranging from the movement of people, goods, and ideas, to the long-term consequences of colonization. Moreover, like timelines, maps can support students' historical thinking, helping them understand change over time or how phenomena across political units compare with each other. Encouraging students to think *with* maps about key social studies concepts is another important element of developing their spatial thinking.

Let us first return to the common practice of using maps to show location. Teachers usually do this to establish context for students as they study events, processes, activities, or cultures connected to particular places (Brugar, 2017). But context is more than location; it is about understanding the physical, cultural, economic, and social circumstances surrounding an event or phenomenon. This involves imagining the *place* in which events occurred and in which people lived. If the goal of using a map is to help students understand context, then location should be just the starting point. The question that should follow is "What is/was it like here?," thus prompting inquiry into topography, the built environment, climate, flora, fauna, and humans who resided in the place that provides the setting for a topic under investigation (Gersmehl, 2014). Here again, maps, coupled with carefully formulated questions to encourage spatial thinking, can support students' understanding of place or setting (Jo et al., 2010) Indeed, according to Gersmehl (2014), asking questions is a critical geographical habit of mind, including questions like:

- How is/was this place connected to other places?
- How does this place fit within a spatial hierarchy? What larger places is this place inside? What smaller areas are inside of it? What impact does this hierarchy have on the places involved?
- How is/was this place similar to or different than another place?
- What other places are like this place?
- How is this place likely to affect or influence another place?
- How can this place be grouped with other places?
- How do things change when you move from this place to another, or from another place to this place?

Questions such as these, in addition to questions that ask students to use a map to draw inferences, will go further in helping students understand context than pointing out location alone.

Consider a lesson on the Transcontinental Railroad. A social studies teacher might include in instruction a map like the one in Figure 7.6, featured in a National Endowment for the Humanities EDSITEment (https://edsitement

Maps for Spatial Thinking and Problem Solving                                123

**Figure 7.6. Map of the Transcontinental Railroad Lines, 1880s**

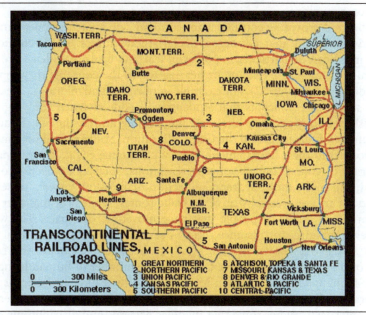

*Source:* "Map: Transcontinental Railroad Lines, 1880s," from *America: A Narrative History, Fourth Edition, Volume Two,* by George Brown Tindall and David E. Shi. Copyright © 1996, 1992, 1988, 1984 by W. W. Norton & Company, Inc. Used by permission of W. W. Norton & Company, Inc.

.neh.gov/) lesson, which shows railway lines ten years after the completion of the Transcontinental Railroad. The map is useful because it shows the extensiveness and connectedness of railways across the United States and could be used to prompt questions about the number and locations of different railway lines. However, beyond showing students the states the railways crossed, the map does little to help students understand what it was like in the places where the railways were built, which does little to help them understand how impactful the building of the Transcontinental Railroad was. The teacher might therefore supplement it with Google Earth images to help students visualize the terrain, and draw upon the concepts of distance and magnitude to help them understand the backbreaking labor undertaken by Chinese immigrants and other minority groups. In addition, a teacher could use a map showing the homelands of indigenous tribes who were displaced when the railways were built (see, for example, the Native Land Digital map at https://native-land.ca/), asking students to draw inferences about the impact of the railways on indigenous people and their way of life. Such maps, in addition to primary source documents and photographs, could provide a fuller and more accurate context for students than maps focused on showing location alone.

Beyond providing context, maps can also help students understand substantive concepts that cut across social studies topics. Research indicates that maps can be particularly powerful learning tools if students are asked to study them *before* reading or hearing about the concepts they represent (Verdi & Kulhavy, 2002). For example, movement and migration are important substantive concepts that students will address when studying topics in history and geography like early human migrations, the Silk Roads, the Columbian Exchange, and the Great Migration. Students will take in information about these human movements with language (e.g., by reading or in lectures) of course, but visual representations, such as connection or flow maps, can make them clearer. Connection maps allow viewers to see how locations are connected by travel or trade routes, while flow maps represent quantities of goods or people that have moved across space. The website Slavevoyages.org, for instance, utilizes several connection and flow maps, such as the one shown in Figure 7.7, to help people understand the extent of the trans-Atlantic slave trade and the number of human beings that were kidnapped from different locations and then unwillingly transported to strange places across the ocean, where they were forced into slavery.

Any social studies topic that involves patterns and distributions should be supplemented by a map as well. Connection, choropleth, and dot maps

**Figure 7.7. D. Eltis & D. Richardson, Flowmap showing volume and direction of the trans-Atlantic slave trade**

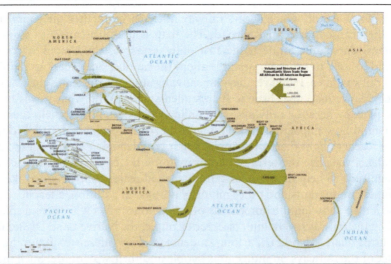

*Source*: Eltis and Richardson, 2022. https://www.slavevoyages.org/blog/volume-and-direction-trans-atlantic-slave-trade

Maps for Spatial Thinking and Problem Solving 125

can help students visualize spatial patterns and distributions that are otherwise difficult to imagine, such as settlement patterns, distribution of resources, and concentrations of trading connections. Just think about the significance of population growth and distribution in history and its influence on historical developments, including technological innovation, concentrations of power, and emergence of conflict. Maps that show population distribution help students grasp these ideas. In addition, interactive maps or sequences of static maps are useful for helping students understand how distributions or patterns have changed over time (Liben, 2001). For example, the website World Population History (https://worldpopulationhistory.org) uses an interactive, animated dot distribution map coupled with a timeline (with each dot representing one million people) to show, not only how quickly the population has grown throughout time, but where it has grown (see Figure 7.8).

Maps are also helpful for making comparisons, and for showing proportions or relationships. Choropleth maps, such as the one in Figure 7.9, display political units or other geographic divisions that are colored, shaded, or patterned in relation to data variables. These maps allow readers to easily compare data across geographic units. In social studies, you will often come across choropleth maps that display population data such as the share of people living in urban areas (see Figure 7.9), election data, literacy and poverty rates, and other variables. Proportional bubble or symbol maps use circles or other symbols to show data over a geographic space, with the size of the symbols proportional to their values within a dataset. In Figure 7.10, for example, the size of each symbol represents the number of 2016 presidential election votes cast within each state. Making comparisons with maps such

Figure 7.8. Dot distribution map showing distribution of the world population over time

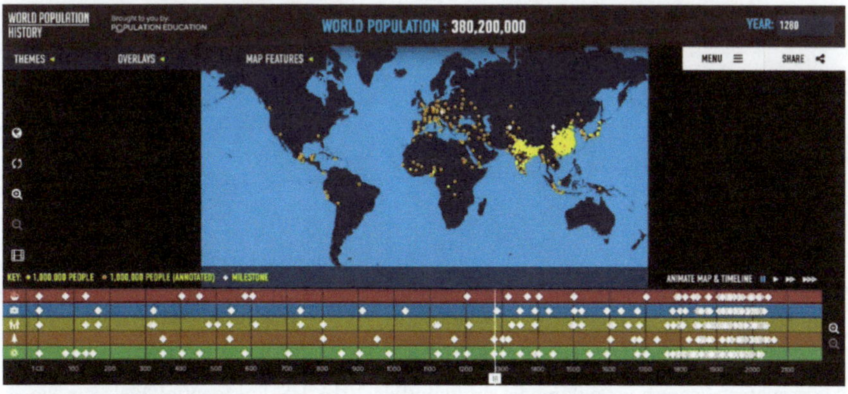

*Source:* Population Education, n.d.

**Figure 7.9. Choropleth map showing share of people living in urban areas, 2021**

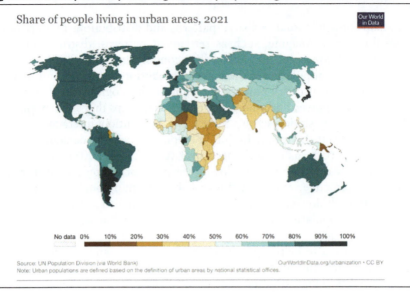

*Source:* Our World in Data, 2022. https://ourworldindata.org/grapher/share-of-population-urban

**Figure 7.10. Proportional symbol map that uses different-sized pie charts to compare the number of votes across states and display the proportion of votes that went to each candidate in each state**

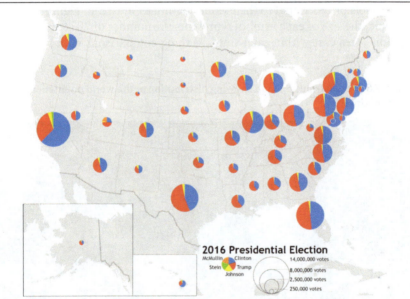

*Source:* https://commons.wikimedia.org/wiki/File:2016_US_Presidential_Election_Pie_Charts.png

as these helps prompt inquiry, leading students to ask questions about what accounts for observed differences.

Learning to think with maps is also important because maps are used so widely as evidence for arguments in history and other social studies disciplines (Shreiner, 2023; Shreiner & Zwart, 2020). For example, in their influential study *Salem Possessed: The Social Origins of Witchcraft,* Boyer and Nissenbaum (1976) made significant use of a map of Salem Village in 1692, which showed the locations of virtually all the households in Salem Village. Boyer and Nissenbaum plotted the locations of the accusers and the accused in the village, and used the map to argue that economic differences divided the village geographically into two conflicting groups—poorer agrarian householders with Puritan sensibilities on the western side of the village versus more prosperous and commercially minded neighbors in the eastern part of the village. According to Boyer and Nissenbaum, the clash led the frustrated westerners to respond by charging the easterners with witchcraft. *Salem Possessed* succeeded so well in explaining the witchcraft episode in Salem Village, partially through the use of the map as evidence, that it was not significantly challenged by another scholarly account until Norton's (2002) innovative and more comprehensive work, *In the Devil's Snare.* Anyone who struggles to think about and with maps would also struggle to fully understand—or critique—spatially based arguments like that of Boyer and Nissenbaum.

To fully realize the power of maps, though, students should be able to do with maps what scholars like Boyer and Nissenbaum did, or the NCRC did with maps like the one in Figure 7.1. That is, in addition to thinking *about* and *with* maps, students should learn to think *through* maps. They should be able to address political or social issues and solve political and social problems via maps and mapping technologies.

## THINKING THROUGH MAPS

Throughout history, maps have been tools of action. Too often, they have been used as tools in acts of empire, oppression, or, as was the case with the HOLC maps described earlier in this chapter, discrimination (Mitchell & Elwood, 2012; Williams, 2020). Yet maps have also served as tools for social and political justice and for activism in the interest of the public good (Williams, 2020). For example, in 1919, the National Association for the Advancement of Colored People (NAACP) included the map shown in Figure 7.11 in their report *Thirty Years of Lynching in the United States* to promote awareness of acts of terrorism against Black people in the United States. The seminal study provided information on the lynching of 3,224 African Americans between 1889 and 1918. By using a map, the NAACP study contributors were able to highlight important regional differences in

**Figure 7.11. NAACP, *Lynchings of Last Ten Years, 1909–1918***

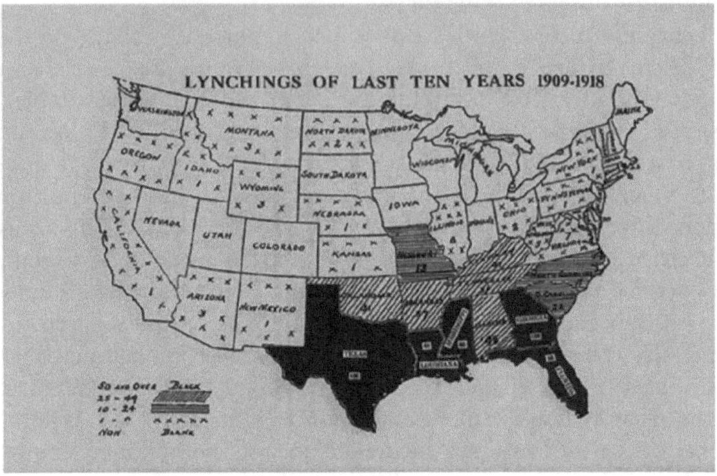

*Source:* National Association for the Advancement of Colored People, 1919.

the incidents of lynching, and, through the anti-lynching campaign that accompanied the report, persuade several Southern newspapers to take an anti-lynching stance (National Association for the Advancement of Colored People, 2023). In 2017, the Equal Justice Initiative (EJI) published an expanded report on lynching, accompanied by an interactive map, with the intention of raising awareness about the history of lynching in the United States by providing information upon which citizens and citizen groups could act within and for their local communities (Equal Justice Initiative, 2017). Their interactive choropleth map (see Figure 7.12) allows viewers to see county-level numbers of reported lynchings across the country and, in some cases, read about the individuals who were murdered.

Both the NAACP and EJI maps represent instances of people thinking through maps. They are the products of people compiling data related to an issue that concerns them and their communities, and using resources available to them to create spatial visualizations that reveal patterns upon which they can act, even if their action is simply raising public awareness. Through maps, particularly counter-maps, participatory GIS, and other web-based mapping tools, students too can think critically about social and political problems (Bednarz et al., 2006; Mitchell & Franco, 2018). They can make visible people and places that other maps make invisible, reveal spatial patterns that contribute to inequities, and uncover how people have lost or won space through political struggle. And students can think through maps with others, sharing knowledge, discussing issues and how different people are affected by them, and collaborating to take action for the common good

Maps for Spatial Thinking and Problem Solving

**Figure 7.12. EJI, Lynching in America interactive map**

*Source:* Equal Justice Initiative, 2017. https://lynchinginamerica.eji.org/explore

(Mitchell & Franco, 2018). Thinking through maps in social studies allows students to move beyond simply learning content, fulfilling the democratic goals of social studies by planning for and taking informed action to address local, regional, national, and global problems (National Council for the Social Studies, 2013).

One way for students to think through maps is to explore and use the multitude of "counter-maps" that are now available online to investigate social and political issues surrounding them. As Mitchell and Franco (2018) have argued, counter-maps begin with the premise that "maps are never neutral or objective but rather reflect existing and/or previous power relations in society" (p. 136). They are cartographic efforts to reveal the experiences and knowledge of marginalized groups in society (Bliss, 2019). Several examples of counter-maps have already been shared in this chapter, including the Digital Scholarship and NCRC map (see Figure 7.1), the NativeLands map (https://native-land.ca/ ), the NAACP map (see Figure 7.11), and the EJI map (see Figure 7.12). But there are more. The project American Panorama (https://dsl.richmond.edu/panorama/), for example, has created maps on Native American land dispossession brought about by the Homestead Act, redlining in the United States, family displacements brought about by urban renewal, the forced migration of enslaved people, and many more. Another project, Million Dollar Blocks (https://chicagosmilliondollarblocks.com/), maps the social cost of incarceration, the concentration of incarcerated individuals from certain urban neighborhoods, and the flows of people from city to prison to city.

Students can use GIS and other mapping tools to create their own maps that will help them think through and discuss social and political issues. The project Mapping Self in Society (https://www.maselfs.org/), for example, has created open-source software and a series of lessons that has students collecting and visualizing their physical movement data over thematic maps to explore relations between people and the social and cultural life of neighborhoods and communities. As will be discussed in Chapter 12, there are also multiple online mapping tools, including Google Earth and Maps, that allow students to spatially represent data in answer to a social or political issue in their community.

Data collection need not be extensive or overly sophisticated for students to address social and political issues. They can collect data through observations of infrastructure, goods and services, and green space in their communities, or by finding information in newspapers, brochures, or websites. Take a topic like the condition of the roads in the local community. Road conditions can have huge financial and safety consequences for people in a community, and it is an issue that can affect people daily. Students can discuss and rate the conditions of roads around where they live, play, access goods and services, and go to school, and then use a tool like Google Maps to visualize the roads they have rated (see Figure 7.13). They can then use the maps they produce to discuss the overall condition of roads in their community and create an action plan to ensure that the roads they travel on are safe and well-maintained.

And finally, students can use maps to simulate spatially based political decision-making. Using and creating maps to learn about the implications

**Figure 7.13. An example of a Google Maps project that students can create to display collected data about their communities**

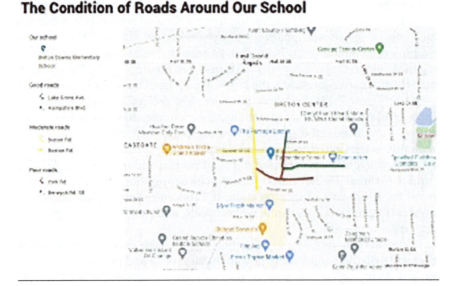

of the political process of redistricting is just one example. Redistricting is the process of drawing lines of districts from which public officials are elected in each state and can have far-reaching consequences for political action at both the state and federal levels. When done fairly, district lines reflect population shifts and racial diversity. But states can also draw district lines to give one party political advantage—a process known as partisan gerrymandering. Politically partisan gerrymandering techniques often target minority populations as a proxy for political parties (Bullock, 2021; Keena et al., 2021). Techniques include dividing the minority population among districts so they have a majority in none, packing districts in order to minimize the number of seats one party can win within a state, stacking very large districts that have multiple representatives so that minority interests can be voted down by the majority of representatives, or redrawing district lines to separate incumbents from the people they have represented. While many states' district lines are drawn by the state legislature—giving the dominant party an advantage—other states have appointed independent commissions to redraw district lines (Bullock, 2021). Several existing organizations, including Politico (https://www.politico.com/interactives/2022/congressional-redistricting-maps-by-state-and-district/), FiveThirtyEight (https://projects.fivethirtyeight.com/redistricting-2022-maps/), and Princeton (https://gerrymander.princeton.edu/) allow viewers to track redistricting across the country, and FiveThirtyEight's Gerrymandering Project (https://fivethirtyeight.com/tag/the-gerrymandering-project/) allows students to see how district lines change according to different political goals. In addition, there are some websites, such as DistrictR (https://districtr.org/) and DistrictBuilder (https://www.districtbuilder.org/) that allow students to draw district lines, which lend themselves to projects that equip students to think about redistricting and its consequences through maps.

Maps play an important role in all our lives. They help us visualize and find our way through the spaces that surround us. However, students should learn that maps are more than just wayfinding devices. They are used as evidence for arguments and as decision-making tools, and they can make people and their experiences visible or invisible. Therefore, understanding maps is not just about gaining practical life skills for navigation; it is about gaining agency and power. As this chapter has argued, students must think about maps, with maps, and through maps to use them effectively. And social studies may be the only place that students are afforded opportunities and instruction to do so.

CHAPTER 8

# Telling Stories With Graphs and Charts

Hans Rosling (1948–2017) made graphs cool. Born in Uppsala, Sweden, and educated as a physician and statistician, Rosling was the cofounder and chairman of the Gapminder Foundation, dedicated to identifying "systematic misconceptions about important global trends and proportions" and using "reliable data to develop easy to understand teaching materials to rid people of their misconceptions" (Gapminder, n.d.). As he wrote in his posthumously published book, *Factfulness*, Rosling was particularly interested in hunting and dispelling "mega misconceptions" about the world and its development (Rosling et al., 2018, p. 21). Through Gapminder, Rosling developed the Trendalyzer, an information visualization software for animation of statistics. A self-described "edutainer," Rosling did a total of 10 highly popular TED Talks, using his signature animated bubble plot (see Figure 8.1) as well as props ranging from apples to IKEA storage bins to highlight global development issues. As of this writing, his first and most renowned TED talk, "The Best Stats You've Ever Seen" from 2006 (https://www.ted.com/talks/hans_rosling_the_best_stats_you_ve_ever_seen), has had over 15 million views.

One reason Rosling's talks worked was because he was a good teacher. Consider, for example, a BBC video broadcast in 2010 (https://youtu.be/jbkSRLYSojo?si=9Dit2Sg6i17Zdv5f), in which Rosling narrated an animated version of one of his most famous graphs, a bubble plot showing the relationships between countries' incomes and life expectancies (see Figures 8.1 and 8.2, showing a static version of the same graphs with 2022 data). Adding his singular wit and flair to tell a 4-minute story of 200 countries over 200 years, Rosling argued that income and health are related, such that people in richer countries live longer. He began the video by calling viewers' attention to the important visual features of the graph—the axis and labels for health, the axis and labels for wealth, the time variable underpinning the animation, and the multicolored bubbles whose size corresponds to population. Next, he helped viewers connect different elements of the graph to understand the information the graph conveys: "I'm going to show you the world 200 years ago," he said, and pointing first to the lower

**Figure 8.1. A static version of Gapminder's animated bubble plot of income and life expectancy in 1800**

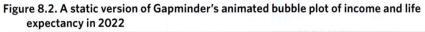

*Source:* Gapminder, 2023.

**Figure 8.2. A static version of Gapminder's animated bubble plot of income and life expectancy in 2022**

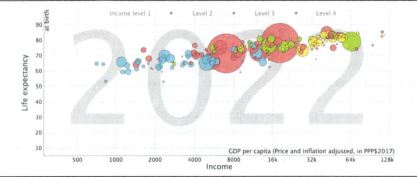

*Source:* Gapminder, 2023.

left corner of the graph and then to the upper right corner (see Figure 8.1), he continued, "Down here is poor and sick. Up here is rich and healthy." Then, with a flourish, he exclaimed, "Now I start the world!" And as the animated bubbles bounced up and across the graph, Rosling told his story, discussing elements that are both apparent and not so apparent in the graph. For instance, he peppered in historical contextual information like the effects of the industrial revolution on countries' wealth, and the impact of the 1918 flu pandemic and World War I on life expectancies. He also paused at the end to disaggregate some of the data, calling attention to huge income and health disparities among regions within countries, before finally offering his conclusions, including his projections for the future. He ended:

And yet, despite the enormous disparities today, we have seen 200 years of remarkable progress. That huge historical gap between the West and the rest is now closing. We have become an entirely new converging world. And I see a clear trend into the future. With age, trade, green technology, and peace, it's fully possible that everyone can make it to the healthy wealthy corner.

Rosling employed effective instructional techniques to help his audience make sense of and draw inferences from his graphs. First, through the steps described above, he employed a hierarchical approach to graph comprehension, signaling key visual elements of the graph, making logical connections between the elements, and providing context to explain changes in the data. At the same time, Rosling used cognitive aids to support graph comprehension, using words and gestures to signal viewers about where to focus attention, and priming them for learning by addressing relevant graphical conventions and content (Mautone & Mayer, 2007).

In this chapter, I argue that these same techniques can and should be incorporated into social studies instruction with graphs. The techniques not only scaffold skills for graph comprehension, but also offer the potential to unlock *data-based stories* about past and present. Indeed, part of Rosling's appeal was that he was good at telling stories with graphs. And for our purposes, the stories that graphs can tell—or, more accurately, that can be told with graphs—are germane to social studies. Graphs can help us tell stories about causes and consequences, similarities, differences, and change over time. Graphs distill huge amounts of data, clarify complex variations and relationships, and allow comparisons of peoples, places, and conditions that would otherwise require years of study (Braun, 2022). Writing in 1878, French polymath Étienne-Jules Marey argued that graphs "capture nuances which would escape other means of observation" and "when it comes to exposing the course of a phenomenon, the graphic method translates phases with a clarity that language does not have" (Hattab & Andrews, 2022, p. 29). We use graphs in the disciplines of social studies and as citizens to help us understand some of the biggest, most complex process and problems that confront us: population changes, agricultural production, economic conditions, the prevalence of poverty, the spread of disease, climate change, the impact of war, and the severity of inequalities (Braun, 2022; Shreiner, 2023).

While just about anyone can show and even create graphs, not everyone can tell good stories with graphs. Not everyone can put into words what graphs show us. But social studies teachers can—and they should. Researchers (e.g., Barton & Levstik, 2004; Combs & Beach, 1994; Levstik & Barton, 2015; Wertsch, 2004, 2008) have long argued that stories and storytelling are powerful tools for learning in social studies, and more recently, there has been growing interest in the power of storytelling for learning from and making decisions with graphs (e.g., Denbo, 2015; Lee et al.,

2015; Pfannkuch et al., 2010; Segel & Heer, 2010). I contend that storytelling is already part of what many social studies teachers do, and there is good reason to employ these skills with graphs as well, not least because social studies teachers are especially equipped to help students see beyond the data in the way that Rosling so aptly demonstrated. That is, they are equipped to teach about economic, political, and social concepts represented in graphs, to share the experiences and firsthand accounts of individuals quantified in the graph, and to dig deeply into the historical and geographic context for the data. Even with concepts that might fall within the purview of science, such as climate and disease, social studies teachers are still equipped to talk about their social, economic, and political ramifications.

However, as I will also argue, social studies teachers should not be the only ones interpreting and telling stories with graphs. Students should have these opportunities as well. This can include developing counternarratives about graphs that misrepresent their personal experiences, reinforce stereotypes, or omit them altogether (Navarro & Howard, 2017; Salinas et al., 2012; Shreiner & Martell, 2022). Only by engaging in such activities with the data in graphs can students develop the critical, humanistic data literacy skills. Only then can they counter dominant narratives that do not match their experiences and observations, or that spread misconceptions— just like Hans Rosling did.

## MAKING SENSE OF GRAPHS AND CHARTS

Graphs are a type of data visualization that use spatial characteristics like height, length, size, area, or angle to represent or encode quantities (Friel et al., 2001; Quadri & Rosen, 2022). As discussed in Chapter 1, some scholars (e.g., Börner et al., 2016; Börner & Polley, 2014; Knaflic, 2015) distinguish between *graphs* (visualizations with a well-defined reference system, like bar and line graphs) and *charts* (visualizations with no inherent reference system, such as pie charts). For simplicity's sake, I use the term "graph" in this chapter to encompass both the former and the latter.

All graphs (including charts) share three structural components: some sort of a *framework* to provide information about the data and measurements being used (e.g., axes, grids, polar coordinates); *specifiers* or geometries (e.g., bars, lines, wedges); and *labels* to indicate what the graph is about, the measurement being made, or the data to which the measurement applies (e.g., title, legends, axis labels) (Friel et al., 2001). Beyond these components, though, graphs come in a variety of forms and serve a variety of functions. There are bar graphs, stacked bar graphs, line graphs, multiline graphs, area graphs, stacked area graphs, pie charts, population pyramids, scatterplots, bubble plots, word clouds, tree maps, and more. Different graphs fulfill different functions. Some graphs, like bar graphs and population pyramids, are useful for making comparisons, while others, such as area and line graphs, are helpful for tracing changes or trends over time. Pie charts and stacked bar graphs show us proportions, and scatterplots show us distributions. Most graphs serve multiple functions. The bubble plots that Rosling used, for example, are good for showing distributions, correlations, and change over time, and for making comparisons (Ribecca, 2016).

Students will encounter a variety of graphs in their social studies classes. Almost all states require that students study or use graphs or charts in social studies at some point in their school career, and social studies textbooks are full of them (Shreiner, 2018, 2020). Indeed, the variety of graphs students will encounter as they move through school is dizzying. In using a typical elementary social studies textbook, for example, students are likely to see pie charts, bar graphs, line graphs, and even the occasional area graph as they read, but as soon as middle school, they will encounter these same types of graphs, plus more complex ones such as population pyramids, stacked bar graphs, and those that combine different kinds of graphs into one display (Shreiner, 2018). And this does not even include the variety of graphs students will see in other social studies resources or online, many of which are multilayered, complex, and interactive (Myers, 2022).

Although people often assume graphs make information easier to understand, interpreting graphs is actually quite effortful, and it is common for both children and adults to make systematic errors when trying to interpret them (Shah & Hoeffner, 2002). As scholars from fields such as mathematics education and psychology (e.g., Friel et al., 2001; Maltese et al., 2015; Shah & Hoeffner, 2002; Shah et al., 1999) have argued, reading graphs is a complex process with several mediating factors. First, viewers must identify important visual encodings of a graph such as the shape and direction of a line, the size and distribution of bubbles, or the numbers and units on an axis (Friel et al., 2001; Shah & Hoeffner, 2002; Shah et al., 1999). Looking at the stacked area graph in Figure 8.3, viewers would need to take note of the title and source in the display, the numbers and labels on the $y$-axis, the years on the $x$-axis, and the colors and labels separating the segments of the area graphed.

Second, readers must map between visual encodings to determine their conceptual relations, such as recognizing that an upward sloping line indicates an accelerating relationship (Friel et al., 2001; Shah & Hoeffner, 2002). The recognition of conceptual relations is dependent on a viewer's perception of visual encodings, but it is also largely dependent upon the viewer's experience with and knowledge of different graphs (Friel et al., 2001; Shah et al., 1999). Viewers looking at Figure 8.3 would need to recognize that the upward slope indicates an increase, and that stacked area graphs like this show total quantity and the portions that make up the whole—in this case, the different kinds of fossil fuels.

Finally, a viewer must be able to make associations between the graphic representation and its context, including a conceptual understanding of the referents that are being quantified (Friel et al., 2001; Shah & Hoeffner, 2002). In Figure 8.3, viewers would need to recognize that gas, oil, and coal are different types of fossil fuels, which we use as energy sources, and that the graph is quantifying fossil fuel usage over time, measured in terawatt-hours, which are a unit of energy used for expressing the amount of produced energy.

All told, three factors seem to mediate an individual's comprehension of a graph: Understanding common graphical conventions, understanding the conventions of the specific representation with which they are working, and understanding the context or content related to the data in the representation (Friel et al., 2001; Maltese et al., 2015; Shah & Hoeffner, 2002). A breakdown in any one of these factors can hinder comprehension. In addition, comprehension can be affected by how closely data in a graph are related to the task a student is trying to carry out. For example, Strobel et al. (2018) found in a controlled experiment with university students that task-irrelevant details in graphs increased error rates and processing time. They also found that, as measured by participants' rating of task difficulty, irrelevant data points and series also increased the cognitive load of the task, making it more effortful and difficult to complete.

**Figure 8.3. Stacked area graph of global fossil fuel consumption**

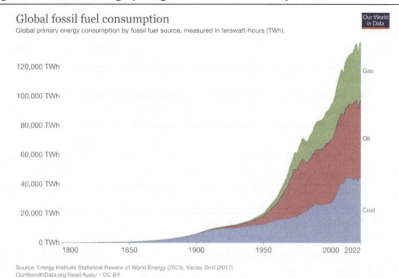

*Source:* Ritchie et al., n.d. https://ourworldindata.org/grapher/global-fossil-fuel-consumption

In short, students need instruction in how to read graphs, and they need such instruction in social studies. First and foremost, context and content matter when trying to make sense of graphs, which is why experts recommend that students study graphs in the subject areas for which they are relevant (Shah & Hoeffner, 2002). Second, there is little doubt that whether a teacher intentionally introduces students to graphs or not, students will encounter graphs in their social studies classes beginning in elementary school and that these graphs will only become more frequent and more complex as students move through school (Shreiner, 2018). If students have not acquired basic understanding of different graphical forms and conventions in elementary and middle school, they will have trouble making sense of the more complex graphs they encounter in their high school social studies classes, where other cognitive demands will also increase. Moreover, if students do not acquire basic graph comprehension skills, they will be ill-equipped to use graphs to draw inferences and make decisions—that is, they will struggle to do the kind of work that is required of them in the social studies disciplines and in civic life.

## TEACHING GRAPH COMPREHENSION

If reading graphs is complex, multistepped, and effortful, how can we teach students to make sense of them? How can we prepare them for the important work of using graphs to make decisions and communicate? Nearly 40 years ago, Curcio (1987) suggested that graph comprehension could be summed up as a hierarchy of skills he called *reading the data*, *reading between the data*, and *reading beyond the data*. Since then, other scholars (e.g., Cohen & Cohen, 2021; Friel et al., 2001; Galesic & Garcia-Retamero, 2011; Harsh et al., 2019; Sharma, 2006) have expounded upon the hierarchy and used it as a framework for instruction and assessment of graph comprehension in a variety of contexts. *Reading the data* is an elementary skill about taking stock of visual elements of a graph and lifting the most obvious information from data points or specifiers. This level of comprehension might be compared to decoding and defining the words that constitute a sentence. Reading the data is important not only because it provides a foundation for higher-level graph comprehension, but also because it can help students spot manipulations of data, such as irregular intervals on the horizontal axis of a graph (Friel et al., 2001).

*Reading between the data* is an intermediate skill about making connections across data points to interpret the information presented in the graph. It entails making comparisons or recognizing trends or patterns. This might be viewed as similar to making connections between words in a sentence in order to comprehend the message it conveys (Friel et al., 2001). Signaling, or making graph elements or relevant relationships between graph elements more salient, is one technique to help students read the data and read between the data (Mautone & Mayer, 2007). Signaling includes using cues such as arrows or shading to highlight features or segments of a graph, or presenting a graph in a layered fashion, showing key components one by one until the whole graph is visible (see also Chapter 11). Another technique is priming students' knowledge of both the graphical conventions relevant to the graph under study and the subject matter content of the graph, including vocabulary words and contextual information. Students' prior knowledge matters and should be addressed in order to support meaning-making and to avoid misconceptions (Mautone & Mayer, 2007).

However, reading the data and reading between the data do not go far enough, particularly within a social studies context. Just as we want people to think deeply about the implications of a sentence or argument, we want students to connect, extend, and question what they read in a graph. We want them to move beyond what is displayed in the graph to critically evaluate it and think about its broader meaning or implications. This is *reading beyond the data,* and involves steps like connecting the concepts addressed in a graph (e.g., gross domestic product, immigration, poverty) to prior knowledge or other sources of information, considering the implications of a graph for individuals or for the future, and questioning the categories, groupings, or omissions in a graph (Friel et al., 2001).

Unfortunately, as extant research (e.g., Galesic & Garcia-Retamero, 2011; Harsh et al., 2019; Maltese et al., 2015; Sharma, 2006) suggests, a significant number of people across age groups have trouble even reading between the data and this affects their ability to read beyond the data and to use graphs effectively as evidence or for decision-making. Clearly, social studies teachers cannot count on students learning everything they need to know about graphs in math or science classes. And because content knowledge is also a critical component of graph comprehension, learning to make sense of graphs that deal with economic, political, and social issues belongs in the social studies classroom.

Researchers (e.g., Cohen & Cohen, 2021; Friel et al., 2001; Galesic & Garcia-Retamero, 2011; Harsh et al., 2019) who have implemented the graph comprehension framework described above emphasize the use of carefully crafted questions to support comprehension. Cohen and Cohen (2021) found, for example, that introducing students to questions guided by the framework and then asking them to pose similar questions to their classmates resulted in improvements in students' graph comprehension skills. The questions that one can ask within the framework provide opportunities to teach substantive concepts that students encounter in social studies, as well as to discuss connections to broader issues.

To illustrate all these strategies, let us imagine a scenario in which students are studying the human use of fossil fuels, whether from a historical perspective, as part of a geography unit on humans and the environment, or

Telling Stories With Graphs and Charts                                    141

as a public policy issue in a civics class. The teacher presents them with the graph in Figure 8.4, perhaps even in conjunction with the graph in Figure 8.3, both found on the website Our World in Data (https://ourworldindata.org/), to help them compare fossil fuel consumption across the globe. In line with research on signaling and the importance of addressing background knowledge (Mautone & Mayer, 2007) the teacher provides a handout or slide with definitions of *fossil fuels, consumption, per capita,* and *kilowatt-hours* prior to introducing the graph. In addition, the teacher provides a map of the geographic regions displayed in the graph. Then the teacher poses questions focused on reading the data, including:

- Where does this data come from? What is the source?
- What, in your own words, does fossil fuel consumption per capita mean?
- How many kWh of fossil fuels did the average person in the United States consume in 2022? In about 1970?
- How many kWh of fossil fuels did the average person in China consume in 2022? In about 1970?

All these questions are designed primarily to ensure that students are paying attention to all the important visual elements and that they have the

**Figure 8.4. Multiline graph of fossil fuel consumption per capita**

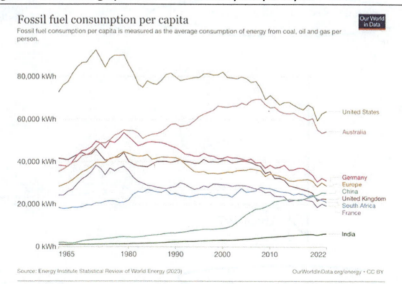

*Source:* Ritchie et al., n.d. https://ourworldindata.org/grapher/fossil-fuels-per-capita ?time=1965..2022

necessary background knowledge to decode language and labels in the graph, and to help them extract basic information. Following this line of questioning, the teacher discusses responses with students, using signaling techniques such as circling or arrows to focus attention on important visual features (see Figure 8.5).

Then, moving to the next level of comprehension, the teacher poses questions to encourage students to read *between* the data, including:

- Which country's per capita fuel consumption has been the highest since 1965?
- Which countries' per capita fuel consumption have risen over the last 20 years? Which country's consumption has risen the fastest?
- How much more does the highest consuming country consume than the lowest consuming country?

These questions are aimed at helping students make comparisons among data points or helping them understand how the data have changed over time. They are also about information extraction, but at a higher and more holistic level.

Figure 8.5. Multiline graph of fossil fuel consumption per capita overlaid with examples of signaling cues to help students read the data

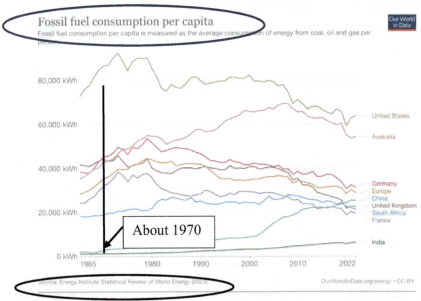

*Source*: Ritchie et al., n.d.

# Telling Stories With Graphs and Charts

Once students can read the graph and understand the information it conveys, the teacher asks questions or encourages students to ask their own questions focused on reading beyond the data. Questions at this level include:

- Is the source for the data reliable? What makes you think so?
- How might the graph look different if we were quantifying total fossil fuel consumption instead of per capita fossil fuel consumption?
- Why is per capita consumption so high in the United States and Australia?
- What accounts for China's per capita increase over the last 20 years?
- What different types of fossil fuels are countries using the most? For example, what would we see if we isolated coal, the greatest producer of $CO_2$? What energy sources besides fossil fuels are countries using?

The idea is for students to draw inferences and connect to the larger issues of fossil fuel consumption, $CO_2$ emissions, and climate change. Students might also pose their own questions to each other, or develop questions with plans to research historical context, dig into country-level data, or search for related graphs.

Although the ability to answer specific questions about graphs is useful and important for graph comprehension, it is also important for students to learn to communicate with data, infusing data with meaning for themselves and others (Pfannkuch et al., 2010; Rodríguez et al., 2015). For example, while reading between and beyond the data might teach students to draw inferences from and think about the broader implications of a graph in Figure 8.4, it does not necessarily prepare them to do something with the knowledge they have acquired. Therefore, the teacher might go a step further by having students compose and deliver a speech on a policy recommendation or create an action plan for reducing their own fossil fuel usage. In doing so, students would need to transform the information from the graph into words that persuade or inform. As will be discussed in the next section, telling data-based stories is a promising way to uncover broader meaning from data and use it to communicate with others. Merging graph comprehension with storytelling techniques helps students unlock the communicative and evidentiary power of graphs and provides ways for students to challenge and personalize graphs.

## TELLING STORIES WITH GRAPHS

Telling stories with graphs is certainly not new. As discussed in Chapter 2, Florence Nightingale was an early innovator in telling stories with graphs when she used a rose diagram (now widely known as a Nightingale rose chart) to help tell a story about the impact of hospital sanitation measures on the mortality rates of soldiers in the Crimean War. Then there is, of course, Rosling, who was described as a master storyteller with graphs. Another storytelling innovator, Neil Halloran, has created several "data documentaries" with graphs, including his award-winning 2015 film *The Fallen of World War II* (http://www.fallen.io/ww2/). Historians too have been combining narrative techniques with graphs for decades (Denbo, 2015; Shreiner, 2023). In one of the early issues of *The American Historical Review*, historian Ulrich B. Phillips, who was considered a trailblazer in the social and economic study of slavery (albeit a controversial one), used multiple graphs (for one example, see Figure 8.6) to tell a story about how the system of slavery in the United States concentrated wealth "within the hands of a single economic class and within certain distinctive geographical areas" (Phillips, 1906, p. 798).

**Figure 8.6. An example of a graph in a 1906 issue of *The American Historical Review***

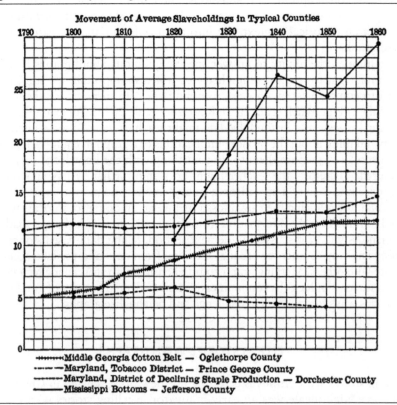

*Source:* Phillips, 1906.

Graphs carry elements of story because they help us understand relationships, similarities, differences, and change over time—all concepts that play a central role in social studies as well. Yet, to my knowledge, telling stories with graphs is not a regular part of social studies classrooms. Even the idea of transforming the expository texts commonly used in a social studies classroom into narratives that will better engage students is relatively new (Martino, 2019; Sanchez & Mills, 2005). Still, it has long been argued that narrative can be a powerful pedagogical device in social studies (Arias-Ferrer et al., 2019; Combs & Beach, 1994; Levstik & Barton, 2015; Shreiner, 2014; VanSledright & Brophy, 1992). Stories have a privileged status in learning and memory (Willingham, 2004, 2009), and they are an integral part of the social studies disciplines, particularly in history (Combs & Beach, 1994; Levstik & Barton, 2015; Willingham, 2004). Storytelling helps students remember details and offers opportunities for them to add their own personal anecdotes.

Scholars and educators in STEM fields (e.g., Chick et al., 2005; Meyer, 2007; Pfannkuch et al., 2010; Sinclair et al., 2009) have explored storytelling as a powerful way for people to work with and understand graphs. One suggested strategy from math education has been to help students understand how graphs can tell a story by giving them a written story and asking them to try to graph it, and then giving them a graph and asking them to write a story from it. In one online mathematics lesson, for example, students are asked to use the following story to create a graph with time on the horizontal axis and speed on the vertical axis:

> My dad drove me to school this morning. We drove for 10 minutes at about 30 mph. We then slowed to half that speed for the next 5 minutes before stopping at a stoplight for 2 minutes. We got on the highway and drove at 50 mph for 20 minutes. We got off the highway and stopped at a stop sign for a minute. We drove at 20 mph for another 10 minutes, then turned into the school's driveway and stopped. (WGBH Educational Foundation, 2021)

Then the lesson asks students to write their own story from a graph they or their teacher has created about everyday topics like bake sales, weekly weather, or money earned over the summer (WGBH Educational Foundation, 2021).

Such "graph stories" activities could be easily modified for social studies lessons. Let us consider a lesson on industrialization. Students throughout the United States learn about the period of industrialization in world history coursework, typically in high school. Part of their studies most likely includes references to the various prime movers, or devices that convert energy into work, that were improved upon or invented during the Industrial Revolution, such as water wheels, steam engines, and steam turbines. Students would likely learn about how these prime movers set humans on course to harness more and more energy throughout the industrialized era and contributed to a greater demand for fossil fuels. During their studies, students might see a graph like the one in Figure 8.7. It shows how the quantities of power humans could harness for work from prime movers changed over time while also showing them how prime movers overlapped, with early prime movers persisting even as new technologies were adopted. The graph reminds students that, even as technologies emerged and improved, we still depended on humans and domesticated animals for work, and that industrialization also involved efforts to harness their energies more efficiently.

Smil (2018) used this graph to tell a story about how humans' ability to harness energy has transitioned over time, and suggests that such a story can help people understand the evolution of material culture, economic growth and development and social organization in world history. The graph could

**Figure 8.7. V. Smil, graph of prime mover power capacity**

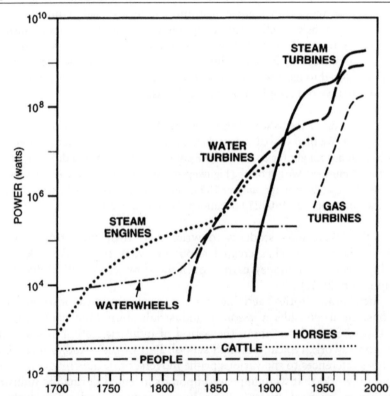

*Source:* Smil, 2018.

be useful in helping students understand this story as well, but it could also easily overwhelm them. Without support, students might infer from it only that power capacities have changed over time, missing the nuances in the story of industrial era power the graph presents.

Imagine a scenario, though, in which students learn how to tell a story with the graph. The teacher supports this endeavor by first having students transform the following story into a graph:

> Throughout history, there have emerged "peak prime movers." Prime movers are machines that can convert energy into work. Peak prime movers are the animate beings or machines that have the highest power capacity, measure in watts, at a particular point in history. Before the domestication of animals, humans had to depend on their own power to do work. In other words, humans themselves were the peak prime movers for a portion of our history. Sustained human labor produces roughly 100 watts of power. However, peak prime mover capacities moved to about 300 watts for draft animals sometime during the third millennium B.C. The line rose to about 5000 watts in horizontal waterwheels by the end of the first millennium A.D. By 1800 it had reached at least 100,000 watts in steam engines, and it was 100 times higher in water turbines a century later. Finally, it has reached a plateau at more than 1 billion watts in the largest steam turbines after 1960. (adapted from Smil, 2018, pp. 228–229)

Using this story, students might produce a graph something like the one shown in Figure 8.8, with a logarithmic scale for power on the vertical axis and time (not to scale) on the horizontal axis.

The idea here is that creating a graph from a preexisting narrative can help students see the connection between graph and story, priming them to create their own graph story. Imagine, then, that students return to the graph in Figure 8.7, now with a clearer recognition of connections between graphs and narrative. The teacher asks them to craft a story from the graph, perhaps getting them started with a prompt such as:

> Throughout history, humans have been dependent on themselves and other humans as a source of power. Humans convert energy they get from plant and animal food sources into energy for labor. However, humans' power capacity is limited. Even the strongest humans can only generate about 100 watts of power through sustained labor. This is why the domestication of draft animals was an important steppingstone in our ability to harness power and use if for work. Cattle, for example, . . .

This last phrase cues students to turn to the information provided in the graph to continue the story, before moving on to include horses, waterwheels, steam engines and more.

**Figure 8.8. Graph produced from a story of increasing peak prime mover power**

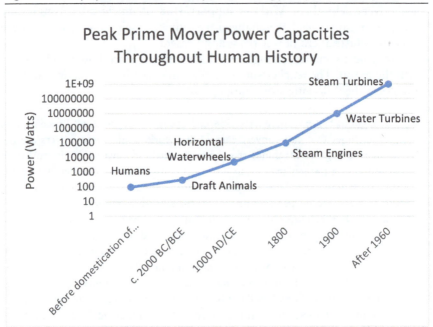

Imagine further that students tell a story using not only the information provided in the graph, but also data from their own knowledge and experiences. With respect to Figure 8.7, they might discuss energy exerted by themselves or their family members working in the present day. Or they might supplement the story with information on present-day inanimate prime movers and fuel sources with which they are familiar or that are fundamental to their local economy and their daily lives. Developing the skills they need for projects like these can empower students to challenge graphs they encounter inside and outside of school. When they see graphs related to health and mortality, jobs and income, and safety and security, they can supplement stories about trends and patterns in the aggregate with personal stories, experiences, and concerns that counter or problematize assumptions or stereotypes the graphs might perpetuate.

Telling stories with graphs invites students to engage with graphs in a deeper and more meaningful way than activities aimed primarily at information extraction. It asks them to transform graphical representations into everyday language in a way that will support their efforts to communicate with data, while also teaching them about different ways that graphs can be interpreted.

However, students must also learn about the human choices inherent in the data themselves. Not only has someone made choices about how to visualize the data, they have also made choices about what data to include and exclude. Moreover, someone has made choices about how and from whom to gather the data in the first place. To understand the nature of data, and the factors that can influence data choices, we must help students work with the data themselves. As will be argued in the next chapter, we must allow students to produce, wrangle, and visualize data on their own.

CHAPTER 9

# Producing, Wrangling, and Transforming Data
## Pathways to Critical, Humanistic Data Literacy

When Georgia Lupi and Stefanie Posavec first met at a conference in 2014, they had no idea they had so much in common. They were the same age, grew up as only children, and were each living in a country that was foreign to them. They also both loved data. Over the course of a year, they wrote postcards to each other every week, getting to know each other by visualizing data from their daily lives according to mutually agreed-upon themes. Sharing the belief that "everything can be mapped, measured, and counted," Lupi and Posavec (2016, p. xi) visualized everyday observations or experiences ranging from how often they said thank you, to the content of their closets, to the doors they passed through (see Figure 9.1). In the process, they learned not only about each other, but also that data can be used "to become more humane and to connect with ourselves and others at a deeper level" (Lupi & Posavec, 2016, p. xi).

Figure 9.1. G. Lupi and S. Posavec, postcards made for the Dear Data project

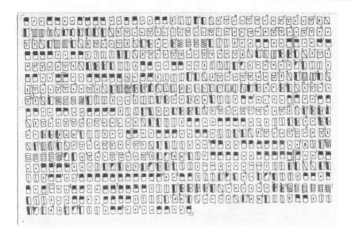

### Figure 9.1. (Continued)

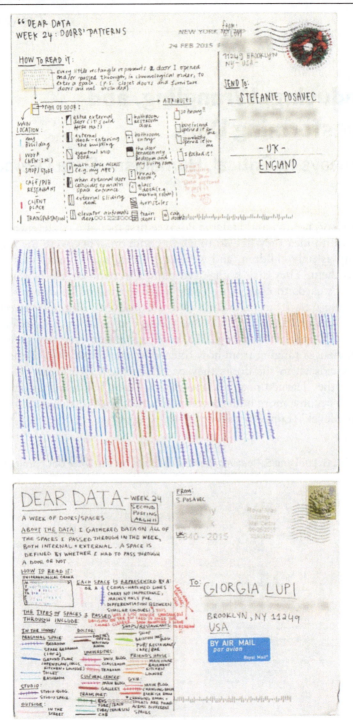

*Source:* Lupi & Posavec, n.d. http://www.dear-data.com/all

Lupi and Posavec's journey to express themselves through data in what they dubbed their "Dear Data" project is an inspiring tale. All of us, including students, are most often consumers of data, interpreting and trying to draw insight and meaning from the visual representations of data others have produced. These data visualizations usually aggregate, filter, and simplify individual human characteristics and experiences with the intent of helping us better and more efficiently understand the very complex individuals from whom or about whom the data were produced. However, through their highly individualized, slow, analog, data-producing and -visualizing process, Lupi and Posavec celebrate "the infinitesimal, incomplete, imperfect, yet marvelously human details through which we wrest meaning out of the incomprehensible vastness of all possible experiences that is life" (Popova, 2016, p. vii). In one respect, by going through the exercise of defining what to measure and how to measure it, attempting to capture and quantify both the nebulous and complex, and visualizing it for others to understand, Lupi and Posavec have peeled back the curtain on data work. Yet in another respect, they have added an element to their data work that is too often missing. As Sorapure and Fauni (2020) have argued, the approach to data in the Dear Data project "facilitates a particularly humanistic approach to data literacy, incorporating interpretation at all levels and focusing on data as a human-made artifact to be examined rather than a value-free given to be accepted" (n.p.).

Producing, organizing, and visualizing data as Lupi and Posavec have, whether through analog or digital means, is an important part of acquiring critical, humanistic data literacy. In previous chapters, most of what has been discussed with respect to critical, humanistic data literacy has been about comprehension and critique of existing data visualizations, with only brief mentions here and there of giving students opportunities to create their own data visualizations. But critical, humanistic data literacy should include *participation* with data. Students should learn to harness the power of data so that they can use them in civic and political spheres for issues that matter most to them and, in the process, they should learn the true nature of data—that is, that data do not simply exist, but are produced by human action and through human intent (Noushad et al., 2022).

This chapter argues that students can come to understand the nature of data through foundational data work—that is, by working with data before it is organized and visually represented as timelines, maps, or graphs. There are three separate but interconnected components of fundamental data work that I discuss in this chapter—producing data, wrangling data, and, finally, visualizing data. In the following sections, I define each component and provide a few examples of what it might look like to apply the component in a social studies classroom with the goal of participating with data. As has been the case in other chapters, my goal here is not to provide an exhaustive list of activities. Rather, I wish only to plant a seed with suggestions that will inspire data work, and with it, critical, humanistic data literacy instruction in the social studies classroom.

**PRODUCING DATA**

Students produce data every day. Indeed, the amount of data that humans generate overall is mind-boggling. It is estimated that 2.5 quintillion bytes of data are created every day and that the number is likely to only increase with time (CIO Bulletin, 2022). We generate data when we conduct searches on the internet, use social media, make purchases on Amazon, order food, use a fitness app, send money over Venmo, and so much more (Marr, 2018). Unfortunately, though, we have little knowledge of or control over how our data is being used. Giving students power over the data they produce, as well as the power to produce data for purposes that interest them, is both an important and enlightening experience, and a way for students to enhance their economic, geographic, or political understanding.

I borrow the term *producing data* from Hardy, Dixon, and Hsi (2020) who argue that educators should "stop talking about data collection, as if data were sand dollars waiting on a beach" (p. 124). Instead, they should acknowledge with students that data are (1) created, captured, and packaged in pursuit of human goals and purposes; (2) part facts, part artifacts of human-designed tools, surveys, protocols, or other devices; and (3) theory-laden, in that humans must determine how they will design said tools, surveys, protocols, or other devices to reduce complex people and phenomena into useful forms of data (Hardy et al., 2020).

Some computer application developers and educators have already produced tools that allow students to generate and use their own data. For example, there are multiple age-differentiated computer and phone applications to help students learn about personal finance, develop budgets, and track spending. In addition, projects like Mapping Self in Society (see Chapter 7) take advantage of applications that track our movements in space, asking students to use such a tool to capture and visualize their own physical movement over thematic maps, and allowing them to explore relations between themselves and the social and cultural life of the neighborhoods and communities that surround them. However, while such computer applications are innovative and beneficial, they still limit students' choices. The application developers have already determined what data will be collected, under what categories to organize data, and, essentially, what questions need answering. Therefore, students miss out on opportunities to engage in fundamental data production work.

Data production work can begin as early as elementary school. Although producing data is not explicitly required in the *C3 Framework*, the document does recommend that even early elementary students learn about measurable phenomena, such as weather or goods and services (National Council for the Social Studies, 2013). Students can quantify or measure such phenomena with the help of their teachers, and in doing so engage in the data work of identifying, categorizing, and recording information. If they are tracking weather, for example, they would have to determine how to identify weather conditions (e.g., sunny, cloudy, or rainy; hot, cold, or mild) and what to do when weather does not fit neatly into their predetermined categories. In addition, elementary students who, per recommendations of the *C3 Framework*, explore and try to explain local issues (e.g., the need for better roads, improving playground equipment at local parks, etc.), can produce data by conducting opinion polls at their school to assess classmates' viewpoints. Again, this requires that they identify what information they are interested in, how they will question people, and how to record and organize the information.

By middle and high school, students' data production work can be more involved. Journell, Beeson, and Ayers (2015) have argued convincingly that critically evaluating polling data and conducting polls are important skills for developing students' political thinking and understanding. Opinion polls are highly influential in public policy debates, but few students understand how they work and what information can be reasonably gleaned from them. Students can better understand the polling process if they develop their own questions and discuss how one phrasing may be more biased than another, administer polls within their school or community while acknowledging the limitations of different sampling procedures, and then organize and analyze the data accordingly (Wilson & Journell, 2011).

## WRANGLING DATA

*Wrangling data* is another important aspect of data work. Data wrangling is the process of iterative data exploration and transformation with the goal of making data useful for analysis. This process includes identifying data that is relevant to a particular question, interest, or investigation, and putting them into a usable form in spreadsheets, statistics packages, or visualization tools (Kahn & Jiang, 2021; Kandel et al., 2011). From a critical, humanistic perspective, data wrangling also allows people to take data from large, community or open datasets and make them useful for themselves or other people or organizations (Shapiro et al., 2022). For example, Kahn and Jiang (2021) designed activities for middle and high school students to explore datasets from the websites Gapminder and Social Explorer and connect them to their families' personal migration stories. They found that students approached these large complex datasets by exploring data indicators that represented populations matching some of their demographic characteristics or focused on geographic areas they lived and knew. As students processed and modeled this data, they aligned their personal or family experiences to the trends they found in the data, either using the large-scale data to make sense of their histories or challenging it as unrepresentative of their histories.

Data wrangling can be a time-consuming and messy process, but in a social studies context, it also gives students access to social, political, and historical information that might otherwise remain hidden to them. Historical data, for example, despite being more widely digitally available, are not always digitized in a format that is easy to analyze. For example, the U.S. Census Bureau (1909) published information on early colonial censuses conducted before the official federal census of 1790, but the information is not aggregated. Rather, it is scattered across tables with different dates, reflecting the decentralized nature of early census-taking in the American colonies (see examples from two colonies in Figures 9.2 and 9.3). Students could wrangle such data into a usable form to determine what questions it can answer and how they can compare or aggregate data from across the colonies. Would it make sense to look across the tables and create a new table with all the years recorded, but a mismatch of data available in particular years? Or would it be better to simply make comparisons during years for which there is common data, such as in 1761 and 1790? In the process of making these decisions, students will not only learn about challenges of taking data from different sources, but also about similarities and differences in administration of government across the colonies, problems created by lack of a central government, and the role of population estimates in the discipline of history.

**Figure 9.2. Population data for New Hampshire from administered colonial censuses and experts' estimates**

| YEAR. | Estimates. | Censuses. |
|---|---|---|
| 1641 | 1,000 | |
| 1675 | 4,000 | |
| 1680 | 6,000 | |
| 1716 | 9,000 | |
| 1721 | 9,500 | |
| 1732 | 12,500 | |
| 1742 | 24,000 | |
| 1749 | 30,000 | |
| 1761 | 38,000 | |
| 1767 | | 52,70 |
| 1773 | | 72,09 |
| 1775 | | 81,00 |
| 1786 | | 95,7£ |
| 1790 | | 141,8९ |

*Source:* U.S. Census Bureau, 1909. https://www.census.gov/history/pdf/colonialboston pops.pdf

**Figure 9.3. Population data for Maryland from administered colonial censuses and experts' estimates**

| YEAR. | Estimates. | Censuses. |
|---|---|---|
| 1660 | 8,000 | |
| 1676 | 16,000 | |
| 1701 | 32,258 | |
| 1712 | | 46,073 |
| 1715 | 50,200 | |
| 1719 | 61,000 | |
| 1748 | 130,000 | |
| 1755 | | 153,564 |
| 1761 | 164,007 | |
| 1775 | 200,000 | |
| 1783 | 254,000 | |
| 1790 | | 319,728 |

*Source:* U.S. Census Bureau, 1909. https://www.census.gov/history/pdf/colonialbostonpops.pdf

Of course, students can also make decisions about how to organize data like the colonial population estimates in Figures 9.2 and 9.3 based on how they would like to visualize it. In fact, their decisions about organizing data might very well start with their goals for visualization. In any case, visualizing data is another important part of data work, primarily because it helps students understand the full complement of choices that go into data work.

## VISUALIZING DATA

Students should have opportunities to *visualize data* through both analog and computer-aided processes, experimenting with different forms so that they can better understand how different representations of data can influence people's interpretations of them. Some websites can support students manipulating data visualizations to see how different visualizations tell different stories. These include Gapminder, Our World in Data, USAFacts, and Data USA. However, it is also useful for students to create analog data visualizations—that is, to draw data visualizations by hand using simple tools like paper and colored pencils or pens.

As illustrated by the data visualizations drawn by Lupi and Posovec, and throughout time by innovators like Charles Minard, Florence Nightingale, and W.E.B. Du Bois, handmade data visualizations can have an unfettered inventiveness that the convenient presets available in computers may forestall. Many of the programs available in schools produce only conventional bar graphs, line graphs, pie charts and the like, whereas hand drawn data visualizations allow more experimentation with design, shape, and color.

158    How Can Data Literacy Support Student Learning in Social Studies?

Students can create their own data visualizations in the style of Lupi or Posovec, using topics they identify as interesting or those related to social studies concepts. Such topics include tracking goods and services used in a day or week, recording times they see or are affected by government, or mapping the origin of the foods they eat. Students might also experiment with unconventional data visualization formats by choosing a favorite Du Bois visualization and then using local data to create their own in the same style as Du Bois (see Figure 9.4).

Another way for students to experiment with data visualization is by transforming tables from historical monographs or other scholarly papers related to social studies into data visualizations. Historians use tables extensively, perhaps because they prefer visualizations that are more precise and available for analysis than graphs, inviting their peers and other readers to "read" the data itself rather than the patterns and trends conveyed by data visualizations (Shreiner, 2023). However, there is some evidence to suggest that students may struggle more with tables than with graphs (Sharma, 2006). Considering data in both tabular and graphical form can provide students with opportunities to consider advantages and disadvantages of both.

**Figure 9.4. A hand-drawn data visualization in the style of DuBois, using local data**

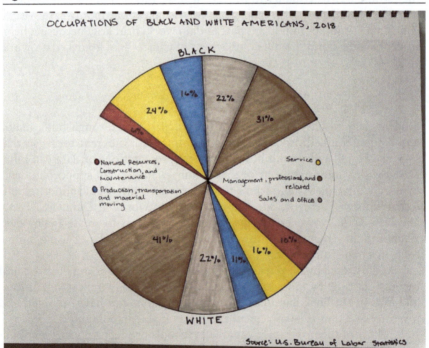

*Source:* Ms. P, 2020.

For example, in an article from the *Journal of World History*, Van Rossum (2020) uses the Dutch East India Company (VOC) as a case study to illustrate the importance of commodified slavery in the Indian Ocean and Indonesian archipelago. This topic would be important for students to consider in a world or global history course that examines slavery and slave trade beyond the trans-Atlantic slave trade. Van Rossum includes the table shown in Figure 9.5 to help illustrate how crucial slavery became in the VOC trading system's Dutch-controlled territories, in the eastern as well as the western hemisphere, and how it expanded especially in the second half of the 17th century, continuing to grow in importance through the 18th century. While the table is useful for seeing exact numbers year over year, as well as totals, students might have a better sense of its expansion, and how expansion in the Dutch East Indies compared to expansion in the Dutch West Indies, by converting the table to a graph like the one shown in Figure 9.6. The process of moving from Figure 9.5 to 9.6 would require students to select data they would like to visualize, organize the data in spreadsheets (e.g., Google Sheets or Excel), and play around with different outputs to decide which format is optimal for their purposes (see Figure 9.7 for an alternative graph format). For teachers who wish to both expand the information they teach beyond that provided in the textbook by turning to historical monographs, and to support students' data literacy through examination of quantitative evidence, such exercises can be informative and useful.

**Figure 9.5. Table used to illustrate the growth of the slave trade to Dutch-controlled territories**

TABLE 2. Slave trade needed to sustain enslaved populations, Dutch East and West Indies (estimates for specific years)

|  | Dutch East Indies | | Dutch West Indies | |
| --- | --- | --- | --- | --- |
|  | Minimum | Maximum | Minimum | Maximum |
| 1625 | 500 | 850 | 50 | 100 |
| 1650 | 1,950 | 3,350 | 800 | 1,350 |
| 1675 | 3,350 | 5,800 | 1,050 | 1,800 |
| 1700 | 4,200 | 7,300 | 1,500 | 2,600 |
| 1725 | 4,450 | 7,700 | 2,350 | 4,050 |
| 1750 | 4,650 | 8,050 | 4,100 | 7,100 |
| 1775 | 4,900 | 8,450 | 6,400 | 11,050 |
| 1800 | 4,200 | 7,250 | 7,400 | 12,800 |
| Total for entire period (1600–1800) | 660,000 | 1,135,000 | 495,000 | 850,000 |

Source: van Rossum, *Kleurrijke tragiek*, 26; idem, "Vervloekte goudzugt," 42.

*Source:* Van Rossum, 2020.

**Figure 9.6. A graph that visualizes data from the table in Figure 9.5.**

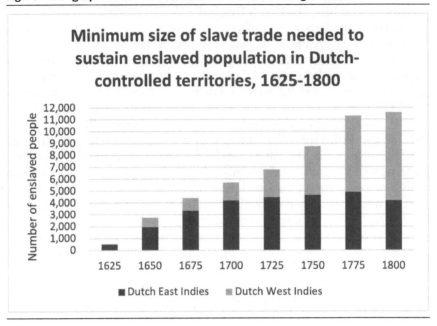

**Figure 9.7. An alternative way to visualize data from the table in Figure 9.5.**

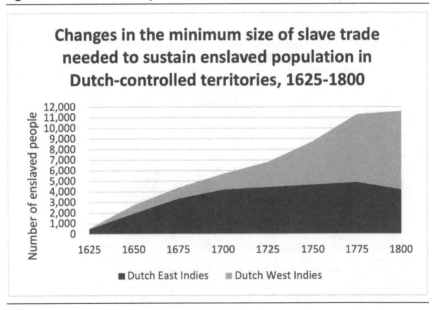

The data work described in this chapter not only gives students skills they can use outside of social studies, but also provides them insight into the ways that data are produced, selected, cleaned, and visually represented. Such work is crucial for critical, humanistic data literacy. Though teaching data literacy in this way is time-consuming, it is possible. In the next section of this book, I provide some practical guidelines for implementing data literacy into the social studies curriculum across grade levels, including the work of producing, wrangling, and visualizing data.

# Part IV

# INCORPORATING DATA LITERACY INTO THE SOCIAL STUDIES CURRICULUM

CHAPTER 10

# Teaching Data Literacy Across Grade Levels

Acquiring data literacy, particularly a critical, humanistic form of data literacy, takes time and practice. Ideally, students will receive data literacy instruction in social studies beginning in kindergarten and such instruction will continue through elementary, middle, and high school, with each grade-level teacher both reinforcing and building upon students' knowledge and skills. Unfortunately, there is little guidance to help social studies teachers figure out what they should be teaching with respect to data literacy at different grade levels. Standards documents are perhaps closest to a curricular guide for teaching, but as discussed in Chapter 3, standards are generally vague and inconsistent with respect to data literacy (Shreiner, 2020).

To address the lack of readily accessible guidance for teaching data literacy in social studies, this chapter synthesizes scholarly and standards-based recommendations for teaching data literacy at different grade levels. I pull together recommendations included in scholarship referenced throughout this book and, knowing teachers' obligations to meet academic standards, I reference recommendations from the *C3 Framework* and, where appropriate, the *Common Core State Standards for English Language Arts & Literacy in History/Social Studies, Science, and Technical Subjects* (hereafter, CCSS-ELA) and the *Common Core State Standards for Mathematics* (hereafter, CCSS-Math).

The chapter is organized by sections corresponding to the grade levels in the *C3 Framework*: kindergarten through 2nd grade, 3rd through 5th grade, 6th through 8th grade, and 9th through 12th grade. Within each section, I address each major type of data visualization and include a summary table, organized according to the kind of work students should do with data and data visualizations to develop critical, humanistic data literacy. As discussed in Chapter 5, such work includes comprehending and critiquing data and data visualizations; using data and data visualizations to draw conclusions, build arguments, and communicate with others; and creating data and data visualizations (see also Shreiner & Martell, 2022).

Two caveats must be noted here: First, although all recommendations are based on scholarship and national curricular guidance, not all are based on empirical research. In other words, I cannot always cite observed evidence that exercises or lessons have yielded positive results. This speaks to the need for additional empirical research regarding data literacy in social studies. Secondly, my decision to align each section with the grade levels in the *C3 Framework* is to acknowledge that teachers need flexibility in what they teach due to contextual factors including their state, local, and school curricula and students' readiness to learn. Nonetheless, the goal here is to provide some explicit guidance for incorporating data literacy across the social studies curriculum.

## KINDERGARTEN THROUGH SECOND GRADE

Early elementary school likely will be students' first exposure to any kind of data visualizations beyond navigational maps, and at this stage of emergent literacy, it is important to attend to students' "concept of graphics," including their understanding of how timelines, maps, and graphs function in a text (Duke et al., 2013). Students should learn, for example, that data visualizations are representations of reality that someone has created to communicate information (Duke et al., 2013), and to that end, students can look for the maker, date, and place of origin in data visualization displays (National Council for the Social Studies, 2013). Students should further learn that when data visualizations and other graphics appear in multimodal texts, they are related to the written text, but may not include all the same information. At the same time, students should know that data visualizations and other graphics can provide additional information not found in the written text (Duke et al., 2013). Finally, they should learn how to extract information from the data visualizations, while also recognizing that some information in a data visualization can be more important than other information (Duke et al., 2013).

Students will develop understanding of these concepts of graphics at different stages, but intentional instruction around data visualizations and other graphics in early elementary grades can help ensure that these concepts are secure for students when they move to the next school level. And of course, because different kinds of data visualizations have different purposes, properties, and conventions, it is important to provide specific instruction around each type of data visualization.

### Timelines

Instruction with timelines in early elementary school should concentrate on establishing students' chronological understanding, particularly their understanding of sequence. Teachers can show students simple timelines that use pictures to depict events, and can work with them to describe sequences of events using temporal vocabulary like *before* and *after* (Dawson, 2004; Stow & Haydn, 2012). As the *C3 Framework* recommends, students can also construct chronological sequences with timelines of their own lives, as well as of their family and local histories (National Council for the Social Studies, 2013). These timelines can include words and dates when students are ready, but students can also construct timelines with drawings and printed images, or by creating human timelines whereby students are assigned events and asked to position themselves in chronological order (Dawson, 2004; Stow & Haydn, 2012).

Using their own timelines or those from texts and websites, students can also compare timelines with one another, discussing similarities and differences and possible reasons behind creators' choices. Such an activity would not only create a foundation for students' understanding of the concept of significance, but also align with CCSS-ELA standards that recommend students compare chronologies in texts (National Governors Association Center for Best Practices & Council of Chief State School Officers, 2010a). By the end of early elementary, students are also supposed to begin constructing simple narratives, and timelines could serve as prompts to help them sequence the events in their narratives (National Governors Association Center for Best Practices & Council of Chief State School Officers, 2010a) (see Table 10.1).

## Maps

Instruction around maps at this level of schooling should focus on helping students learn about features of maps and their purposes. That is, students should learn *about* maps. Students may enter school already knowing that maps can be used for navigation, but they should learn that maps have other purposes as well, including helping us learn about places from the past and present we cannot see. Introducing students to primary source maps of their city or state can help them understand how maps can change over time and according to people's knowledge, as well as expose them to the different kinds of sources people use to understand the past (National Council for the Social Studies, 2013).

Students should also spend time studying large, simple maps of familiar places and learning about key elements that help us read maps, including titles, legends, scale, and directional indicators. They should learn how to identify and distinguish between different geographic features depicted on maps (e.g., landmasses, bodies of water, political units), perhaps using large floor maps to move to different parts of a map in response to teacher prompts (Mohan & Mohan, 2013; Mohan et al., 2015). Such prompts might include directions that allow them to apply the concept of magnitude as well, such as "locate the biggest body of water," or "find the smallest state." Visitor or tourist maps can help students distinguish between cultural and environmental features depicted on maps, which is a benchmark of the *C3 Framework* (National Council for the Social Studies, 2013). They can also practice using maps to locate familiar places, such as their home or school, and describe places in relations to one another using terms like *near*, *far*, and *next to*. Although scale might be a difficult concept for students at this age to grasp, they could be ready by 2nd grade (depending on their mathematical knowledge) to take measurements with a ruler or other tool and use the scale on a map to determine distances (National Governors Association Center for Best Practices & Council of Chief State School Officers, 2010b).

Having students construct maps of familiar places is another way to help students learn about maps and how they communicate information (National Council for the Social Studies, 2013). For example, with their teacher's help, students could draw a map of their classroom and share it with an adult at home, investigating the extent to which the adult can accurately describe what the place looks like based on the map. Or they could draw a map of a place in their home, like their bedroom or living room, and ask classmates to describe the room based on the map. Students can also create maps to help others navigate to a hidden object in the classroom or school, which not only helps them understand the importance of visual elements of a map, such as symbols and a legend, but also allows them to practice applying the concept of direction (Mohan & Mohan, 2013) (See Table 10.1).

**Graphs and Charts**

Students in early elementary school need to gain some familiarity with different kinds of graphs and charts and their conventions. Picture graphs and bar graphs with up to four categories that they can use for comparisons are the best choices for students at this school level; they should focus on social studies topics specific to state and local standards (Friel et al., 2001; National Governors Association Center for Best Practices & Council of Chief State School Officers, 2010b). Bar graphs with gridlines can be particularly helpful, so students can keep track of the quantities encoded in the bars. Students can also create three-dimensional graphs using blocks or other objects (Friel et al., 2001). Regardless of the form of the graph, students will need guidance in identifying and naming the different visual elements of the graphs (e.g., title, $y$- or vertical axis, $x$- or horizontal axis) and learning how to both read the data (e.g., what are the categories being compared in the bar graph?) and read between the data (e.g., which category's value has the largest?) to extract information.

Students can also begin producing and categorizing data at this school level. For example, in accordance with recommendations for "taking informed action" in the *C3 Framework* students might learn how to gather survey data to address a classroom issue, and create simple line plots, which they can then use to make decisions, to keep track of how many students have voted for a particular solution or object (National Council for the Social Studies, 2013). Such activities will prepare students for more in-depth action projects as they move into upper elementary (see Table 10.1).

Table 10.1. Overview of data literacy instruction recommendations for kindergarten through 2nd grade

|  | Timelines | Maps | Graphs/Charts |
|---|---|---|---|
| Comprehension | • Discuss functions of timelines in texts (i.e., concepts of graphics).<br>• Comprehend simple timelines.<br>• Discuss choices of events in timelines.<br>• Describe event sequence, using temporal vocabulary (e.g., before, after). | • Discuss functions of maps in texts (i.e., concepts of graphics).<br>• Comprehend simple maps (e.g., large floor maps).<br>• Discuss different purposes for maps.<br>• Describe similarities and differences between different maps.<br>• Identify key map elements (i.e., title, legend, scale, directional indicator, source).<br>• Understand and apply primitive spatial concepts of identity, location, and magnitude.<br>• Understand and apply simple spatial concept of distance in terms of proximity. | • Discuss functions of graphs/charts in texts (i.e., concepts of graphics).<br>• Comprehend simple picture graphs and bar graphs with up to four categories.<br>• Identify visual elements of graphs. |
| Use |  | • Use maps to locate familiar places and describe their physical and human characteristics. | • Use graphs to make and discuss comparisons.<br>• Use graphed data to deliberate and make decisions about classroom issues. |
| | • Use timelines to assist in telling stories in correct sequence. | | |
| Creation | • Create simple timelines of personal, family, or local history.<br>• Construct human timelines of local history. | • Create maps of familiar places to represent the place for others.<br>• Create maps of familiar places to help others navigate. | • Create simple and three-dimensional graphs about social studies topics.<br>• Produce data about classroom topics (e.g., votes on class pet) and construct simple line plots. |

## THIRD THROUGH FIFTH GRADE

Although many students will have grasped basic concepts of graphics when they enter upper elementary school (Duke et al., 2013), it is important to continue assessing and building their understanding of such concepts in multimodal informational texts. By the end of elementary school, students will probably use multimodal social studies textbooks and trade books more extensively and will therefore be exposed to data visualizations more frequently. While this may present some challenges for young readers, there is also abundant research (e.g., Ainsworth, 1999; Carney & Levin, 2002; Mayer, 2009; Schnotz, 2002; Schnotz et al., 2022; Schnotz et al., 2017) to suggest that students learn better from integrating verbal text and visuals, including data visualizations, than from verbal text alone. In fact, CCSS-ELA benchmarks suggest that students at this level should be able to interpret information in different kinds of data visualizations and "explain how the information contributes to an understanding of the text in which it appears" (National Governors Association Center for Best Practices & Council of Chief State School Officers, 2010a, p. 14).

Unfortunately, though, social studies textbooks and published curricular materials often provide few supports to encourage or scaffold integration of data visualizations with written text (Finholm & Shreiner, 2022; Shreiner, 2018). Textbooks rarely include references to data visualizations in the verbal text or use captions that connect the data visualizations back to the verbal text. Similarly, online lesson plans that include data visualizations frequently lack instructional recommendations for integrating them with verbal text in the same lesson (Finholm & Shreiner, 2022). Not surprisingly, then, students across school levels, including at the upper elementary level, tend not to read data visualizations in multimodal texts unless prompted to do so (Shreiner, 2019). Therefore, teachers need to design instruction to ensure that students attend to the data visualizations in multimodal texts and that they are well equipped to make meaning of them (Duke et al., 2013).

### Timelines

Upper elementary school students should continue to build their chronological understanding, reading and creating timelines beyond their own personal experience, using more multilayered timelines (e.g., state and national history), and working more regularly to sequence events by date (Blow et al., 2012). Additionally, students should learn the chronological conventions of BCE/CE and BC/AD and how to sequence events with these designations (Blow et al., 2012). Helping students more fully grasp the concept of sequence is important at this school level partly because they are expected to write narratives and explanations with correct sequence in these grades (National Council for the Social Studies, 2013a; National

Governors Association Center for Best Practices & Council of Chief State School Officers, 2010a). Asking them to study and create timelines, especially ones with images, as a formative activity prior to writing can help them strengthen their understanding of chronology.

Students at this grade level should also engage in activities with timelines to support their understanding of the concepts of duration and concurrence. The *C3 Framework* recommends students work with timelines with events occurring concurrently at this age level (National Council for the Social Studies, 2013) and, as students are probably learning about time intervals in mathematics (National Governors Association Center for Best Practices & Council of Chief State School Officers, 2010b), they will be ready to learn about and apply terminology that denotes different durations, such as *decade* and *century*. Having students engage with timeline activities like using different colors to separate specific intervals of time on a timeline gives them practice in applying and visualizing the concepts (Blow et al., 2012). Moreover, knowing these concepts and their implications for relationships among events will be important for students as they attempt to decipher and describe causal links between events in reading and writing, as the CCSS-ELA guidelines recommend (National Governors Association Center for Best Practices & Council of Chief State School Officers, 2010a).

Teachers can also work with students at this school level to begin developing a sense of period, particularly as they are likely studying both state and national history. To ensure consistency across grade levels, it is a good idea to look at the periodization scheme used in state standards, as well as in any textbooks that have been adopted by the school or district, and discuss the periodization with students. Such discussions also provide opportunities to address historical significance, and how dividing time is dependent upon determinations of historical significance. To further support such historical thinking, teachers could use timelines marked with historical periods and have students engage in picture sorting exercises using images of clothing, homes and buildings, technologies, and major events or historical figures (Dawson, 2004). Posting a visual of the periodization scheme in the classroom will also serve as an easy reference for students as they learn content throughout a year (see Table 10.2).

## Maps

Upper elementary students should read and construct more complex maps than those they worked with in lower grades, including maps of unfamiliar places and at different scales (e.g., country and continent level) (Mohan & Mohan, 2013; National Council for the Social Studies, 2013). At the same time, recognizing and using important visual features of maps, including title, legend, scale, and directional indicator, should be reinforced. Students in upper elementary should use maps with a grid system and, by the end of this stage, learn latitude and longitude as a means for determining absolute location, and how to use cardinal directions (Mohan & Mohan, 2013). They can also begin learning about map projections and distortions, examining how the apparent sizes and shapes of landmasses change with different projections. Most students can understand abstract symbolism in maps at this level but will still need guidance to understand what the symbols mean. Primary source maps should be used more frequently as well, and will be helpful for teaching students about the importance of considering the source of a map, as well as how the perspectives, intentions, and geographic knowledge of mapmakers shape their maps (National Council for the Social Studies, 2013).

By this school level students should be equipped to identify and locate places and landscapes on maps, and to distinguish between cultural and environmental characteristics (Mohan & Mohan, 2013). While they may need to review these concepts, they also should spend more time thinking *with* maps about the places, patterns, developments, and movements they represent. They should learn to read dot, connection, and flow maps that will support their understanding of content recommended in the *C3 Framework*, such as population distribution, movement of people, goods, and ideas, and spatial patterns (National Council for the Social Studies, 2013). When a single map does not contain all the layers of information students need to reason about places they are studying, teachers should have them gather information from two or three maps that together provide the necessary data. To help students grasp the realities that maps represent, students should also learn to calculate distances on maps. However, since students do not typically receive formal instruction in ratios until middle school, at this stage they may lack the background knowledge that will help them think about scale. (Mohan & Mohan, 2013; National Governors Association Center for Best Practices & Council of Chief State School Officers, 2010b). Introducing students to tools like Google Earth will also help them better understand what unfamiliar places look like in reality and prime them for creating their own projects with such tools either at the end of elementary school or in middle school (see Table 10.2).

## Graphs and Charts

Students should learn to comprehend a wider variety of graphs and charts in upper elementary school, including stacked and multiset bar graphs, and bar graphs with more than four categories (Friel et al., 2001; National Governors Association Center for Best Practices & Council of Chief State School Officers, 2010b). Relevant social studies topics the graphs address could include population, war casualties, imports and exports, industrial output, employment numbers, and more (National Council for the Social Studies, 2013). Because change over time will be an increasingly important concept for students to grasp, having them use graphs that compare variables over time will be helpful. Students can also learn about pie charts, but while CCSS-Math guidelines recommend students learn about fractions and angles in upper elementary school, they do not recommend percentages until middle school (National Governors Association Center for Best Practices & Council of Chief State School Officers, 2010b). Therefore, it may be better to discuss pie charts with students using terms like *larger*, *smaller*, or *equal* parts of a whole, rather than in terms of percentages, and to focus on reading pie charts rather than creating them (Friel et al., 2001). As in early elementary school, it will be helpful to use signaling techniques to point out and name for students the different visual elements of graphs and charts, and to formulate questions that will help students read the data and read between the data.

Students can also continue to produce and visualize data at this school level. For example, they can produce survey data related to local issues and, with teacher support and modeling, organize it into tables and then draw bar graphs (National Council for the Social Studies, 2013a). Students may also be ready to explore existing local datasets to address local issues, track change over time, or make comparisons, and they can convert such data into simple bar or line graphs with help from their teacher (Wilkerson & Laina, 2018). Reading tables can be difficult for some students at this age (Roberts & Brugar, 2017), so using tables to convert data into graphs is a good opportunity to help them better understand how to read tables both vertically and horizontally. Working with data in this way also will help students better understand civic issues, and will support them in discussing ways such issues could be addressed (National Council for the Social Studies, 2013; see Table 10.2).

## SIXTH THROUGH EIGHTH GRADE

Middle school students could see nearly double the number of data visualizations in social studies textbooks and other curricular materials as they saw in elementary school (Shreiner, 2018), but they are also likely to ignore them in their readings (Shreiner, 2019). Therefore, it is important for teachers to direct students to data visualizations in the multimodal informational texts they read and, as CCSS-ELA guidelines suggest, help them integrate visual information with surrounding verbal text and with any other sources of information they use to study a topic or address a question (National Governors Association Center for Best Practices & Council of Chief State School Officers, 2010a).

Students in middle school should also learn to integrate data visualizations in presentations and writing to share information and provide explanations (National Council for the Social Studies, 2013a; National

Table 10.2. Overview of data literacy instruction recommendations for 3rd through 5th grade

| | Timelines | Maps | Graphs/Charts |
|---|---|---|---|
| Comprehension | • Discuss functions of timelines in texts, especially their relationship to other sources of information.<br>• Comprehend simple and multi-layered timelines.<br>• Discuss choices about significant events in timelines.<br>• Describe event sequence, duration, and concurrence using chronological conventions (e.g., BCE/CE, BC/AD) and temporal vocabulary (e.g., decades, centuries). | • Discuss functions of maps in texts, especially their relationship to other sources of information.<br>• Comprehend simple and layered maps of familiar and unfamiliar places, including dot distribution, connection, and flow maps, maps with abstract symbolization, and primary source maps.<br>• Discuss the importance of a map's source and purpose.<br>• Analyze and explain possible reasons for similarities and differences between maps.<br>• Identify and explain the importance of key map elements.<br>• Understand and apply primitive spatial concepts of identity, location, and magnitude.<br>• Understand and apply simple spatial concepts of direction and distance, including calculating distances and using cardinal directions. | • Discuss functions of graphs/charts in texts as necessary (i.e., concepts of graphics).<br>• Comprehend bar graphs with more than four categories, multi-set and stacked bar graphs, and pie charts.<br>• Discuss the importance of a graph/chart's source and purpose.<br>• Identify visual elements of graphs/charts. |

|  |  |  |  |
|---|---|---|---|
|  | • Characterize and distinguish between historical periods for local, state, and national history. | • Understand complex spatial concepts of latitude/longitude, projections, and distortion. |  |
| Use | • Use timelines to assist in writing narratives and explanations with correct sequence and connections among events.<br>• Use timelines to diagram and describe causal links among events. | • Use maps and GIS (e.g., Google Earth) to locate places and describe their physical and human characteristics.<br>• Use maps to explain distributions, movement, and patterns related to grade-specific social studies topics. | • Use graphs/charts to make comparisons and describe change over time.<br>• Use datasets and graphed data to deliberate and make decisions about local and national civic issues. |
| Creation | • Create simple and multi-layered timelines of local, state, and national history.<br>• Create timelines with dates, words, pictures, and color-coding to indicate sequence, duration, concurrence, and periodization. | • Create maps of familiar and unfamiliar places.<br>• Create simple map projects with GIS tools (e.g., Google Earth). | • Create bar graphs with survey and/or other produced data.<br>• Create bar graphs from data in tables or datasets. |

Governors Association Center for Best Practices & Council of Chief State School Officers, 2010a). However, since students do not typically receive formal instruction in ratios until middle school, at this stage they may lack the background knowledge that will help them think about scale. Middle school students should also experiment with digital publication media (e.g., blogs and websites) which will also allow them to include web-based and interactive data visualizations to support their arguments or explanations (National Governors Association Center for Best Practices & Council of Chief State School Officers, 2010a). To integrate information from data visualizations well, students will need continued support in comprehending and evaluating different kinds of data visualizations.

**Timelines**

Standards documents often stop including recommendations for working with timelines at the middle school level (Shreiner, 2018). However, instruction about and with timelines should not stop just because standards cease to include them. Students will continue to see timelines in textbooks and other curricular materials, and some students will still need considerable support in developing chronological understanding and a sense of historical time (Stow & Haydn, 2012). Furthermore, students in middle school will likely engage in more focused, in-depth historical study at different scales, including both national and global history, so it will be important that they can decode chronological terminology and visualize temporal relationships. Teachers should therefore ensure that students know chronological conventions such as BCE/CE and BC/AD, and that they can use such designations to determine the duration of events or civilizations and how many years ago an event occurred or how long a person lived (Dawson, 2004). Timelines can serve as a useful visual to support students' understanding of sequence and can assist them in calculating durations.

Teachers can also continue using timelines to show and discuss the periodization schemes that frame historical content, and students will still benefit from picture sorting activities that help them distinguish between different time periods. Because middle-school instruction will likely move between different scales of history (e.g., world history one year and national history the next), it is also beneficial to provide students with a big picture of the past and to nest national and state historical narratives within a world-historical narrative. Indeed, the *C3 Framework* recommends that students at this level "analyze connections among events and developments in broader historical contexts" (p. 46), which speaks to the importance of a nested understanding of historical time. Timelines can be useful visual aids for such temporal connections, and students would benefit from seeing timelines at different scales posted in the classroom.

Students at this grade level are also expected to engage more deeply with historical concepts that are integral to historical narratives, such as change, continuity, and causation (National Council for the Social Studies, 2013). Understanding sequence, duration, and concurrence is a prerequisite for understanding relationships among events in historical narratives, and timelines can serve as visual aids. Students can create color-coded and multilayered timelines to demonstrate their understanding of sequence, duration, and concurrence, and they can transform written narratives into timelines, isolating events and marking significant historical changes, or using connecting lines, arrows, and color coding to show how events on a timeline are related to one another.

Understanding and evaluating historical significance is also important at this level of school (National Council for the Social Studies, 2013). Teachers can take advantage of timelines at the beginning of textbook chapters or units by having students examine them before they read, and then again after they have studied relevant content, to critically evaluate the timeline creator's or textbook author's choices (Dawson, 2004). Having students create their own timelines of the periods under study is another way for teachers to assess students' understanding of historically significant events or developments and for students to make their own determinations about historical significance. Such exercises could also help prepare students for writing historical narratives that establish historical sequence and highlight relationships among events (National Governors Association Center for Best Practices & Council of Chief State School Officers, 2010a) (see Table 10.3).

## Maps

Middle school students will need to comprehend a greater variety of maps at different scales, and maps that are more complex and multilayered than those they dealt with in elementary school (Shreiner, 2018). Hopefully, they will already have a grasp of primitive and simple spatial concepts of identity, location, magnitude, distance, and direction when they enter middle school, but teachers may need to repeat some of the instruction recommended for earlier grades. Regardless, students will need to continue learning about maps to secure an understanding of more complex spatial concepts, including scale, projection, and symbolization (Mohan & Mohan, 2013).

At this level of school, students should more often think *with* maps about social studies content and historical and contemporary places. They will most likely study both national and global history and will have more instructional time dedicated to learning social studies content. If they have not already, students should learn to read choropleth maps, as they will likely see more maps displaying quantitative data in their textbooks and through research. In addition, topographical, dot distribution, connection, flow maps, and other map types, as well as GIS representations, will help them understand concepts included in standards, such as human and physical characteristics of places, spatial connections among places, population distributions, population settlement and movement, patterns of conflict and cooperation, patterns of trade, and spatial growth and change (National Council for the Social Studies, 2013). Students can also analyze maps to investigate the causal role that geographic factors may have played in historical change and developments and can benefit from their teacher modeling how to analyze and use maps for such purposes.

Middle school students should use primary source maps in history whenever possible. Primary source maps may help them investigate causal factors, and provide insight into "how and why perspectives of people have changed over time" (National Council for the Social Studies, 2013, p. 47). Students also should develop habits in sourcing and contextualizing maps, investigating the origins of maps even when the information is not easily accessible (National Council for the Social Studies, 2013). Because primary source maps can be complex, unconventional, or otherwise difficult to read, teachers should regularly use signaling techniques to help students read them (Mayer & Moreno, 2003).

Finally, middle school students should construct maps to engage with social studies content, continuing to use paper-based maps where appropriate, but also constructing or manipulating electronic maps. They can also construct maps as part of civic action projects, exploring topics such as spatial patterns of social inequities, environmental issues, resource access, political belief or voting patterns, or resource access at the local, national, or global level (National Council for the Social Studies, 2013; see Table 10.3).

**Graphs and Charts**

Students should be able to read and analyze all types of graphs and charts by the end of middle school. Starting in 6th grade, they should learn about line graphs, area graphs, population pyramids, scatterplots, and any other kinds of graph or chart they encounter through their studies. As they learn about percentages in mathematics, students also will be better equipped to use and construct pie charts. With each type of data visualization they introduce, teachers should review visual elements of the graph or chart, helping students to read the data and read beyond the data.

According to the *C3 Framework*, students should study data and data visualizations related to public policies, which might include immigration, poverty, gun control, employment and unemployment, inflation, production, economic growth, and more (National Council for the Social Studies, 2013). Much of this data will be displayed in graphs, and students should be equipped not only to understand the information such graphs provide, but also tto read beyond the data in the graphs to reason about their implications and omissions. Graphs can then serve as evidence in arguments and explanations students construct for writing, presentations, and action projects (National Council for the Social Studies, 2013).

Students in middle school should spend time constructing graphs as well. To analyze change and continuity over time as is recommended by the *C3 Framework* (National Council for the Social Studies, 2013a), they might extract data from historical narratives to create graphs, or transform tables into graphs. Students can create graphs by hand, but by the end of middle school, they should start using programs to create or manipulate electronic graphs with the support and modeling of their teachers. Students at this level will likely spend some class time addressing local, national, or global issues, so producing, wrangling, and visualizing data also may be appropriate (see Table 10.3).

## NINTH THROUGH TWELFTH GRADE

High school social studies textbooks and other curricular resources are full of data visualizations, and students who do not read them may miss a substantial amount of information that is not covered in the written text (Shreiner, 2018). Therefore, it is important to impress upon students that paying attention to the data visualizations in the texts they read is essential. High school students should also develop the habit of not just extracting information from data visualizations, but also analyzing and evaluating data visualizations as they integrate them with other information (National Governors Association Center for Best Practices & Council of Chief State School Officers, 2010a). At this stage, students should critically evaluate data visualizations regularly, fully recognizing by the time they graduate that data visualizations are authored interpretations that reflect the intentions and biases of the creators.

Integrating data visualizations into written narratives, explanations, and arguments should also ramp up at this level of school. Teachers should encourage students to look for data and data visualization sources in their research and they should have opportunities to write multimodal digital texts (National Governors Association Center for Best Practices & Council of Chief State School Officers, 2010a). Students should also learn to attend to disciplinary norms in writing, using data visualizations to provide context or as evidence for change and continuity, similarities and differences, and relative impact or significance (Shreiner, 2023). Critical evaluation of data visualizations also should be apparent in their writing, and they and should learn to introduce and reference data and data visualizations fluidly (Shreiner, 2023).

Table 10.3. Overview of data literacy instruction recommendations for 6th through 8th grade

| | Timelines | Maps | Graphs/Charts |
|---|---|---|---|
| Comprehension | • Treat timelines as important but limited sources of information in texts that contribute to the text's overall meaning.<br>• Comprehend simple and multi-layered timelines and their chronological conventions.<br>• Critically evaluate timeline creators' choices of significant events.<br>• Describe event sequence, duration, and concurrence using chronological conventions (e.g., BCE/CE, BC/AD) and temporal vocabulary (e.g., centuries, eras).<br>• Characterize and distinguish between historical periods for national and global history.<br>• Develop a "big picture" understanding of the past and make connections between different scales of history. | • Treat maps as important but limited sources of information in texts that contribute to the text's overall meaning.<br>• Comprehend complex, multi-layered maps, including topographical, dot distribution, connection, flow, and choropleth maps, maps with abstract symbolization, and primary source maps.<br>• Discuss the importance of map's source and purpose.<br>• Analyze and explain possible reasons for similarities and differences between maps.<br>• Identify and explain the importance of key map elements.<br>• Understand and apply primitive spatial concepts of identity, location, and magnitude.<br>• Understand and apply simple spatial concepts of direction and distance, including calculating distances.<br>• Understand and apply complex spatial concepts, projections, distortion, and scale. | • Treat graphs/charts as important but limited sources of information in texts that contribute to the text's overall meaning.<br>• Comprehend all types of graphs and charts (e.g., bar graphs, pie charts, line graphs, area graphs, population pyramids, scatterplots)<br>• Discuss the importance of a graph/chart's source and purpose.<br>• Identify visual elements of all graphs/charts. |

|  | | | |
|---|---|---|---|
| Use | • Use timelines to assist in writing narratives and explanations with correct sequence and connections among events.<br>• Use timelines to diagram and describe causal links among events.<br>• Use timelines in multimodal presentations and writing. | • Use maps and GIS (e.g., Google Earth) to locate places and describe their physical and human characteristics.<br>• Use maps to explain distributions, movement, and patterns related to grade-specific social studies topics.<br>• Use maps in multimodal presentations and writing. | • Use graphs/charts to make comparisons and describe trends, patterns, and change over time.<br>• Use graphs and charts to reason about and make decisions regarding public policy. |
| Creation | • Create simple and multi-layered timelines of national and global history.<br>• Create timelines with dates, words, pictures, and color-coding to indicate sequence, duration, concurrence, and periodization.<br>• Create timelines to synthesize and show relationships among significant events in written narratives. | • Create state, national, and world maps.<br>• Create map projects with GIS tools to reflect social studies concepts or as part of civic action projects. | • Create graphs/charts using paper/pencil and computer programs with data from narratives, explanations, and tables.<br>• Produce, wrangle, and visualize data about local, national, and global issues, especially those that can be connected to personal stories. |

## Timelines

High school students should have chronological conventions well in hand and should be able to calculate durations spanning from BCE or BC to CE or AD. If they cannot, revisiting the exercises described for middle school students would be beneficial. Students should also have a solid understanding of sequence and concurrence so that they easily can fold these concepts into narratives, explanations, and arguments. High school students are expected to develop a more sophisticated understanding of causation, distinguishing between "long-term causes and triggering events" and analyzing "multiple and complex causes and effects of events in the past" (National Council for the Social Studies, 2013, p. 49), and timelines could be used as tools to help them distill historical narratives into component events and analyze causal relationships.

Further developing students' sense of historical time is critical during this time. They should examine how broader contexts shaped historical events, so using a series of nested timelines at different scales, or multilayered, color-coded timelines, will be helpful. They also need to analyze change and continuity in historical eras, and again timelines may be useful for scaffolding such analyses. Moreover, high school students are expected to examine how people's perspectives shape their interpretations of history (National Council for the Social Studies, 2013a), so they should also spend time critically evaluating choices of significant events on timelines, including those in their textbooks. Students might also create their own multilayered, annotated timelines to demonstrate their own determinations of historically significant events within a specified timeframe (see Table 10.4).

## Maps

Students should be equipped to work with all kinds of maps in high school, including dynamic interactive maps, maps that are multilayered or that are combined with graphs, charts, and timelines, and primary source maps (Shreiner, 2018). High school students should also regularly use maps to think spatially about social studies content, moving beyond location to think not only about what a place is like, but also how a place is related to, influences, and is influenced by other places and human activities. The *C3 Framework* recommends that students use maps to analyze the political, cultural, and economic relationships between places; variations in spatial patterns of cultural and environmental characteristics; and the reciprocal relationships among the diffusion of ideas, technologies, and cultures, population distribution, and migration patterns. Furthermore, students should draw upon their knowledge of economic activities, political decisions, climate changes, and cultural changes to evaluate their impact on human migration, settlement, interactions, and other spatial patterns that they observe on maps (National Council for the Social Studies, 2013).

High school students also should have opportunities to think *through* maps—that is, to think spatially and critically about real-world contexts and problems by manipulating and creating maps. In accordance with recommendations from the *C3 Framework*, they can use maps to identify and examine local, regional, and global problems from a spatial perspective, and evaluate how place-based characteristics might create challenges or opportunities for people trying to address a problem (National Council for the Social Studies, 2013). GIS technologies afford students opportunities to explore spatial characteristics and relationships in ways that static, paper-based maps cannot, and online tools for creating map-based projects allow students to map phenomena and write annotations that reveal patterns and relationships for themselves and others (see Table 10.4).

## Graphs and Charts

High school students should be prepared to make sense of a wide range of graphs and charts, including those with multiple variables, such as bubble charts. They will study national and global developments in history, politics, and economics in high school, and graphs and charts will serve as useful sources of information about trends over time or to make state-level, regional, or national comparisons. For graphs that are particularly complex, students can practice telling graph stories that weave in contextual factors as well. Students should also be regularly encouraged to critically evaluate graphs and charts, thinking beyond the data to consider their economic, political, and social implications, contextual factors that explain trends and changes, and a graph's distortions and omissions.

Students in high school should also have opportunities to produce, wrangle, and visualize data to address local, national, and global issues and problems (National Council for the Social Studies, 2013). When students study U.S. history, for example, they can look at census reports from the period under study to view the data tables and convert them into graphs, and when they study world history, they can utilize online datasets about conflict, trade, population, or other topics. High school students can also conduct surveys, gather data from multiple websites and reports, and create graphs to include in evidence-based arguments in presentations, essays, blogs, websites, or policy recommendations (National Governors Association Center for Best Practices & Council of Chief State School Officers, 2010a; see Table 10.4).

For some teachers, incorporating recommendations from this chapter may be overwhelming. Perhaps they have not thought of themselves as teachers of data literacy, or perhaps they feel they lack techniques for teaching data literacy because it was not a part of their own education and

Table 10.4. Overview of data literacy instruction recommendations for 9th through 12th grade

| Timelines | Maps | Graphs/Charts |
| --- | --- | --- |
| • Treat timelines as important but limited sources of information in texts that contribute to the text's overall meaning.<br><br>• Comprehend simple and multi-layered timelines and their chronological conventions.<br><br>• Critically evaluate timeline creators' choices of significant events.<br><br>• Describe event sequence, duration, and concurrence using chronological conventions (e.g., BCE/CE, BC/AD) and temporal vocabulary (e.g., centuries, eras).<br><br>• Characterize and distinguish between historical periods for national and global history.<br><br>• Secure a "big picture" understanding of the past and make connections between different scales of history. | • Treat maps as important but limited sources of information in texts that contribute to the text's overall meaning.<br><br>• Comprehend complex, interactive, multi-layered maps, including topographical, dot distribution, connection, flow, and choropleth maps, maps with abstract symbolization, and primary source maps.<br><br>• Analyze maps for biases and distortions.<br><br>• Utilize key map elements and spatial concepts to extract information from maps, recognizing the limitations of the map. | • Treat graphs/charts as important but limited sources of information in texts that contribute to the text's overall meaning.<br><br>• Comprehend all types of graphs and charts, including those with multiple variables such as bubble charts.<br><br>• Provide context for trends, patterns, or variations in a graph/chart.<br><br>• Evaluate a graph for biases, distortions, and omissions. |

- Use timelines to assist in writing narratives and explanations with correct sequence and connections among events.
- Use timelines to analyze change over time and causal relationships among events.
- Use timelines in multimodal presentations and digital writing projects.

---

- Create simple and multi-layered timelines of national and global history.
- Create timelines, including digital timelines, with dates, words, pictures, and color-coding to indicate sequence, duration, concurrence, and periodization.
- Create timelines to synthesize and show relationships among significant events in written narratives.

| | |
|---|---|
| • Use maps and GIS (e.g., Google Earth) to locate places and describe their physical and human characteristics.<br>• Use maps to explain distributions, movement, and patterns related to grade-specific social studies topics.<br>• Use maps to analyze relationships between places, variations in spatial patterns, and the influence of geography on human developments.<br>• Use maps in multimodal presentations and digital writing projects. | • Use graphs/charts to make state-level, regional, or national comparisons and analyze trends, patterns, and change over time.<br>• Use datasets and graphed data to deliberate and make decisions about national, civic, and global issues.<br>• Use graphs or charts to draw inferences about implications or consequences.<br>• Use graphs/charts in multimodal presentations and digital writing projects. |
| • Create state, national, and world maps.<br>• Manipulate and create digital maps to identify and address local, regional, and global problems from a spatial perspective. | • Create graphs/charts using paper/pencil and computer programs with data from narratives, explanations, and tables.<br>• Produce, wrangle, and visualize data about local, national, and global issues. |

preparation (Shreiner & Dykes, 2021). While it is one thing to say that helping students comprehend and critique different kinds of data visualizations is a goal of social studies instruction, it is quite another to design instructional methods to accomplish this goal. And while creating data visualizations is a worthy objective, finding ways to help students do it is more easily said than done. However, as the next two chapters will argue, there are several relatively simple techniques that can be used to help students comprehend and create data visualizations, and they can be incorporated at multiple levels of school, and with timelines, maps, and graphs alike.

CHAPTER 11

# Helping Students Comprehend and Critique Data Visualizations

The ability to comprehend data visualizations is an essential condition of data literacy. One cannot possibly be a data literate person if they cannot even decode the information data visualizations provide or draw inferences from them that will be useful for formulating evidence-based arguments or making decisions. Yet people too often include or show data visualizations in presentations and texts under the assumption that little to no explanation is needed—that with no more than a minute of studying a data visualization the information will somehow just "sink in" (Shreiner & Guzdial, 2022). Of course, this is simply not the case, especially for learners who have little experience with data visualizations in general, or who see a particular type of data visualization for the first time. Add to that data visualizations that include multiple variables, assume background knowledge about concepts or vocabulary, or are just poorly designed, and the notion of a learner making sense of them on their own becomes laughable.

At the same time, teaching students only to comprehend data visualizations risks implicitly teaching them that data and data visualizations are neutral and objective and that we need only unpack what the data visualization is telling us to learn the "facts." Therefore, we must also provide opportunities for students to question and critique data visualizations—to express their own wonderings and interpretations, and to push back on information they deem incorrect or misrepresentative of human experiences.

So how can you teach learners to make sense of data visualizations in a systematic manner? Certainly, questioning strategies that have been suggested in this book (see Chapters 7 and 8) and encourage students to, for example, think *through* maps or see *beyond* the data are useful, as are see-think-wonder strategies such as those used by the *New York Times*' "What's Going On in This Graph?" series (https://www.nytimes.com/column/whats-going-on-in-this-graph). However, students may sometimes need more heavily scaffolded instruction that breaks down the reading and sense-making process. Therefore, this chapter details two computer-aided techniques to help students focus their attention on the component parts of data visualizations and provide opportunities for them to think through and beyond the information presented in the graphic. These techniques, which I refer to as "slow analysis" and "slow reveal," are both grounded in research on multimedia learning (e.g., Alpizar et al., 2020; Lin & Atkinson, 2011; Mayer & Moreno, 2003). Such research suggests that signaling techniques, which have been mentioned in previous chapters and involve providing visual and verbal cues to focus students' attention on different components of an information source, may reduce cognitive load and help learners more effectively process information. Alpizar, Adescope, and Wong (2020) point out that signaling can be beneficial for learners who struggle to identify critical information on their own, can support the organization and integration of information with prior knowledge, and can help ensure that relations between concepts are explicit, allowing learners to draw better inferences and conclusions about a topic. In the techniques I describe here, signaling also affords the teacher opportunity to slow down the process of comprehending the data visualization so they can support students in questioning and critiquing the data visualization.

It is important to note that while slow analysis and slow reveal techniques can be applied to all types of data visualizations and with all grade levels of students, they are not meant to replace attention to the visualization-specific concepts and skills discussed in previous chapters. Students still need to learn the visual elements and conventions specific to timelines, maps, and graphs, and the temporal and spatial concepts that underlie each type of data visualization. Indeed, far from replacing these visualization-specific aspects, slow analysis and slow reveal allow for their careful examination. They are, in fact, powerful complements to teaching the skills and knowledge for critical, humanistic data literacy already discussed throughout this book.

## SLOW ANALYSIS TECHNIQUE

The "slow analysis" technique is, as the name implies, a mechanism for slowing down the otherwise quick cognitive processes involved in expertly decoding a data visualization's message. It helps learners who might be overwhelmed, or unsure of how to methodically process information in a data visualization, by addressing each of its visual components one by one in an order that makes sense for optimal comprehension. The technique uses signals in the form of circles, arrows, or highlighting to call students' attention to encoded information in the data visualization. This process ensures not only that students pay attention to all the important visual features, but also that there is ample opportunity for the teacher to address terminology or conceptual vocabulary, connect the information to students' prior knowledge, get ahead of possible misconceptions, and answer students' questions.

Helping Students Comprehend and Critique Data Visualizations 189

Consider for example, the graph in Figure 11.1, which was featured in a 2020 Pew Research Center article (Budiman, 2020). A version of this graph is also featured in the National Issues Forums' deliberation guide on the issue of immigration in the United States (National Issues Forums and the Kettering Foundation, 2020), which could be used with students to support an evidence-based deliberative discussion. Some students might be able to glean accurate and useful information from this graph relatively quickly, but other students might struggle to make sense of it or, worse, draw inaccurate inferences from it.

Using shape tools in presentation programs such as Google Slides or Microsoft PowerPoint to superimpose arrows, circles, and highlights onto data visualizations, the teacher can signal students to focus attention on one visual component of the data visualization at a time. In the case illustrated here, students are first cued with a superimposed circle to look at the title and the subtitle of the graph, a common first step in making sense of a graph (see Figure 11.2). After cueing students, the teacher might point out that the subtitle tells us what the graph is showing—the percentage of the U.S. population that is foreign born—while the title in larger print is interpretive, pointing out what the author believes is the most important information to gather from the graph. The teacher might also use this an opportunity to make sure students understand who makes up the foreign-born population—that is, naturalized citizens, unauthorized immigrants, lawful

**Figure 11.1. Pew Research Center, graph depicting changes in the percentage of the foreign-born population in the United States**

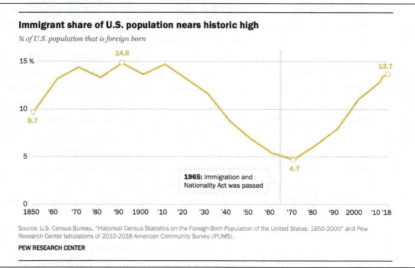

*Source:* Budiman, 2020.

**Figure 11.2. Modified version of Pew Research Center graph, using presentation program shape tools to cue students to read the title**

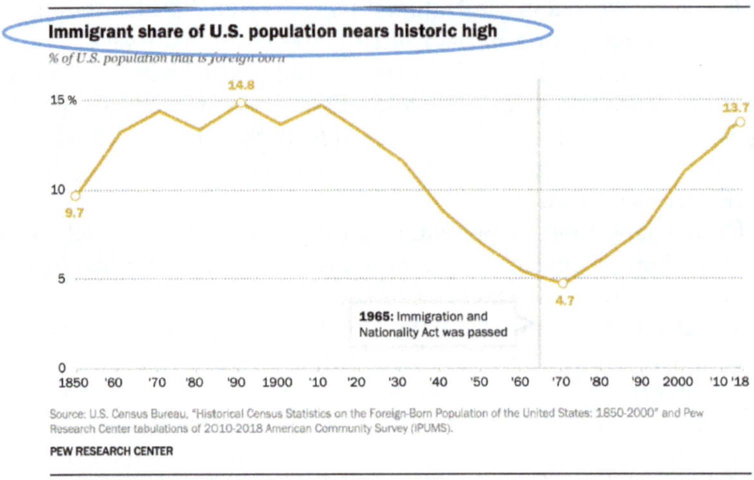

*Immigrant share of U.S. population nears historic high*
% of U.S. population that is foreign born

- 14.8 (1890)
- 9.7 (1850)
- 4.7 (1970)
- 13.7 (2018)

1965: Immigration and Nationality Act was passed

Source: U.S. Census Bureau, "Historical Census Statistics on the Foreign-Born Population of the United States: 1850-2000" and Pew Research Center tabulations of 2010-2018 American Community Survey (IPUMS).

PEW RESEARCH CENTER

*Source:* Budiman, 2020.

permanent residents, and temporary lawful residents, thereby avoiding possible misconceptions about whom the graph represents.

The teacher can then draw students' attention to other visual components in a sequence that best supports comprehension. For example, they might cue students to read the source at the bottom of the graph, then the horizontal axis and labels, then the vertical axis and labels, and then the line that encodes changes over time. At this point, the teacher might pause to show students how each point on the line represents the percentage of the total U.S. population that is foreign born during a particular year. This might also be an opportunity to call students' attention to the highest point labeled on the graph, 14.8% in 1890, not only making sure students can see how the number corresponds with the labels on the axes, but also providing students with historical context for such a high percentage in 1890. Providing historical context also will be important for explaining the vertical line marking when the Immigration and Nationality Act was passed, which abolished the existing immigrant quota system, and thus helps explain the associated rise in the percentage of foreign-born population from its historic low in 1970 to the most recent data on the graph.

Some interactive data visualizations have features built in that allow students to focus on certain elements, lending themselves to slow analysis as well. For example, Figure 11.3 shows a screenshot of one of several interactive maps available on the website Our World in Data (https://ourworldindata.org/). Using the map's interactive features on the website allows users to

Helping Students Comprehend and Critique Data Visualizations          191

**Figure 11.3. Our World in Data, map showing literacy rates from 2021, with countries with literacy rates between 20% and 40% highlighted on the interactive version of the map**

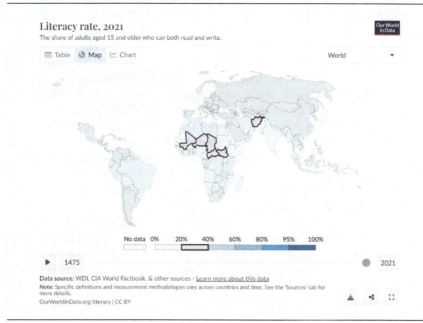

*Source:* Roser & Ortiz-Ospina, 2018. https://ourworldindata.org/grapher/literacy-rate-adults

highlight regions corresponding to the literacy rate ranges shown in the color key below the map. By hovering your cursor over the 20% to 40% color block, for example, the countries that fall within that range will light up. Users can then hover over the highlighted countries to learn their names, the year the data for each country was gathered, and the precise percentage of literate adults in the country. However, it still may be advisable to use slow analysis using screenshots like the one in Figure 11.3 to call students' attention to interactive elements, to discuss terminology such as the title and the meaning of literacy, or to discuss how the map displays "binned" data, which entails grouping relatively continuous data values into a smaller number of categories (e.g., values greater than 60% but less than or equal to 80%, and values greater than 80% but less than or equal to 95%).

## SLOW REVEAL TECHNIQUE

While the slow analysis technique involves showing all the components of a data visualization at once and using circles, arrows, and highlighting to cue students to pay attention to a particular element, the slow reveal technique entails covering visual elements of a data visualization to show only the most stripped-down version of the data visualization first, and then slowly revealing additional features one by one (for examples, see https://slowrevealgraphs.com/). All that is visible to students in the initial presentation of the data visualization are the signifiers and colors that encode the data, such as the line and tick marks on a timeline, the color-coded political units on a choropleth map, or the lines or bars on a graph. Teachers then encourage students to engage in discussion about what they notice and wonder about in the stripped-down data visualization. After this initial discussion, the teacher methodically reveals additional visual elements in the data visualization. Each time they uncover an element, they pause and allow students sufficient time for observation, deep thinking, and class discussion, asking "What new information did we learn? How does this change your thinking about the graph? What do you wonder about now? What new information do we need?" (see also Taurence et al., 2022).

For example, let us imagine that instead of a map of world literacy as shown in the previous example, a teacher wants to use a graph, also from Our World in Data, as shown in Figure 11.4. Using solid shape tools from their presentation program, in this case white rectangles, the teacher covers all but the lines and numberless axes on the graph (see Figure 11.5). They discuss the features of the numberless graph with students, encouraging them

**Figure 11.4. Our World in Data, graph of adult literacy rates around the world**

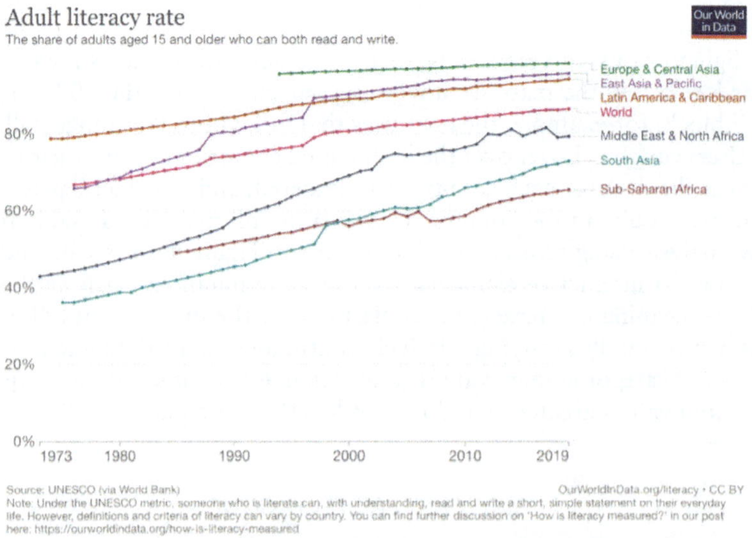

*Source:* Roser & Ortiz-Ospina, 2018. https://ourworldindata.org/grapher/literacy-rate-adults?tab=chart

Helping Students Comprehend and Critique Data Visualizations 193

**Figure 11.5. Our World in Data, graph of adult literacy rates around the world with all but the grid lines and graph lines covered using shape tools**

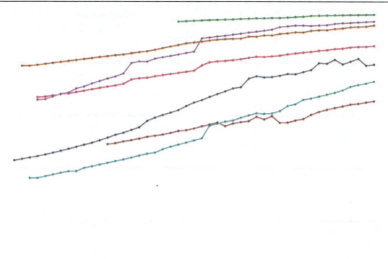

*Source:* Roser & Ortiz-Ospina, 2018.

to notice the horizontal axis line, the horizontal grid lines that are lightly shaded in the background, the number of graph lines, how some lines start in different places at the left, the general slope of each line, and how the slopes of the lines compare to one another. In this way, students are both reading the data and reading between the data, as discussed in Chapter 8, but focusing on only a small, manageable number of encodings at a time.

The teacher might then choose to reveal the years on the horizontal axis, first asking students, "What new information did we just learn?" Hopefully, the students would recognize that these are years, and they might note the slightly irregular intervals, allowing the teacher to discuss how irregularities at the beginning and end of a series of years on a graph can indicate the first and last years of data collected, which does not always fit neatly into a regular pattern of intervals. This would also give them an opportunity to share that this easily explained mild irregularity is far less concerning than is a graph with years out of order or with an irregular pattern of intervals throughout. After these initial discussions, the teacher would ask, "How does the new information change your thinking about the graph?" with the intent that through this prompt and subsequent discussion students understand that the graph shows change over time from 1973 to 2019. They would follow with the question "What do you wonder about now?" or some variation of the question, hoping that students might wonder about what is on the vertical axis, or what the title of the graph is.

**Figure 11.6. Our World in Data, graph of adult literacy rates around the world with years revealed in slow reveal process.**

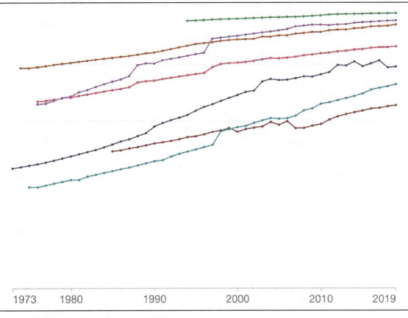

*Source:* Roser & Ortiz-Ospina, 2018.

This process of revealing graph components and asking the same basic questions (i.e., What new information did we just learn? How does this change your thinking about the graph? What do you wonder about now?) would continue for the remainder of the exercise. The sequence of reveals depends on the nature of the data visualization and on the teacher's goals. If the goal in teaching the graph in Figure 11.4, for example, is for students to understand that literacy has generally been improving but there are still regions that are well behind others, it might make sense to show the vertical axis next and then the title. This would allow the teacher to discuss the meaning of "adult literacy rate" and focus students' attention on the changing rates over time for different lines. They might point out, for example, that some lines do not even end as high in 2019 as some lines begin in 1973. The teacher might then show "the world" label next (see Figure 11.7), preparing students to understand disparities among regions. They might first encourage students to state something like, "The estimated (because clearly not all data was available at the time) adult literacy rate throughout the world increased from slightly under 70% in the mid 1970s to over 80% in 2019." And they could use the opportunity to encourage students to read beyond the data (see Chapter 8), considering that the world population also increased over this period, which raises questions about

**Figure 11.7. Our World in Data, graph of adult literacy rates around the world with years and one label revealed in slow reveal process**

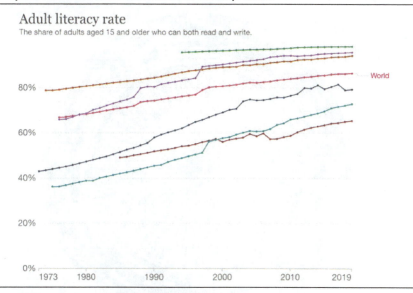

*Source:* Roser & Ortiz-Ospina, 2018.

how the total *numbers* of literate and illiterate adults have changed over time. The teacher also could encourage students to offer conjectures about the other places each line represents, thereby collecting students' preconceptions about places around the world that might have literacy rates below and above the world average, before finally revealing the other labels and further discussing.

The slow reveal graph process can be helpful for analyzing and making sense of primary source data visualizations too, which is the focus of the website Slow Reveal Graphics for Social Studies (https://sites.google.com/view/slowrevealforsocialstudies/home). The website has dozens of primary source data visualizations, particularly maps and graphs, that have been recreated using the program R, so that they easily can be transformed into slow reveal graphics slides. The slow reveal process is particularly useful for primary source data visualizations since they are often complex and unconventional by today's standards. Consider the data visualizations in Figure 11.8, from the 1918 *Woman Voter's Manual*, which was published by the National American Woman Suffrage Association (NAWSA) to educate women about the structure and functions of government in anticipation of universal suffrage (Forman & Shuler, 1918). The intent of the data visualization was to show how states that had already given women the right to vote subsequently passed "good legislation" affecting women and children throughout the United States. The data visualization is useful for teaching

**Figure 11.8. Forman & Shuler, data visualization indicating "good" and "bad" legislation passed in states with women's suffrage, redrawn**

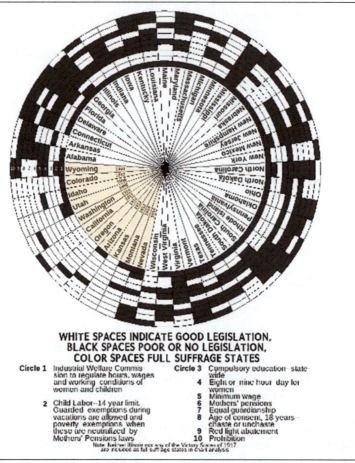

*Source:* Forman & Shuler, 1918 (redrawn). https://www.loc.gov/resource/rbnawsa.n7111/?sp=3&st=image

students about the woman suffrage movement because it demonstrates that the movement started at the state level first and illustrates the issues that leaders of the suffrage movement used to appeal to women. Each circle's label (e.g., "Minimum wage" or "Mother's pensions") also provides insight into social and political issues of the time, making the information in the data visualization ripe for further inquiry. However, the data visualization is complex, and students might be immediately overwhelmed when they first view it. The slow reveal process, illustrated in part by the series of images in Figure 11.9, allows students to engage with each visual element of the data visualizations to better understand its message and intent.

**Figure 11.9. Images from "slow reveal" presentation of the data visualization from Figure 11.8**

WHITE SPACES INDICATE GOOD LEGISLATION.
BLACK SPACES POOR OR NO LEGISLATION.
COLOR SPACES FULL SUFFRAGE STATES

Using techniques like slow analysis and slow reveal, teachers can help students better comprehend otherwise complex data visualizations. Such methods may better prepare students to use existing data visualizations, including primary source data visualizations, as evidence and illustration in discussion, presentations, and writing.

Students should also be prepared to create their own data visualizations or data visualization projects, engaging with data and their meaning more actively, and with more agency. While there are many existing tools to help students do this, students need help in approaching and using such tools for their own purposes. The next chapter provides some ideas to help teachers tackle this problem.

CHAPTER 12

# Using Technology to Manipulate and Visualize Data

Data work is often thought of falling solely within the purview of "unicorns" and "wizards"—rare individuals who have advanced technical skills beyond the reach of ordinary people (D'Ignazio & Bhargava, 2020). Subscribing to such views, though, only perpetuates an unequal system of power, in which most people are relegated to the role of data consumers while a select few have the power to manipulate and use data to influence people's beliefs, decisions, and actions. In fact, everyone can work with data, and in doing so, people are empowered not only to communicate their own messages but to critique the messages of others. As D'Ignazio and Bhargava (2020) have argued, we have a choice as educators with respect to teaching data literacy. We can facilitate the integration of students into the "logic of the present system and bring about conformity to it," or we can provide students with the means to "participate in the transformation of their world" (Freire, 2014, p. 34).

This chapter aims to support the latter choice. It is premised on the idea that students are fully capable of working with and visualizing data, but that they must practice such data work to gain a sense of efficacy. It is further premised on the idea that students should work with data within a space that is contextually rich and purposeful and that social studies classes, especially ones that privilege inquiry, disciplinary literacy, and civic action, can provide this space.

However, social studies teachers need resources and support for such data work to happen, particularly when the work also involves using computing technologies. Technology plays a critical and necessary role in working with the copious amounts of data that are available in our datafied society. It is simply unrealistic for people to manage the data available to them without the aid of computing tools. Thankfully, there are a multitude of freely available, open-access tools that students can use to process data and create data visualizations on their own. Yet, with few exceptions (e.g., Naimipour et al., 2020), most of these tools were not created specifically for social studies teachers and students, and do not necessarily provide teachers with guidance on how they can use them to support social studies instruction. This chapter begins to remedy this problem.

In what follows, I describe some existing tools that are particularly useful for addressing social studies questions and topics and are also uncomplicated enough for teachers and students to work with after minimal practice. I differentiate between tools that are primarily aimed at *manipulating* data visualizations, which can then be used for narratives, explanations, or arguments, and tools that allow users to *create* data visualizations using data they have generated or gathered from online databases. As part of this section, I briefly address sites students can use to find and prepare datasets, or to wrangle data, in preparation for visualization.

Knowing where to find tools and datasets, though, does not address the challenges of teaching with them. Data visualization tools can be complicated and finicky, and some teachers judge them as lacking in usefulness and usability (Shreiner & Guzdial, 2022). I propose that designing and using "minimal manuals" may offer one solution to these challenges. The concept of minimal manuals is borrowed from the field of human-computer interaction (Carroll et al., 1987). Unlike lengthy general-purpose manuals or video instructions, minimal manuals concentrate on a specific task and provide step-by-step instructions to help users carry it out. In what follows, I summarize characteristics of minimal manuals and show an example I created to accompany a data visualization tool. While such step-by-step instructions are equally useful for helping students draw data visualizations with pencil and paper, I focus on computing tools useful for organizing and visualizing data to encourage the use of data processing and visualizing technologies with students. By using such technologies, students can take advantage of large online datasets that are widely available to them and become better equipped to understand the choices behind the mostly computer-generated data visualizations they are likely to see in their everyday lives.

## DATA VISUALIZATION TOOLS

Many tools for preparing and visualizing data are accessible online. As just one illustration, since 2010, data visualization expert Andy Kirk has been collecting and curating data visualization resources on his website Visualising Data (https://visualisingdata.com/resources/). At this writing, there are 309 total tools featured on his website, loosely organized around categories like "Charting," "Mapping," and "Data." The website is a good reference to learn about existing tools, and to explore their usefulness on one's own. However, many of these sites have a paywall, require users to download an application to their computers, or require users to sign in with their email addresses—all of which might prevent their use in school. While schools might already subscribe to some of Kirk's featured tools (e.g., ArcGIS) I

Using Technology to Manipulate and Visualize Data                               201

focus here on tools that are free, open, and web-based, or that can at least be used on a trial run for free.

Tools that are useful for social studies generally fall into two broad categories: those that allow students to choose from included datasets and manipulate the digital data visualizations the tool generates, and those that allow students to add or upload their own data or datasets and create data visualizations. In the first category are tools like DataUSA (https://datausa.io/), Data Visualization for Literacy (DV4L; http://historyindata.org/dv4l/), Gapminder (https://www.gapminder.org/), USAFacts (https://usafacts.org/), and the Federal Reserve Economic Database (FRED; https://fred.stlouisfed.org/). I briefly describe each of these tools below.

**Manipulating Data Visualizations**

DataUSA (https://datausa.io/) is a website focusing on data visualizations of U.S. public data. The VizBuilder tool on the site allow students to select from data concerning a range of topics, including demographics, government spending, healthcare access and quality, industry output, and more. After choosing a topic, students will see default data visualizations, allowing them to consider differences in the stories the data visualizations tell and to choose the most effective data visualization to communicate information to others. Students can also add their own groupings and filters to change the output based on their unique inquiries, which yields even more data visualizations for them to consider. In addition, students can view and download the source for the data visualizations, an important component for teaching students to critically evaluate data and data visualizations. One disadvantage of the tool, though, is there is no built-in function for students to download or share their data visualizations, so they would have to rely on screenshots or on describing what they learned from the data visualizations they produce.

DV4L (http://historyindata.org/dv4l/) is one of just a few tools built with and for social studies educators (Naimipour et al., 2020). The tool supports inquiry by allowing students to enter a driving question or choose from a list of predetermined questions and then explore data visualizations generated from suggested or chosen datasets. The tool always displays two bar graphs as the output so that students can make comparisons and derive inquiries from observations of similarities and differences in trendlines. Students can also save the graphs and write notes about their observations, both of which can be exported to their teacher. In addition, students can view the source of the data in the graph and are given the URL so they can visit it themselves. One thing to watch out for on the tool is that the variable ranges displayed on the graphs can differ greatly, so students must pay attention to ranges and intervals on both axes. Regardless, the tool is great for helping them observe and compare trends.

The tools section of the Gapminder website (https://www.gapminder.org/tools/#$chart-type=bubbles&url=v1), a website introduced in Chapter 8, allows students to explore data through a variety of graphs and maps. On the site's bubble and line graphs students can change the data on the $x$- and $y$-axes based on their inquiries, and they can choose regions or countries to focus on in the maps, income graphs, and population pyramids. In the rankings graph section, students can choose to see country rankings for population, life expectancy, unemployment, and a variety of other topics. All data visualizations on the site are color coded by world regions so students can easily track them across multiple data visualizations. Once students create a data visualization based on their inquiries and interests, there is an option for them to download or share it.

USAFacts (https://usafacts.org/), a website run by a team of career researchers, data analysts, statisticians, and communication professionals, provides U.S. government data and data visualizations on topics including crime, the economy, education, health, and population in the United States. The site also has data visualizations grouped by questions, such as "What is the role of government in health?" or "Is the cost of living rising?" When students click on a topic of interest, they can choose from several graphs and download the associated data. There is also an Explorer tab that allows students to interact with the data, including by choosing different graph types to display the data differently or to toggle different data categories on and off. As in DV4L and Gapminder, all graphs can be downloaded to include in presentations, papers, or websites, or to simply share with a teacher.

FRED (https://fred.stlouisfed.org/) is a powerful tool for visualizing and manipulating current and historical economic data. The site allows users to graph, manipulate, and download 823,000 U.S. and international time series from 114 data sources. You can search for economic data of interest or filter available data by concepts (e.g., unemployment, poverty, GDP) or by geography (e.g., county-level or state-level data) and choose a time series line graph of data to display. Where the data has a geographic component, you can display the data in a map. Once the data visualization is displayed, users can edit the graph by choosing different units, modifying the frequencies, or adding a time series with different data. For example, I could view a graph of the unemployment rate in the United States over time, and then add a line with children between 5 and 17 in poverty to analyze the relationship between the two. Users can then download their graphs as an image, pdf, or Powerpoint slide, or the data as an Excel or CSV file.

While the tools described in this section are highly useful in social studies, none of them provide opportunities for students to enter data found outside of the tool's website and create their own data visualizations. For certain inquiries and activities, particularly those involving large datasets from government and other largescale databases, this is completely appropriate, but students should also have opportunities to dirty their hands in the messy work of selecting and organizing data. The tools I describe below provide such opportunities.

Because many schools use Google products, I begin with Google Sheets (https://www.google.com/sheets), Google Maps (https://www.google.com/maps), and Google Earth https://earth.google.com/web). Then I describe three tools designed for journalists that have proved popular among the pre-service and practicing teachers with whom I have worked: Knight Lab's Storyline.JS (https://storyline.knightlab.com/), Storymap.JS (https://storymap.knightlab.com/), and Timeline.JS (https://timeline.knightlab.com/).

**Creating Data Visualizations**

Google Sheets is probably the best place to start, partly because Google spreadsheets are used in several of the other tools described in this section, but also because it is integrated with Google Charts so students can create data visualizations within the application, ranging from simple line graphs to complex hierarchical tree maps. Students can enter their own data rows and columns from data they have produced, data from text or tables in readings, or data they are pulling from disparate texts or webpages. Alternatively, students can upload or copy existing datasets from websites such as UNData (https://data.un.org/), Data.gov (https://data.gov/), U.S. Census Bureau (https://www.census.gov/data.html) Pew Research Datasets (https://www.pewresearch.org/download-datasets/), World-Historical Dataverse (https://www.dataverse.pitt.edu/) or local community data sites (e.g., Data Driven Detroit, https://datadrivendetroit.org/). Preparing and visualizing data within Google Sheets is useful for building critical data literacy skills because it asks students to think about the purposes and functions different data visualizations serve, and the different stories they can tell with data.

It should be noted here that using datasets from library databases or from websites will likely require that students reorganize and prepare the data for visualization. There may be columns or rows they want to delete entirely, codes they need to make more comprehensible, or inconsistencies in data entry that need to be corrected. Giving students scaffolded opportunities to practice this data preparation before they are required to do so independently is critical. Beginning with an existing dataset provides students an opportunity to work with and prepare data for visualization, which will help build skills in selecting data most relevant to a question or topic, and thinking about how data need to be reorganized or cleaned.

Google Maps is another useful tool for entering and visualizing data. Although many people are familiar with Google Maps as a navigational tool, you can also use the "My Maps" function to create your own maps (see also Chapter 7). Users can change the base map and add thematic layers to their maps, and within each layer, they can decide which places they would like to add to their map and add location markers, to which they can add color-coding, text descriptions, images, and videos. They can also add lines as routes or connectors and polygons to mark off a specific area, and then explain their significance on the map with color-coding and descriptions. By selecting media to accompany a place marker, line, or polygon, they can practice integrating multimedia to tell a story. The finished map can then be embedded on a website, exported, or printed.

Google Earth has similar features (i.e, tagging locations, adding lines and polygons, adding images and media), but it also generates an interactive slideshow that walks viewers through a 3-dimensional tour of the places highlighted on the map, and provides a narrative explanation of each place's relationship to the topic. It also allows users to import map overlays, including historical maps, from numerous third-party sources, and to toggle on lines of latitude and longitude or timelapse photos showing how an area has changed over time.

Northwestern University Knight Lab provides another set of useful tools. According to their website, "Northwestern University Knight Lab is a community of designers, developers, students, and educators working on experiments designed to push journalism into new spaces" (Knight Lab, 2023). They offer several interactive, open-source tools that were developed with journalists in mind, but three of their tools are useful for teaching aspects of data literacy in social studies as well: StoryLine.JS, StoryMap.JS, and Timeline.JS. All the tools have users enter data into Google spreadsheets and then transform them into annotated interactive displays. Through the data entry process, students can learn about the choices behind data visualizations and the care that must be taken to enter data carefully.

Storyline.JS enables users to create an annotated, interactive temporal line graph by entering data into a date/time column and a data column to produce their graph. By adding columns with titles and content, users can add "cards" that tell a story about datapoints and trends in the graph. The tool is limited in a few ways: the $x$-axis will accept only time/date formats, it allows no more than 12 limited-text cards per story, and it works best with fewer than 800 data points. Still, the output is beautiful, and the tool allows students to create projects that engage their understanding of historical significance, change and continuity over time, and graphical elements, trends, and patterns. Teachers can also use the tool's annotation capabilities to challenge students to see beyond the data in the graph and engage with the data's deeper meaning, significance, and shortfalls.

Knight Lab's StoryMap.JS is similarly powerful. Like StoryLine.JS, it begins with a Google sheet and forces users to make choices about events or developments to include in their display. Unlike StoryLine.JS, it is focused on telling a spatial story by highlighting up to 20 locations of events and annotating the locations with cards that provide context. The site can also pull media from Twitter, Flickr, YouTube, Vimeo, Vine, Dailymotion, Google Maps, Wikipedia, SoundCloud, Document Cloud, and more, allowing students to add static maps or other visuals, primary source documents, and background videos. It provides a useful tool for students to create projects that engage their spatial reasoning about events of historical significance and can assist students in supporting an argument with spatial dimensions.

Finally, Timeline.JS allows users to build visually rich, interactive timelines that display duration and concurrence, as well as sequence of events. It focuses users' attention on making choices about historical significance, while affording students the opportunity to support their choices of events or people through the annotation feature. Teachers can also use the annotation feature to encourage students to explain change and continuity over time as they add events. And as in StoryMap.JS, Timeline.JS allows users to add media from a variety of sources to provide more contextual details.

All the tools I have described in this section may be useful in a social studies classroom, but they must also be *usable* for teachers and students. Teachers and students may very well be able to figure out how to use these tools on their own, but they may also run into issues and errors that leave them bored or frustrated. In the next section, I propose that developing so-called minimal manuals to support the use of data visualization tools can minimize risks associated with using them.

## MINIMAL MANUALS

The concept of the minimal manual was introduced by Carroll et al. (1987) in recognition of the difficulties non–computer experts often have in learning how to use complex computer applications with only the help of general-purpose self-instruction manuals. Minimal manuals are task-specific and succinct. They share three characteristics. First, they support the user in getting started right away on the task they wish to accomplish. This works in a social studies context when the goal is not *learning about* the tool but *using* the tool to learn about or engage with content, or to learn cross-cutting data literacy skills. There may be functions of a tool that are not useful in a typical social studies classroom, and a minimal manual simply ignores such features and focuses students' attention on the features they will need to carry out a task. For example, the minimal manual for Timeline.JS in Figure 12.1 encourages users to begin creating their project right away. It does not explain any of the features or functions of the application before students need to use them. This prevents boredom and lets the students immediately start using the tool.

Second, minimal manuals do not provide explanations beyond those that are needed to complete the task. Readers tend to skip over information that is not directly related to what they are trying to accomplish anyway, so minimal manuals slash unnecessary verbiage. For example, in the minimal manual for Timeline.JS, there is no explanation of how the website interface works, and it only briefly mentions columns in the spreadsheet template

**Figure 12.1. Example of a minimal manual for Timeline.JS**

Create a Timeline using Timeline.JS

1. Open Timeline.JS on your computer by visiting: https://timeline.knightlab.com/.
2. Begin creating your timeline by clicking on the "Make a Timeline" button.
3. You should be redirected further down the page where you will see an option to "Get the Spreadsheet Template." Click on that button.

4. This will redirect you to a page like this:

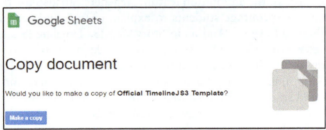

5. Select "Make a copy" and you will be taken to your main timeline data sheet.
6. This Google Sheets template already has some sample headings and timeline data in it. To get started, you should clear the template by selecting cell 2A to cell 9R. This is done by clicking and dragging the translucent box from the top left to the bottom right and deleting the contents using the delete key. This can also be done in multiple smaller selections based on your available device.

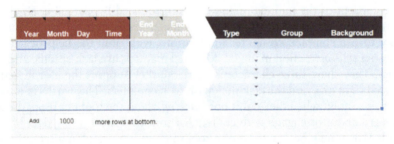

*NOTE: Do **not** delete any of the data in row 1 of the spreadsheet.

7. Now that you have a blank template to create your timeline, you may notice that row 2 has a light blue background color. That distinguishes what will be the title slide for your timeline. Don't add any date information to this row, but instead add a title of your choice to the "Headline" column and some descriptive text for your project to the "Text" column. (See the example on the American Revolution below.) Finally, in the "Type" column, choose "title" from the drop-down menu.

In the next four cells (Media to Media Thumbnail) you can add accepted media types (Youtube, Vimeo, Soundcloud, Dailymotion, Instagram, Twitter status, Wikipedia, or an image) to your title. This process will be explained in step 10 so you can skip this step for now.

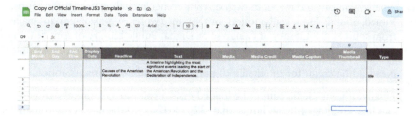

8. You can now begin creating your timeline events in the subsequent rows. First, add date information to your event. An event only needs to have a "Year" to be displayed, so if you don't have any other date information, you can leave additional date fields on the sheet blank. However, if you have an end year to input, your timeline will show the duration of the event. Months need to be input as their number equivalent (e.g., December would be 12 and January would be 1).

> *NOTE: Timeline.JS will only display the start year on your timeline by default. To overwrite the Timeline.JS date formatting and add your own format (e.g., an event's start and end date), type the date you want displayed in the "Display Date" cell. Otherwise, leave this cell empty. See the example below.

9. Next, add a name for the event to the "Headline" column and text explaining the event and an explanation of its significance to the "Text" column. This can be done by filling out the cells with the relevant information from your research. At this point, your timeline should look something like this:

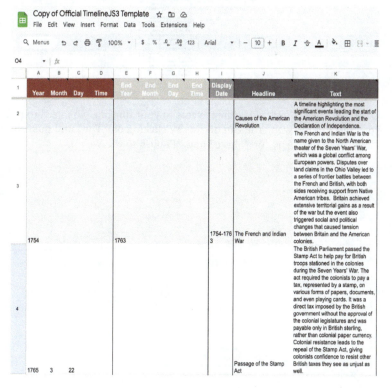

207

10. Finally, you can add media to each of your events, including links to YouTube, Vimeo, SoundCloud, Dailymotion, Instagram, Twitter, Wikipedia, or an image from sources like Library of Congress or Digital Public Library of America. In the media cell for the respective event, paste the link to the accepted media format.

Next, add a credit for the media (if applicable) and an optional caption.

Finally, if your media cannot be loaded or is displayed as a thumbnail you can link an **image** file, no larger than 32px × 32px, in the media thumbnail cell which will appear in place of your media. A finished timeline event should look something like this:

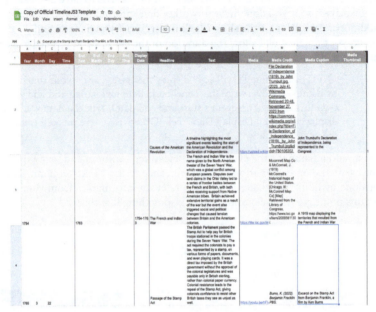

11. Once you have completed adding events to your timeline, you need to publish your sheet to the web. You can do this by clicking on "File" and then choosing "Publish to the Web" (or "Share" and "Publish to the Web").

12. You should now see a window that looks like the one below. In the left box under Link select "od1" and leave the right box as "web page." Then click "Publish." You may see a window pop-up asking you to confirm. Select **OK**. Then close out of the Publish window.

> NOTE: You do **not** need to copy the URL in the publish box.

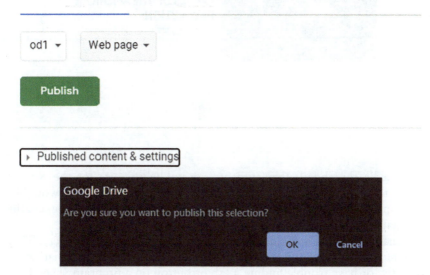

13. After you have closed the Publish window, copy the link for the Google sheets in the address bar of the browser window. Then head over to https://timeline.knightlab.com/#make and scroll down to step 3. Paste the URL link you just copied into the field there, as shown below.

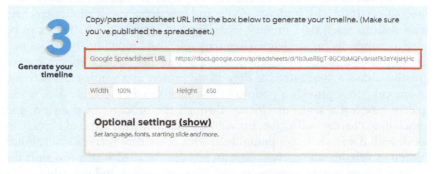

> NOTE: Do **not** use the link that is generated in the "Publish to the web" window. Use the URL of the page from the address bar at the top of your browser.

14. Finally, to submit your completed project, scroll down to step 4 on the Timeline.JS website. You can either submit the direct link to your project or use the embed option to post your project to a website. The finished project will look something like the image below.

(e.g., media thumbnail) that students are unlikely to use for the type of project they are being asked to create. Even though these features would be useful in some contexts, teaching students to use them or providing lengthy explanations for their inclusion would only waste precious time.

Finally, minimal manuals support error recognition and recovery. They account for the fact that a tool user might miss a step, enter information incorrectly, or have trouble finding a tab or button on a program. Therefore, they might include warnings to prevent errors in the future or tell users how to walk back their mistakes before moving on. The minimal manual displayed in Figure 12.1 includes notes to users when errors are likely to occur.

Minimal manuals such as the one displayed in Figure 12.1 have been used successfully with both preservice and practicing social studies teachers who wish to teach data literacy (Shreiner & Guzdial, 2022). They can be used as handouts for students when they use a tool individually or in small groups, or as a script for teachers to walk students through the process of creating a data visualization or data-based project as a whole-class activity. In any case, they provide a pathway for students to do authentic data work, and to develop a sense of efficacy through the process. As the next and concluding chapter will argue, providing students with a sense of efficacy to work with data, while equipping them with other data literacy skills, holds promise to change the current narrative in our datafied world—to shift the balance between data consumers and data influencers and contribute to a more just society.

Part V

# CONCLUSION

# CHAPTER 13

# The Data Stories Students Will Tell

Mimi Onuoha collects missing datasets. Since 2015, the New York City-based, Nigerian American researcher has curated a project entitled *The Library of Missing Datasets* (https://mimionuoha.com/the-library-of-missing-datasets-v3), which highlights the "blank spots that exist in spaces that are otherwise data-saturated" (Onuoha, 2022, n.p.). Examples of missing datasets she has identified include "People excluded from public housing because of criminal records," "Muslim mosques/communities surveilled by the FBI/CIA," and "Undocumented immigrants currently incarcerated and/or underpaid" (Onuoha, 2022, n.p.). In an introduction to her project, Onuoha (2022) writes:

> The word "missing" is inherently normative. It implies both a lack and an ought: something does not exist, but it should. That which should be somewhere is not in its expected place; an established system is disrupted by distinct absence. That which we ignore reveals more than what we give our attention to. It's in these things that we find cultural and colloquial hints of what is deemed important. Spots that we've left blank reveal our hidden social biases and indifferences. (n.p.)

Other scholars (e.g., D'Ignazio & Klein, 2020; Maier & Imazeki, 2013; Perez, 2019) have also documented the problems with absences in data, and the ambiguities in the data we do have. In the wake of the Flint water crisis, for example, *Wired* reporter Issie Lapowsky (2017) decried the woeful absence of adequate data on drinking water quality that exists across the country, concluding from the lack of data, "You have no real way of knowing if your town, your family, or your children face the kind of water contamination that exposed everyone in Flint, Michigan, to lead poisoning" (n.p.). In their book *The Data Game: Controversies in Social Science Statistics*, Maier and Imazeki (2013) summarize the perennial problem of incomplete demographic and education data, and inaccuracies and ambiguities in crime, wealth, poverty, and employment data—some of which are difficult to avoid, but should nonetheless temper the conclusions we draw from them. In *Invisible Women*, Perez (2019) points to much more unequivocally avoidable data exclusions and prejudices. She cites numerous examples of women being excluded from data stories, including how women's travel patterns have been ignored in city infrastructure and zoning plans, how the actual incidence of crimes against women versus reported crimes has resulted in conclusions that women's fears of crime are irrational and overblown, and how the impact of modern warfare on female civilians has been largely ignored even though domestic violence against women and maternal death rates increase during conflict.

Yet the reverence for data as representing unadulterated truth about our world continues to flourish. And from this reverence flow policies, beliefs, and assumptions that too often ignore the realities of individual human beings who are affected by both our action and our inaction. This is not by any means to dismiss the great value of data. I agree with Our World in Data founder Max Roser's (2023) assertion that it would be a mistake to "believe that we can simply rely on personal experience to develop our understanding of the world" (n.p.). As he argues, "The world is large, and we can experience only very little of it personally. To see what the world is like, we need to rely on other means: carefully-collected global statistics" (n.p.). At the same time, I agree with the sentiment, the origin of which can be traced to sociologist William Bruce Cameron (1963): "Not everything that can be counted counts, and not everything that counts can be counted" (p. 4).

I believe teaching data literacy as part of social studies education is our best hope for instilling both these perspectives in future generations. Teaching data literacy in social studies can equip more people with the knowledge and skills to analyze and use data with power, and the wisdom to recognize the limitations of data. The teaching of data literacy can give people the capability to see the stories that data tell, and to change those stories.

Consider the work of the Detroit Geographic Expedition, a project by the Society for Human Exploration that was formed not long after the 1967 Detroit Riot. The goal of the expedition was to join academic geographers with "folk geographers," or people without formal geography training, and members of the African American community to create "oughtness maps"—maps of how things are and maps of how things ought to be. One of the non-geographer leaders in the expedition was Gwendolyn Warren, a Black community leader and activist. Warren participated in several arms of the project, but important among them were studies she conducted on the "geography of children" in Detroit.

One such study investigated children's deaths caused by automobile drivers passing through Black communities on their commute from the affluent white suburbs to downtown Detroit. When Warren began the study, no data or detailed records of the deaths were publicly available, and it was difficult to get them from authorities. Eventually, Warren and her team used "political people" to get information from the police department describing the drivers and reporting where, how, and at what time the children

**Figure 13.1. G. Warren, *Where Commuters Run Over Black Children on the Pointes-Downtown Track*, Map from the Detroit Geographic Expedition**

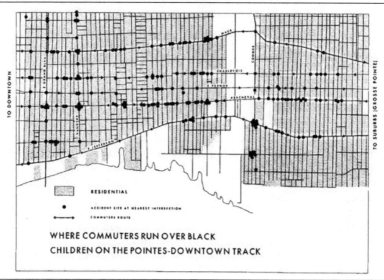

*Source:* Kanarinka, 2013.

were killed. At the culmination of the project, the team created a map provocatively entitled "Where Commuters Run Over Black Children on the Pointes-Downtown Track" (see Figure 13.1) that proved that the children's deaths were not isolated incidents but part of a pattern of spatial and racial injustice affecting the most vulnerable members of society. Warren used the maps, and others she and her team created, to demonstrate that Detroit's urban planning and transportation system were unjust for the Black community. At the time she helped lead the project, Warren was just 18 years old (Kanarinka, 2013).

John Snow, Florence Nightingale, W. E. B. Du Bois, Ida B. Wells-Barnett, Gwendolyn Warren. Though they were different ages, had different expertise, and lived at different times, they were all people who used data with power. They knew that data were not the whole of the stories they wanted to tell, but they recognized that data could make their stories more convincing. And they understood that the stories they could tell with data—data others ignored, misinterpreted, or did not care to produce—could shift the dominant narratives of the time and place in which they lived.

These are the kinds of data stories our students should be able to tell. And, as I have tried to establish throughout this book, these are the kinds of stories social studies teachers—*all* social studies teachers—can help them tell. We need only give them the confidence and tools to do it.

# References

Ainsworth, S. (1999). The functions of multiple representations. *Computers and Education*, *33*(2–3), 131–152. https://doi.org/https://doi.org/10.1016/S0360-1315(99)00029-9

Akerman, J. R., & Karrow, R. W. (Eds.). (2007). *Maps: Finding our place in the world*. The University of Chicago Press.

Allen, J., Howland, B., Mobius, M., Rothschild, D., & Watts, D. J. (2020). Evaluating the fake news problem at the scale of the information ecosystem. *Science advances*, *6*(14). https://doi.org/10.1126/sciadv.aay3539

Allen, W. L. (2021). The conventions and politics of migration data visualizations. *New Media & Society, 25*(2), 1–22.

Alpizar, D., Adesope, O. O., & Wong, R. M. (2020). A meta-analysis of signaling principle in multimedia learning environments. *Educational Technology Research and Development*, *68*(5), 2095–2119. https://doi.org/10.1007/s11423-020-09748-7

Amit-Danhi, E. R., & Shifman, L. (2022). Off the charts: user engagement enhancers in election infographics. *Information, Communication & Society, 25*(1), 55–73. https://doi.org/10.1080/1369118X.2020.1761858

Anderson, K. C., & Leinhardt, G. (2002). Maps as representations: Expert novice comparison of projection understanding. *Cognition and Instruction, 20*(3), 283–321. https://doi.org/https://doi.org/10.1207/S1532690XCI2003_1

Anderson, M. J. (2015). *The American Census: A social history* (2nd ed.). Yale University Press.

Andrews, R. J. (Ed.). (2022). *Florence Nightingale: Mortality and health diagrams*. Visionary Press.

Arias-Ferrer, L., Egea-Vivancos, A., & Levstik, L. S. (2019). Historical thinking in the early years: The power of image and narrative. In K. J. Kelly-Moran & J.-A. Aerila (Eds.), *Story in children's lives: Contributions of the narrative mode to early childhood development, literacy, and learning* (pp. 175–198). Springer.

Austen, R. A. (2010). *Trans-Saharan Africa in world history*. Oxford University Press.

Bain, R. B. (2000). Into the breach: Using research and theory to shape history instruction. In P. N. Stearns, P. C. Seixas, & S. S. Wineburg (Eds.), *Knowing, teaching, and learning history: National and international perspectives* (pp. 331–352). New York University Press.

Bain, R. B. (2012). Challenges of teaching and learning world history. In D. Northrop (Ed.), *A companion to world history* (pp. 111–127). John Wiley & Sons, Ltd.

# References

Bain, R. B., & Harris, L. M. (2009). A most pressing challenge: Preparing teachers of world history. *Perspectives on History*, *47*(7). https://www.historians.org/publications-and-directories/perspectives-on-history/october-2009/a-most-pressing-challenge-preparing-teachers-of-world-history

Ball, D. L., Thames, M. H., & Phelps, G. (2008). Content knowledge for teaching: What makes it special? *Journal of teacher education*, *59*(5), 389–407.

Barbour, C., & Wright, G. C. (2015). *Keeping the Republic: Power and citizenship in American politics*. Sage.

Barton, K. C., & Levstik, L. S. (1996). "Back when God was around and everything": Elementary children's understanding of historical time. *American Educational Research Journal*, *33*(2), 419–454. https://eric.ed.gov/?id=ED370716

Barton, K. C., & Levstik, L. S. (2004). *Teaching history for the common good*. Lawrence Erlbaum Associates.

Battle-Baptiste, W., & Rusert, B. (Eds.). (2018). *W. E. B. Du Bois's data portraits: Visualizing Black America*. Princeton Architectural Press.

Bausmith, J. M., & Leinhardt, G. (1998). Middle-school students' map construction: Understanding complex spatial displays. *Journal of Geography*, *97*(3), 93–107. https://doi.org/10.1080/00221349808978834

BBC. (2010, November 26). *Hans Rosling's 200 Countries, 200 Years, 4 Minutes*. BBC. https://youtu.be/jbkSRLYSojo?si=9Dit2Sg6i17Zdv5f

Bednarz, S. W., Acheson, G., & Bednarz, R. S. (2006). Maps and map learning in social studies. *Social Education*, *70*(7), 398.

Beezley, W. H. (2011). *Mexico in world history*. Oxford University Press.

Bender, T. (2006). *A nation among nations: America's place in world history*. Hill and Wang.

Bentley, J. H. (2000). Cross-cultural interaction and periodization in world history. In R. E. Dunn (Ed.), *The New World History: A Teacher's Companion* (pp. 376–383). Bedford/St. Martin's.

Bergstrom, C. T., & West, J. D. (2021). *Calling bullshit: The art of skepticism in a data-driven world*. Random House Trade Paperbacks.

Bienen, L. (2012). *Homicide in Chicago 1870–1930: The maps*. Chicago Historical Homicide Project, Northwestern University School of Law. https://homicide.northwestern.edu/pubs/hullhouse/maps/

Black, E. (2012). *War against the weak: Eugenics and America's campaign to create a master race*. Dialog Press.

Bliss, L. (2019). *The power of counter-maps*. Bloomberg MapLab. https://www.bloomberg.com/news/articles/2019-12-04/maplab-the-power-of-counter-maps

Blow, F., Lee, P., & Shemilt, D. (2012). Time and chronology: Conjoined twins or distant cousins? *Teaching History*, *147*, 26–34.

Bond, L. F., Elias, M. J., & Nayman, S. J. (2021). Empowering students for social action in social studies. *Phi Delta Kappan*, *102*(5), 42–46.

Börner, K., Maltese, A. V., Balliet, R. N., & Heimlich, J. (2016). Investigating aspects of data visualization literacy using 20 information visualizations and 273 science museum visitors. *Information Visualization*, *15*(3), 198–213. https://doi.org/10.1177/1473871615594652

Börner, K., & Polley, D. E. (2014). *Visual insights: A practical guide to making sense of data*. MIT Press.

boyd, D., & Crawford, K. (2012). Critical questions for big data: Provocations for a cultural, technological, and scholarly phenomenon. *Information, Communication & Society*, *15*(5), 662–679. https://doi.org/10.1080/1369118X.2012.678878

Boyer, P., & Nissenbaum, S. (1976). *Salem possessed: The social origins of witchcraft*. Harvard University Press.

Braun, M. (2022). From the atoms to the heavens. In G. Hattab & R. J. Andrews (Eds.), *Étienne-Jules Marey, The Graphic Method* (pp. 13–26). Visionary Press.

Breakstone, J., McGrew, S., Smith, M., Ortega, T., & Wineburg, S. (2018). Teaching students to navigate the online landscape. *Social Education*, *82*(4), 219–221.

Breakstone, J., Smith, M., Wineburg, S., Rapaport, A., Carle, J., Garland, M., & Saavedra, A. (2021). Students' civic online reasoning: A national portrait. *Educational Researcher*, *50*(8), 505–515.

British Library. (n.d.). *The World Described by Herman Moll, 1708–20*. British Library Board. Retrieved October 13 from https://www.bl.uk/collection-items/the-world-described-by-herman-moll-1708-1720

Brotton, J. (2013). *A history of the world in 12 maps*. Penguin.

Brotton, J. (2014). *Great maps: The world's masterpieces explored and explained*. DK Publishing.

Brugar, K. A. (2017). "We don't have students colour maps anymore . . ." a survey of social studies teachers use of visual materials. *Journal of Visual Literacy*, *36*(3–4), 142–163.

Bruner, J. S. (1960). *The process of education*. Harvard University Press.

Budiman, A. (2020, August 20). *Key findings about U.S. immigrants*. Pew Research Center. https://www.pewresearch.org/short-reads/2020/08/20/key-findings-about-u-s-immigrants/

Bullock, C. S., III. (2021). *Redistricting: The most political activity in America*. Rowman & Littlefield Publishers.

Bump, P. (2015). Why this National Review global temperature graph is so misleading. *The Washington Post*. https://www.washingtonpost.com/news/the-fix/wp/2015/12/14/why-the-national-reviews-global-temperature-graph-is-so-misleading/

Burkholder, P., & Schaffer, D. (2021). *History, the past, and public culture: Results from a national survey*. https://www.historians.org/history-culture-survey

Cairo, A. (2019). *How charts lie: Getting smarter about visual information*. W. W. Norton & Company.

California Department of Education. (2009). *Sample of California Standards Test questions*. https://www.cde.ca.gov/ta/tg/sa/practicetest.asp

Calvillo, D. P., Rutchick, A. M., & Garcia, R. J. B. (2021). Individual differences in belief in fake news about election fraud after the 2020 U.S. election. *Behavioral Sciences*, *11*(12), 175. https://www.mdpi.com/2076-328X/11/12/175

Cameron, W. B. (1963). *Informal sociology: A casual introduction to sociological thinking*. Random House.

Cannato, V. J. (2010). A home of one's own. *National Affairs*(3). https://www.nationalaffairs.com/publications/detail/a-home-of-ones-own

# References

Carlson, J., Fosmire, M., Miller, C., & Nelson, M. S. (2011). Determining data information literacy needs: A tudy of students and research faculty. *portal: Libraries and the Academy, 11*(2), 629–657.

Carney, R. N., & Levin, J. R. (2002). Pictorial illustrations *still* improve students' learning from text. *Educational Psychology Review, 14*, 5–26. https://doi.org/10.1023/A:1013176309260

Carr, D. (1986). *Time, narrative, and history.* Indiana University Press.

Carroll, J. M., Smith-Kerker, P. L., Ford, J. R., & Mazur-Rimetz, S. A. (1987). The minimal manual. *Human-computer interaction, 3*(2), 123–153.

Center for the Study of the American Constitution. (2023). *Maps of the ratification of the Constitution.* https://csac.history.wisc.edu/multimedia/maps/

Chapman, A. (2003). Camels, diamonds and counterfactuals: A model for teaching causal reasoning. *Teaching History, 112*, 46–53.

Charalambous, C. Y., & Hill, H. C. (2012). Teacher knowledge, curriculum materials, and quality of instruction: Unpacking a complex relationship. *Journal of Curriculum Studies, 44*(4), 443–466.

Chick, H. L., Pfannkuch, M., & Watson, J. M. (2005). Transnumerative thinking: Finding and telling stories within data. *Curriculum Matters, 1*, 87–109.

CIO Bulletin. (2022). How much data is collected every day and how to collect it. *CiO Bulletin.* https://www.ciobulletin.com/big-data/how-much-data-is-created-every-day-and-how-to-collect-it

Cohen, J. D., & Cohen, J. S. (2021). Graph interpretation in a government unit. *Social Education, 85*(1), 50–56.

College Board. (2020). *AP World History: Modern: Course and exam description.* The College Board. https://apcentral.collegeboard.org/pdf/ap-world-history-modern-course-and-exam-description.pdf

Collins, K. (2015). The most misleading charts of 2015, fixed. *Quartz.* https://qz.com/580859/the-most-misleading-charts-of-2015-fixed

Combs, M., & Beach, J. D. (1994). Stories and storytelling: Personalizing the social studies. *The Reading Teacher, 47*(6), 464–471.

Correll, M. (2023). An inconvenient graph. *Medium.* https://mcorrell.medium.com/an-inconvenient-graph-addc218579e9

Council for Economic Education. (2010). *Voluntary national content standards in economics* (2nd ed.). Council for Economic Education. https://www.councilforeconed.org/wp-content/uploads/2012/03/voluntary-national-content-standards-2010.pdf

Crowley, J. E. (2016). Herman Moll's *The World Described* (1720): Mapping Britain's global and imperial interests. *Imago Mundi, 68*(1), 16–34.

Curcio, F. R. (1987). Comprehension of mathematical relationships expressed in graphs. *Journal for Research in Mathematics Education, 18*(5), 382–393.

Digital Scholarship Lab and the National Community Reinvestment Coalition. (2023). Not even past: Social vulnerability and the legacy of redlining. *American panorama* [Website]. University of Richmond. https://dsl.richmond.edu/socialvulnerability

D'Ignazio, C., & Bhargava, R. (2015). *Approaches to building big data literacy.* In Bloomberg Data for Good Exchange 2015. MIT Press. https://www.media.mit.edu/publications/approaches-to-building-big-data-literacy/

D'Ignazio, C., & Bhargava, R. (2020). Data visualization literacy: A feminist starting point. In M. Engebretsen & H. Kennedy (Eds.), *Data visualization in society* (pp. 207–222). Amsterdam University Press. https://www.aup.nl/en/book/97894 63722902/data-visualization-in-society

D'Ignazio, C., & Klein, L. F. (2020). *Data Feminism*. MIT Press.

Dawson, I. (2004). Time for chronology?: Ideas for developing chronological understanding. *Teaching History, 117*, 14.

De Blij, H. (2012). *Why geography matters: More than ever*. Oxford University Press.

De Groot-Reuvekamp, M., Ros, A., & Van Boxtel, C. (2018). Improving elementary school students' understanding of historical time: Effects of teaching with "Timewise." *Theory & Research in Social Education, 46*(1), 35–67.

De Groot-Reuvekamp, M., Ros, A., van Boxtel, C., & Oort, F. (2017). Primary school pupils' performances in understanding historical time. *Education 3–13, 45*(2), 227–242.

De Groot-Reuvekamp, M., Van Boxtel, C., Ros, A., & Harnett, P. (2014). The understanding of historical time in the primary history curriculum in England and the Netherlands. *Journal of Curriculum Studies, 46*(4), 487–514.

De Haan, Y., Kruikemeier, S., Lecheler, S., Smit, G., & Van der Nat, R. (2018). When does an infographic say more than a thousand words? Audience evaluations of news visualizations. *Journalism Studies, 19*(9), 1293–1312.

De La Paz, S. (2005). Effects of historical reasoning instruction and writing strategy mastery in culturally and academically diverse middle school classrooms. *Journal of Educational Psychology, 97*(2), 139–156.

De La Paz, S., & Felton, M. K. (2010). Reading and writing from multiple source documents in history: Effects of strategy instruction with low to average high school writers. *Contemporary Educational Psychology, 35*, 174–192. https://doi.org/10.1016/j.cedpsych.2010.03.001

De La Paz, S., Felton, M., Monte-Sano, C., Croninger, R., Jackson, C., Deogracias, J. S., & Hoffman, B. P. (2014). Developing historical reading and writing with adolescent readers: Effects on student learning. *Theory and Research in Social Education, 42*(2), 228–274.

DeBow, J. D. B. (1853). *The seventh census of the United States*. https://www.census.gov/library/publications/1853/dec/1850a.html

Delaney, J. (2007). *Evolution of the maps of Africa*. Princeton University Library. https://library.princeton.edu/visual_materials/maps/websites/africa/maps-continent/continent.html

Delnero, P. (2018). A land with no borders: A new interpretation of the Babylonian "Map of the World." *Journal of Ancient Near Eastern History, 4*(1–2), 19–37.

Denbo, S. (2015). Data storytelling and historical knowledge. *Perspectives on History, 53*(4). https://www.historians.org/research-and-publications/perspectives-on-history/april-2015/data-storytelling-and-historical-knowledge

deVilla, J. (2014, February 13). Lies, damned lies, and Reuters' graph of Florida firearm deaths before and after "Stand Your Ground." *The Adventures of Accordion Guy in the 21st Century*. https://www.joeydevilla.com/2014/04/14/lies-damned-lies-and-reuters-graph-of-florida-firearm-deaths-before-and-after-stand-your-ground/

# References

deVilla, J. (2020, February 9). Georgia Department of Health's master class on misinforming with statistics. *The Adventures of Accordian Guy in the 21st Century*. https://www.joeydevilla.com/2020/05/17/georgia-department-of-healths-master-class-on-misinforming-with-statistics

Dobbs, C. L., Ippolito, J., & Charner-Laird, M. (2016). Layering intermediate and disciplinary literacy work: Lessons learned from a secondary social studies team. *Journal of Adolescent & Adult Literacy*.

Douglass, F. (1881). The color line. *The North American Review, 132*(295), 567–577.

Drozda, Z., Johnstone, D., & Van Horne, B. (2022). *Previewing the National Landscape of K–12 Data Science Implementation*. National Academies of Sciences, Engineering, and Medicine. https://www.nationalacademies.org/event/09-13-2022/docs/D688ED916E82498DA0E2171A109936D679FD5DE26556

Du Bois, W. E. B. (1900a). [The Georgia Negro] Occupations of negroes and whites in Georgia. From *The Exhibit of American Negroes*. Library of Congress Prints and Photographs Division. https://www.loc.gov/pictures/collection/coll/item/2005679642/

Du Bois, W. E. B. (1900b). [A series of statistical charts illustrating the condition of the descendants of former African slaves now in residence in the United States of America] Comparative rate of increase of the white and Negro elements of the population of the United States. Library of Congress Prints and Photographs Division. https://www.loc.gov/pictures/collection/coll/item/2005679642/

Du Bois, W. E. B. (1900c). [A series of statistical charts illustrating the condition of the descendants of former African slaves now in residence in the United States of America] Illiteracy of the American Negroes compared with that of other nations. Library of Congress Prints and Photographs Division.

Duke, N. K., Martin, N. M., Norman, R. R., Knight, J. A., & Roberts, K. L. (2013). Beyond concepts of print: Development of concepts of graphics in text, preK to Grade 3. *Research in the Teaching of English, 48*, 175–203.

Dunn, R. E. (2000). Redefining world history: Some key statements. In R. E. Dunn (Ed.), *The New World History: A Teacher's Companion* (pp. 109–112). Bedford/St. Martin's.

Eltis, D., & Richardson, D. (2010). *Atlas of the transatlantic slave trade*. Yale University Press.

Engel, P. (2014). This chart shows an alarming rise in Florida gun deaths after 'Stand Your Ground' was enacted. *Business Insider*. https://www.businessinsider.com/gun-deaths-in-florida-increased-with-stand-your-ground-2014-2

Engebretsen, M., & Kennedy, H. (2020). *Data visualization in society*. Amsterdam University Press.

Equal Justice Initiative. (2017). *Lynching in America: Confronting the legacy of racial terror* (3rd ed.). https://lynchinginamerica.eji.org/drupal/sites/default/files/2021-11/report.pdf

Fang, Z., & Coatoam, S. (2013). Disciplinary literacy: What you want to know about it. *Journal of Adolescent and Adult Literacy, 56*(8), 627–632.

Finholm, C. E., & Shreiner, T. L. (2022). A lesson in missed opportunities: Examining the use of data visualizations in online history lessons. *Social Studies Research and Practice, 17*(2), 155–166.

Forman, S. E., & Shuler, M. (1918). *The woman voter's manual*. The Century Co. https://www.loc.gov/item/18007111/

Freire, P. (2014). *Pedagogy of the oppressed: 30th anniversary edition*. Bloomsbury Academic & Professional.

Friel, S. N., Curcio, F. R., & Bright, G. W. (2001). Making sense of graphs: Critical factors influencing comprehension and instructional implications. *Journal for Research in Mathematics Education, 32*(2), 124–158.

Friendly, M., & Wainer, H. (2021). *A history of data visualization and graphic communication*. Harvard University Press.

Gaddis, J. L. (2002). *The landscape of history: How historians map the past*. Oxford University Press.

Galesic, M., & Garcia-Retamero, R. (2011). Graph literacy: A cross-cultural comparison. *Medical Decision Making, 31*(3), 444–457.

Gannett, H. (1894). *Statistics of the Negroes in the United States*. The Trustees of the John F. Slater Fund. https://www.loc.gov/item/06031899/.

Gapminder. (2023). *Bubbles*. Gapminder. https://www.gapminder.org/tools/#$chart-type=bubbles&url=v1

Gapminder. (n.d.). *About*. Gapminder. https://www.gapminder.org/about/

Gersmehl, P. (2014). *Teaching geography*. Guilford Press.

Gibbs, F. W. (2016, February). New forms of history: Critiquing data and its representations. *The American Historian, 7*. http://tah.oah.org/february-2016/new-forms-of-history-critiquing-data-and-its-representations/

Gibbs, F. W., & Owens, T. (2012). The hermeneutics of data and historical writing. In J. Dougherty & K. Nawrotski (Eds.), *Writing history in the digital age*, 4.4. https://writinghistory.trincoll.edu/data/gibbs-owens-2012-spring/

Gilbert, E., & Reynolds, J. T. (2012). *Africa in world hstory*. Prentice-Hall.

Gillborn, D., Warmington, P., & Demack, S. (2018). QuantCrit: education, policy, 'Big Data' and principles for a critical race theory of statistics. *Race Ethnicity and Education, 21*(2), 158–179. https://doi.org/10.1080/13613324.2017.1377417

Gillman, J. M. (1924). Statistics and the immigration problem. *American Journal of Sociology, 30*(1), 29–48.

Gold, H. (2014). *Fox News corrects Obamacare chart*. Politico. https://www.politico.com/blogs/media/2014/04/fox-news-corrects-obamacare-chart-186120

Goldman, S. R., Britt, M. A., Brown, W., Cribb, G., George, M., Greenleaf, C., Lee, C. D., Shanahan, C., & Project READI. (2016). Disciplinary literacies and learning for understanding: A conceptual framework for disciplinary literacy. *Educational Psychologist, 51*(2), 219–246.

Goodwin, N., Nelson, J. A., & Harris, J. M. (2017). *Useful economic tools and concepts*. Global Development and Environment Institute, Tufts University. https://www.bu.edu/eci/files/2019/06/Useful_Macroeconomic_Tools_and_Concepts.pdf

Gray, C., & Lewis, L. (2021). *Use of educational technology for instruction in public schools: 2019–2020*. National Center for Education Statistics. https://nces.ed.gov/pubsearch/pubsinfo.asp?pubid=2021017

Gregg, M., & Leinhardt, G. (1994). Mapping out geography: An example of epistemology and education. *Review of Educational Research, 64*, 311–361.

Grossman, J. (2012). "Big data": An opportunity for historians? *Perspectives on History, 50*(3). https://www.historians.org/publications-and-directories/perspectives-on-history/march-2012/big-data-an-opportunity-for-historians

# References

Guzman, G., & Kollar, M. (2023). *"Income in the United States: 2022.* https://www.census.gov/content/dam/Census/library/visualizations/2023/demo/p60-279/figure2.pdf

Halloran, N. (2015). *The fallen of World War II.* http://www.fallen.io/ww2/

Hansen, M., Levesque, E., Valant, J., & Quintero, D. (2018). *The 2018 Brown Center report on American education: How well are American students learning?* Brown Center on Education Policy, Brookings Institution. https://www.brookings.edu/wp-content/uploads/2018/06/2018-Brown-Center-Report-on-American-Education_FINAL1.pdf

Hardy, L., Dixon, C., & Hsi, S. (2020). From data collectors to data producers: Shifting students' relationship to data. *Journal of the Learning Sciences, 29*(1), 104–126. https://doi.org/10.1080/10508406.2019.1678164

Harris, L. M., & Girard, B. (2014). Instructional significance for teaching history: A preliminary framework. *The Journal of American History, 38*(4), 215–225.

Harsh, J. A., Campillo, M., Murray, C., Myers, C., Nguyen, J., & Maltese, A. V. (2019). 'Seeing' data like an expert: An eye-tracking study using graphical data representations. *CBE Life Sciences Education, 18*(3), 1–12. https://doi.org/https://doi.org/10.1187/cbe.18-06-0102

Hattab, G., & Andrews, R. J. (Eds.). (2022). *Étienne-Jules Marey: The graphic method.* Visionary Press.

Heffron, S., & Downs, R. (Eds.). (2012). *Geography for life: The national geography standards.* National Council for Geographic Education.

Hergesheimer, E. (1861). *Map showing the distribution of the slave population of the southern states of the United States compiled from the census of 1860.* Henry S. Graham. https://www.loc.gov/item/99447026/

Hertzberg, H. W. (1981). *Social studies reform, 1880–1980.* Social Science Education Consortium, Inc.

Hill, H. C., & Charalambous, C. Y. (2012). Teacher knowledge, curriculum materials, and quality of instruction: Lessons learned and open issues. *Journal of Curriculum Studies, 44*(4), 559–576.

Hodkinson, A., & Smith, C. (2018). Chronology and the new National Curriculum for history: Is it time to refocus the debate? *Education 3–13, 46*(6), 700–711. https://doi.org/10.1080/03004279.2018.1483804

Horowitz, W. (1988). The Babylonian map of the world. *Iraq, 50,* 147–165.

Howson, J. (2007). Is it the Tuarts and then the Studors or the other way around? *Teaching History, 127,* 40–47.

Hullman, J., & Diakopoulos, N. (2011). Visualization rhetoric: Framing effects in narrative visualization. *IEEE Transactions on Visualization and Computer Graphics, 17*(12), 2231–2240.

Hunter, B., Crismore, A., & Pearson, P. D. (1987). Visual displays in basal readers and social studies textbooks. In D. M. Willows & H. A. Houghton (Eds.), *The Psychology of Illustration* (pp. 116–135). Springer-Verlag.

Hynd-Shanahan, C. (2013). What does it take? The challenge of disciplinary literacy. *Journal of Adolescent & Adult Literacy, 57*(2), 93–98.

Independent Expert Advisory Group (IEAG).. (2014). *A world that counts: Mobilising the data revolution for sustainable development.* Independent Expert Advisory Group Secretariat, United Nations Secretary-General. https://www.ohchr.org/sites/default/files/Documents/Issues/MDGs/Post2015/WorldThatCounts.pdf

Irgens, G. A., Knight, S., Wise, A. F., Philip, T. M., Olivares, M. C., van Wart, S., Vakil, S., Marshall, J., Parikh, T., Lopez, M. L., Wilkerson, M. H., Gutiérrez, K., Jiang, S., & Kahn, J. (2020). Data literacies and social justice: Exploring critical data literacies through sociocultural perspectives. In M. Gresalfi & I. S. Horn (Eds.), *The interdisciplinarity of the learning sciences, 14th international conference of the learning sciences (ICLS)*, Vol. 1 (pp. 406–413). International Conference of the Learning Sciences.

Jacobson, L. (2015). *Pie chart of 'federal spending' circulating on the Internet is misleading*. PolitiFact. https://www.politifact.com/factchecks/2015/aug/17/facebook-posts/pie-chart-federal-spending-circulating-internet-mi/

Jan, T. (2018, March 28). Redlining was banned 50 years ago. It's still hurting minorities today. *The Wall Street Journal*. https://www.washingtonpost.com/news/wonk/wp/2018/03/28/redlining-was-banned-50-years-ago-its-still-hurting-minorities-today/

Jasanoff, S. (1990). *The fifth branch: Science advisers as policymakers*. Harvard University Press.

Jo, I., & Bednarz, S. W. (2009). Evaluating geography textbook questions from a spatial perspective: Using concepts of space, tools of representation, and cognitive processes to evaluate spatiality. *Journal of Geography*, *108*(1), 4–13.

Jo, I., Bednarz, S. W., & Metoyer, S. (2010). Selecting and designing questions to facilitate spatial thinking. *The Geography Teacher*, *7*(2), 49–55.

Johnson, B., Rydal Shapiro, B., DiSalvo, B., Rothschild, A., & DiSalvo, C. (2021). Exploring approaches to data literacy through a Critical Race Theory perspective. *Proceedings of the 2021 CHI Conference on Human Factors in Computing Systems*, Article no. 706.

Johnson, H., Watson, P., Delahunty, T., McSwiggen, P., & Smith, T. (2011). What it is they do: Differentiating knowledge and literacy practices across content disciplines. *Journal of Adolescent & Adult Literacy*, *55*(2), 100–109.

Johnson, S. (2007). *The ghost map: The story of London's most terrifying epidemic—and how it changed science, cities, and the modern world*. Riverhead Books.

Journell, W., Beeson, M. W., & Ayers, C. A. (2015). Learning to think politically: Toward more complete disciplinary knowledge in civics and government courses. *Theory and Research in Social Education*, *43*(1), 28–67.

Jung, T. (n.d.). *Compare map projections*. https://map-projections.net/imglist.php

Kahn, J. (2020). Learning at the intersection of self and society: The family geobiography as a context for data science education. *Journal of the Learning Sciences*, *29*(1), 57–80.

Kahn, J., & Jiang, S. (2021). Learning with large, complex data and visualizations: youth data wrangling in modeling family migration. *Learning, media and technology*, *46*(2), 128–143.

Kanarinka. (2013). The Detroit Geographic Expedition and Institute: A case study in civic mapping. *Civic media: Creating technology for social change*. https://civic.mit.edu/blog/kanarinka/the-detroit-geographic-expedition-and-institute-a-case-study-in-civic-mapping

Kandel, S., Heer, J., Plaisant, C., Kennedy, J., van Ham, F., Riche, N. H., Weaver, C., Lee, B., Brodbeck, D., & Buono, P. (2011). Research directions in data wrangling: Visualizations and transformations for usable and credible data. *Information Visualization*, *10*(4), 271–288. https://doi.org/10.1177/1473871611415994

# References

Keena, A., Latner, M., McGann, A. J. M., & Smith, C. A. (2021). *Gerrymandering the states: Partisanship, race, and the transformation of American federalism.* Cambridge University Press.

Keirn, T., & Martin, D. (2012). Historical thinking and preservice teacher preparation. *The History Teacher, 45*(4), 489–492.

Kennedy, H., & Engebretsen, M. (2020). Introduction: The relationships between graphs, charts, maps and meanings, feelings, engagements. In M. Engebretsen & H. Kennedy (Eds.), *Data visualization in society* (pp. 19–32). Amsterdam University Press.

Kennedy, H., Engebretsen, M., Hill, R. L., Kirk, A., & Weber, W. (2021). Data visualisations: Newsroom trends and everyday engagements. In L. Bounegru & J. Grey (Eds.), *The data journalism handbook: Towards a critical data practice,*(pp. 162–173). Amsterdam University Press. https://doi.org/10.1017/9789048542079

Kennedy, H., & Hill, R. L. (2018). The feeling of numbers: Emotions in everyday engagements with data and their visualisation. *Sociology, 52*(4), 830–848. https://doi.org/10.1177/0038038516674675

Kennedy, H., Hill, R. L., Aiello, G., & Allen, W. (2016). The work that visualisation conventions do. *Information, Communication & Society, 19*(6), 715–735. https://doi.org/10.1080/1369118X.2016.1153126

Kennedy, J. C. G. (1864). *Population of the United States in 1860; Compiled from the original returns of the eighth census.* Government Printing Office. https://www.census.gov/library/publications/1864/dec/1860a.html

Knaflic, C. N. (2015). *Storytelling with data: A data visualization guide for business professionals.* John Wiley & Sons.

Knight Lab. (2023). *Knight Lab.* Northwestern University. https://knightlab.northwestern.edu/

Kong, H. (2019). *A picture may be worth a thousand words, but words frame a picture.* Multiple views: Visualization research explained. https://medium.com/multiple-views-visualization-research-explained/a-picture-may-be-worth-a-thousand-words-but-words-frame-a-picture-78d4eee1409e

Kong, H.-K., Liu, Z., & Karahalios, K. (2019). Trust and recall of information across varying degrees of title-visualization misalignment. *Proceedings of the 2019 CHI conference on human factors in computing systems*, Paper no. 346. https://dl.acm.org/doi/10.1145/3290605.3300576

Kopf, D. (2016). When did charts become popular? *Pricenonomics.* https://priceonomics.com/when-did-charts-become-popular/

Kracauer, S. (1966). Time and history. *History and Theory, 6*, 65–78.

LaMar, T., & Boaler, J. (2021, July 12). *The importance and emergence of K–12 data science.* Kappan Online. https://kappanonline.org/math-importance-emergence-k12-data-science-lamar-boaler/

Lapowsky, I. (2017). No one has the data to prevent the next Flint. *WIRED.* https://www.wired.com/story/data-lead-poisoning-flint/

Laughlin, H. H. (1923). *Analysis of America's modern melting pot: Hearings Before the Committee on Immigration and Naturalization, House of Representatives, Sixty-seventh Congress, Third Session. November 21, 1922. Serial 7-C.* US Government Printing Office. https://archive.org/details/analysisofameric00unit/page/n1/mode/2up

Lee, B., Riche, N. H., Isenberg, P., & Carpendale, S. (2015). More than telling a story: A closer ook at the process of transforming data into visually shared stories. *IEEE Computer Graphics and Applications, 35*(5), 84–90.

Lee, C., Yang, T., Inchoco, G. D., Jones, G. M., & Satyanarayan, A. (2021). Viral visualizations: How coronavirus skeptics use orthodox data practices to promote unorthodox science online. *Proceedings of the 2021 CHI conference on human factors in computing systems*, Article no. 607. https://dl.acm.org/doi/10.1145/3411764.3445211

Lee, J., & Swan, K. (2013). The C3 Framework and the Common Core State Standards. In National Council for Social Studies (Ed.), *Social Studies for the next generation: Purposes, practices, and implications of the College, Career, and Civic Life (C3) Framework for Social Studies State Standards* (pp. xxi-xxvi). NCSS.

Lee, P. J. (2005). Putting principles into practice: Understanding history. In J. Bransford & S. Donovan (Eds.), *How students learn history, mathematics, and science in the classroom* (pp. 31–78). National Academies Press.

Lee, P. J., & Shemilt, D. (2009). Is any explanation better than none? *Teaching History, 137*, 42–49.

Lee, T. B. (2015). Whatever you think of Planned Parenthood, this is a terrible and dishonest chart. *Vox*. https://www.vox.com/2015/9/29/9417845/planned-parenthood-terrible-chart

Lee, V. R., Pimentel, D. R., Bhargava, R., & D'Ignazio, C. (2022). Taking data feminism to school: A synthesis and review of pre-collegiate data science education projects. *British Journal of Educational Technology, 53*(5), 1096–1113.

Lee, V. R., Wilkerson, M. H., & Lanouette, K. (2021). A call for a humanistic stance toward K–12 data science education. *Educational Researcher, 50*(9), 664–672.

Leetaru, K. (2016). How data and information literacy could end fake news. *Forbes*. https://www.forbes.com/sites/kalevleetaru/2016/12/11/how-data-and-information-literacy-could-end-fake-news/#38fd1fd23399

Leinhardt, G., & Young, K. M. (1996). Two texts, three readers: Distance and expertise in reading history. *Cognition and Instruction, 14*(4), 441–486.

Lévesque, S. (2008). *Thinking historically: Educating students for the twenty-first century*. University of Toronto Press.

Lévesque, S., & Clark, P. (2018). Historical thinking: Definitions and educational applications. In S. A. Metzger & L M. Harris (Eds.), *The Wiley international handbook of history teaching and learning* (pp. 117–148). John Wiley & Sons.

Levitt, S. D. (2022). Data science is the future. Let's start teaching it. *Education Week*. https://www.edweek.org/teaching-learning/opinion-data-science-is-the-future-lets-start-teaching-it/2022/01

Levstik, L. S., & Barton, K. C. (2015). *Doing history: Investigating with children in elementary and middle schools*. Routledge.

Lewis, M. W., Wigen, K., & Wigen, K. E. (1997). *The myth of continents: A critique of metageography*. University of California Press.

Liben, L. S. (2001). Thinking through maps. In M. Gattis (Ed.), *Spatial schemas and abstract thought* (pp. 45–77). The MIT Press.

Lin, L., & Atkinson, R. K. (2011). Using animations and visual cueing to support learning of scientific concepts and processes. *Computers & Education, 56*(3), 650–658. https://doi.org/https://doi.org/10.1016/j.compedu.2010.10.007

Liu, X., Vedlitz, A., Stoutenborough, J. W., & Robinson, S. (2015). Scientists' views and positions on global warming and climate change: A content analysis of congressional testimonies. *Climatic Change*, *131*(4), 487–503. https://doi.org/10.1007/s10584-015-1390-6

Louie, J. (2022). Critical data literacy: Creating a more just world with data. https://www.nationalacademies.org/documents/embed/link/LF2255DA3DD1C41C0A42D3BEF0989ACAECE3053A6A9B/file/D16254F310D01BBDA873920E4EFB8151F2D8334181AA

Lupi, G., & Posavec, S. (2016). *Dear Data*. Princeton Architectural Press.

Lupi, G., & Posavec, S. (n.d.). *Dear Data* [Website]. http://www.dear-data.com/all

Lybrand, H., & Dale, D. (2019, October 2, 2019). Fact checking Trump's "Impeach this" map. *CNN Politics*. https://www.cnn.com/2019/10/01/politics/trump-impeach-this-map-fact-check/index.html

Lyons, B. A., Montgomery, J. M., Guess, A. M., Nyhan, B., & Reifler, J. (2021). Overconfidence in news judgments is associated with false news susceptibility. *Proceedings of the National Academy of Sciences*, *118*(23), e2019527118.

Maher, T. V., Seguin, C., Zhang, Y., & Davis, A. P. (2020). Social scientists' testimony before Congress in the United States between 1946–2016, trends from a new dataset. *PloS one*, *15*(3), e0230104.

Maier, M. H., & Imazeki, J. (2013). *The data game: Controversies in social science statistics* (4th ed.). Taylor & Francis.

Maltese, A. V., Harsh, J. A., & Svetina, D. (2015). Data visualization literacy: Investigating data interpretation along the novice-expert continuum. *Journal of College Science Teaching*, *45*, 84–90.

Manson, S. (2017). *Mapping, society, and technology*. University of Minnesota Libraries. https://open.lib.umn.edu/mapping/

Marr, B. (2018, May 21). How much data do we create every day? The mind-blowing stats everyone should read. Forbes.com. https://www.forbes.com/sites/bernardmarr/2018/05/21/how-much-data-do-we-create-every-day-the-mind-blowing-stats-everyone-should-read

Marshall, T. (2016). *Prisoners of geography: ten maps that explain everything about the world* (Vol. 1). Simon and Schuster.

Martell, C. C., & Stevens, K. M. (2020). *Teaching history for justice: Centering activism in students' study of the past*. Teachers College Press.

Martino, S. (2019). Incorporate narrative expository text in social studies. *Teaching & School Administration* [Blog]. Grand Canyon University. https://www.gcu.edu/blog/teaching-school-administration/incorporate-narrative-expository-text-social-studies

Mautone, P. D., & Mayer, R. E. (2007). Cognitive aids for guiding graph comprehension. *Journal of Educational Psychology*, *99*(3), 640.

Mayer, R. E. (2009). *Multimedia learning*. Cambridge University Press.

Mayer, R. E., & Moreno, R. (2003). Nine ways to reduce cognitive load in multimedia learning. *Educational Psychologist*, *38*(1), 43–52.

McGrew, S. (2020). Learning to evaluate: An intervention in civic online reasoning. *Computers & Education*, *145*, 103711.

McGrew, S., Breakstone, J., Ortega, T., Smith, M., & Wineburg, S. (2018). Can students evaluate online sources? Learning from assessments of civic online reasoning. *Theory & Research in Social Education, 46*(2), 165–193. https://doi.org/https://doi.org/10.1080/00933104.2017.1416320

McGrew, S., Merroth, L., Zuspan, S., Buhrman, S., & Reynolds, E. (2022). Teaching students to evaluate online information through current events. *Social Education, 86*(6), 386–391.

Michigan Department of Education. (2023). Michigan Student Test of Educational Progress: Social Studies; sample items. https://www.michigan.gov/mde/-/media/Project/Websites/mde/Year/2018/01/03/2015_MSTEP_Gr11_SocStudies_Samples_book.pdf

Mitchell, B., & Franco, J. (2018). *HOLC "redlining" maps: The persistent structure of segregation and economic inequality.* National Community Reinvestment Coalition. https://ncrc.org/wp-content/uploads/dlm_uploads/2018/02/NCRC-Research-HOLC-10.pdf

Mitchell, K., & Elwood, S. (2012). From redlining to benevolent societies: The emancipatory power of spatial thinking. *Theory & Research in Social Education, 40*(2), 134–163.

Mohan, A., & Mohan, L. (2013). *Spatial thinking about maps: Development of concepts and skills across the early years.* National Geographic Network of Alliances for Geographic Education. https://media.nationalgeographic.org/assets/file/SpatialThinkingK-5ExSummary.pdf

Mohan, L., Mohan, A., & Uttal, D. (2015). Research on thinking and learning with maps and geospatial technologies. In M. N. Solem, N. T. Hunynh, & R. Boehm (Eds.), *Learning progressions for maps, geospatial technology and spatial thinking: A research handbook* (pp. 9–21). Association of American Geographers. https://groups.psych.northwestern.edu/uttal/documents/Mohanetal2015.pdf

Moje, E. B. (2008). Foregrounding the disciplines in secondary literacy teaching and learning: A call for change. *Journal of Adolescent & Adult Literacy, 52*(2), 96–107.

Moje, E. B. (2015). Doing and teaching disciplinary literacy with adolescent learners: A social and cultural enterprise. *Harvard Educational Review, 85*(2), 254–301. https://psycnet.apa.org/record/2016-18263-005

Moll, H. (1715). *A new and exact map of the dominions of the King of Great Britain on ye Continent of North America, containing Newfoundland, New Scotland, New England, New York, New Jersey, Pensilvania, Maryland, Virginia and Carolina.* London, Tho. Bowles, John Bowles & Son and J. King. https://www.loc.gov/resource/g3300.ct000232/

Monmonier, M. (1996). *How to lie with maps.* University of Chicago Press.

Monte-Sano, C., & De La Paz, S. (2012). Using writing tasks to elicit adolescents' historical reasoning. *Journal of Literacy Research, 44*(3), 273–299.

Monte-Sano, C., De La Paz, S., & Felton, M. (2014). *Reading, thinking, and writing about history: Teaching argument writing to diverse learners in the Common Core classroom, grades 6–12.* Teachers College Press.

Moreland, K., & Rogowitz, B. (2017, February 15). VisLies 2017 gallery. *VisLies.* https://www.vislies.org/2017/gallery/

Morin, K. M. (2012). Geographical literacies and their publics: Reflections on the American scene. *Progress in Human Geography, 37*(1), 3–9.

Morris, A. (2018). American Negro at Paris, 1900. In W. Battle-Baptiste & B. Rusert (Eds.), *W. E. B. Du Bois's data portraits: Visualizing Black America* (pp. 23–36). Princeton Architectural Press.
Meyer, D. (2007, August 17). Graphing Stories. *dy/dan*. https://blog.mrmeyer.com/2007/graphing-stories/
Myers, J. P. (2022). Truth or beauty? Social studies teachers' beliefs about the instructional purposes of data visualizations. *Theory & Research in Social Education*, 1–28.
Nærland, T. U. (2020). The political significance of data visualizations: Four key perspectives. In M. Engebretsen & H. Kennedy (Eds.), *Data visualization in society* (pp. 63–73). Amsterdam University Press.
Naimipour, B., Guzdial, M., & Shreiner, T. (2020). *Engaging pre-service teachers in front-end design: Developing technology for a social studies classroom*. 2020 IEEE Frontiers in Education Conference (FIE). doi: 10.1109/FIE44824.2020.9273908 https://ieeexplore.ieee.org/document/9273908
Nash, G. B., Crabtree, C., & Dunn, R. E. (2000). *History on trial: Culture wars and the Teaching of the past*. First Vintage Books.
National Association for the Advancement of Colored People. (1919). *Thirty years of lynching in the United States, 1889–1918*. National Association for the Advancement of Colored People.
National Association for the Advancement of Colored People. (2023). *History of lynching in America*. https://naacp.org/find-resources/history-explained/history-lynching-america
National Center for History in the Schools. (1996). *World History content standards*. National Center for History in the Schools. https://phi.history.ucla.edu/nchs/world-history-content-standards/
National Council for the Social Studies. (2013). *The college, career, and civic life (C3) framework for social studies state standards: Guidance for enhancing the rigor of K–12 civics, economics, geography, and history*. NCSS. https://www.socialstudies.org/college-career-and-civic-life-c3
National Council for the Social Studies. (2016). A vision of powerful teaching and learning in the social studies. *Social Education, 80*(3), 180–182.
National Council for the Social Studies. (2023). *About NCSS*. National Council for the Social Studies. https://www.socialstudies.org/about
National Education Association Committee of Ten on Secondary School Studies. (1894). *Report of the Committee of Ten on Secondary School Studies: With the reports of the conferences arranged by the committee*. National Educational Association. https://archive.org/details/reportcommittee00studgoog/mode/2up
National Geographic Society. (2016). *What is geo-literacy?* . National Geographic Society. http://nationalgeographic.org/media/what-is-geo-literacy/
National Governors Association Center for Best Practices & Council of Chief State School Officers. (2010a). *Common Core state standards for English language arts & literacy in history/social studies, science, and technical subjects*. National Governors Association Center for Best Practices, Council of Chief State School Officers.
National Governors Association Center for Best Practices & Council of Chief State School Officers. (2010b). *Common Core state standards for mathematics*.

National Governors Association Center for Best Practices, Council of Chief State School Officers.

National Issues Forums and the Kettering Foundation. (2020). *Immigration: Who should we welcome? What should we do?* National Issues Forums Institute. https://www.nifi.org/en/issue-guide/immigration

National Research Council. (1997). *Rediscovering geography: New relevance for science and society.* National Academies Press.

National Research Council. (2005). *Learning to think spatially.* The National Academies Press. https://doi.org/10.17226/11019

Native Land Digital. (2023). *Native land map.* Native Land Digital. https://native-land.ca/

Navarro, O., & Howard, T. C. (2017). A critical race theory analysis of social studies research, theory and practice. In M. M. Manfra & C. M. Bolick (Eds.), *The Wiley handbook of social studies research.* John Wiley & Sons.

New, R., Swan, K., Lee, J., & Grant, S. (2021). The state of social studies standards: What is the impact of the C3 Framework? *Social Education, 85*(4), 239–246.

Newman, N. (2021). *Journalism, media, and technology trends and predictions 2021.* Reuters Institute for the Study of Journalism. https://reutersinstitute.politics.ox.ac.uk/sites/default/files/2021-01/Newman_Predictions_2021_FINAL.pdf

Newman, N. (2023). *Journalism, media, and technology trends and predictions 2023.* Reuters Institute for the Study of Journalism. https://reutersinstitute.politics.ox.ac.uk/sites/default/files/2023-01/Journalism_media_and_technology_trends_and_predictions_2023.pdf

Nobles, M. (2000). *Shades of citizenship: Race and the census in modern politics.* Stanford University Press.

Nokes, J. D. (2012). *Building students' historical literacies: Learning to read and reason with historical texts and evidence.* Taylor and Francis.

Nokes, J. D. (2022). *Building students' historical literacies* (2nd ed.). Routledge.

Norman, S. E. (2023). How data literacy can keep American safe. *Time.* https://time.com/6290684/data-literacy-us-national-security/

Norton, M. B. (2002). *In the Devil's snare: The Salem witchcraft crisis of 1692.* Knopf.

Noushad, N. F., Shim, J., & Yoon, S. A. (2022). Navigating the conceptual and critical demands of data literacy in high school spaces using firsthand data. In C. Chinn, E. Tan, C. Chan, & Y. Kali (Eds.), *Proceedings of the 16th International Conference of the Learning Sciences-ICLS* (pp. 195–202). International Society of the Learning Sciences. https://2022.isls.org/proceedings/

O'Connor, C., & Weatherall, J. O. (2019). *The misinformation age: How false beliefs spread.* Yale University Press.

OER Project. (2023). *Timeline: Big History.* OER Project. https://www.oerproject.com/OER-Materials/OER-Media/Images/SBH/Unit-10/10-0-Looking-Back/Timeline-Big-History

Onuoha, M. (2022). *The Library of Missing Datasets 3.0.* https://github.com/MimiOnuoha/missing-datasets

Our World in Data. (2022). *Share of people living in urban areas, 2021.* Our World in Data. https://ourworldindata.org/grapher/share-of-population-urbanPasse,

J., & Patterson, N. C. (2013). The evolution of a national survey of social studies teachers. In J. Passe & P. G. Fitchett (Eds.), *The status of social studies: Views from the field* (pp. 3–18). Information Age Publishing.

Pawluczuk, A. (2019, August 21). Human rights in the digital age: Data literacy in tackling the big data divide. *Impakter.* https://impakter.com/human-rights-in-the-digital-age-data-literacy-in-tackling-the-big-data-divide/

Pearson Institute & The Associated Press-NORC Center for Public Affairs Research. (2021). *The American public views the spread of misinformation as a major problem.* AP & NORC. https://apnorc.org/wp-content/uploads/2021/10/misinformation_Formatted_v2-002.pdf

Peck, C. L. (2010). "It's not like [I'm] Chinese and Canadian. I am in between": Ethnicity and students' conceptions of historical significance. *Theory & Research in Social Education, 38*(4), 574–617.

Perez, C. C. (2019). *Invisible women: Data bias in a world designed for men.* Abrams.

Perkins, A. (2020, September 22). #MathArtChallenge 92: W.E.B. Du Bois data portraits. *arbitrarilyclose: Musings on math and teaching.* https://arbitrarilyclose.com/2020/07/28/mathartchallenge-92-w-e-b-du-bois-data-portraits/

Pfannkuch, M., Regan, M., Wild, C., & Horton, N. J. (2010). Telling data stories: Essential dialogues for comparative reasoning. *Journal of Statistics Education, 18,* 1–38.

Philip, T. M., Olivares-Pasillas, M. C., & Rocha, J. (2016). Becoming racially literate about data and data-literate about race: Data visualizations in the classroom as site of racial-ideological micro-contestations. *Cognition and Instruction, 34*(4), 361–388. https://doi.org/10.1080/07370008.2016.1210418

Philip, T. M., & Rubel, L. (2019). Classrooms as laboratories of democracy for social transformation: The role of data literacy. In *Shifting Contexts, Stable Core: Advancing Quantitative Literacy in Higher Education.* Mathematical Association of America.

Philip, T. M., Schuler-Brown, S., & Way, W. (2013). A framework for learning about big data with mobile technologies for democratic participation: Possibilities, limitations, and unanticipated obstacles. *Technology, Knowledge and Learning, 18,* 103–120.

Phillips, U. B. (1906). The origin and growth of the Southern Black Belts. *The American Historical Review, 11*(4), 798–816. https://doi.org/10.1086/ahr/11.4.798

Playfair, W. (1801a). *The commerical and political atlas.* T. Burton. https://archive.org/details/PLAYFAIRWilliam1801TheCommercialandPoliticalAtlas/

Playfair, W. (1801b). *The statistical breviary.* T. Bensley. https://archive.org/details/statisticalbrev00playgoog

Popa, N. (2022). Operationalizing historical consciousness: A review and synthesis of the literature on meaning making in historical learning. *Review of Educational Research, 92*(2), 171–208.

Popova, M. (2016). Foreword. In G. Lupi & C. Posavec, *Dear Data* (p. vii). Princeton Architectural Press.

Population Education. (n.d.). *World population history.* Population Connection. https://worldpopulationhistory.org/map/

Porter, A. C., & Smithson, J. L. (2001, December). *Defining, developing, and using curriculum indicators* (CPRE Research Report Series RR-048). Consortium for

Policy Research in Education, University of Pennsylvania Graduate School of Education. http://repository.upenn.edu/cpre_researchreports/69

Posetti, J., & Matthews, A. (2018). *A short guide to the history of "fake news" and disinformation*. International Center for Journalists. https://www.icfj.org/news/short-guide-history-fake-news-and-disinformation-new-icfj-learning-module

Poynar, R. (2023). Exposure: Motion efficiency study by Frank Gilbreth. *Design Observer*. https://designobserver.com/feature/exposure-motion-efficiency-study-by-frank-gilbreth/39272

Qiu, L. (2015). *Chart shown at Planned Parenthood hearing is misleading and 'ethically wrong.'* Politifact. https://www.politifact.com/factchecks/2015/oct/01/jason-chaffetz/chart-shown-planned-parenthood-hearing-misleading-/

Qlik. (2022). *Data Literacy: The Upskilling Revolution*. https://thedataliteracyproject.org/wp-content/uploads/2022/11/Data-Literacy-The-Upskilling-Evolution-Report-1.pdf

Quadri, G. J., & Rosen, P. (2022). A survey of perception-based visualization studies by task. *IEEE Transactions on Visualization and Computer Graphics, 28*(12), 5026–5048. https://doi.org/10.1109/TVCG.2021.3098240

Radinsky, J. (2020). Mobilities of data narratives. *Cognition and Instruction, 38*(3), 374–406.

Radinsky, J., Hospelhorn, E., Melendez, J. W., Riel, J., & Washington, S. (2014). Teaching American migrations with GIS census webmaps: A modified "backwards design" approach in middle-school and college classrooms. *The Journal of Social Studies Research, 38*(3), 143–158.

Reisman, A. (2012). Reading like a historian: A document-based history curriculum intervention in urban high school. *Cognition and Instruction, 30*(1) 86–112. https://doi.org/10.1080/07370008.2011.634081

Residents of Hull House. (1895). *Hull-House maps and papers*. Thomas Y. Crowell & Co. https://homicide.northwestern.edu/pubs/hullhouse/

Ribecca, S. (2016). *The data visualisation catalogue*. The Data Visualisation Catalogue. http://www.datavizcatalogue.com/index.html

Rid, T. (2020). *Active measures: The secret history of disinformation and political warfare*. Farrar, Straus and Giroux.

Ritchie, H., Roser, M., & Rosado, P. (n.d.). *Energy*. Our World in Data. https://ourworldindata.org/energy

Roberts, K. L., & Brugar, K. A. (2014). Navigating maps to support comprehension: When textbooks don't have GPS. *The Geography Teacher, 11*, 149–163. https://doi.org/10.1080/19338341.2014.975143

Roberts, K. L., & Brugar, K. A. (2017). The view from here: Emergence of graphical literacy. *Reading Psychology, 38*(8), 733–777.

Rodríguez, M. T., Nunes, S., & Devezas, T. (2015). Telling stories with data visualization. *Proceedings of the 2015 Workshop on Narrative & Hypertext, Guzelyurt, Northern Cyprus* (pp. 7–11). https://doi.org/10.1145/2804565.2804567

Rogers, B. (2016). Study reveals a new class of data influencers. Forbes. https://www.forbes.com/sites/brucerogers/2016/10/24/study-reveals-a-new-class-of-data-influencers/?sh=1991855f44fd

Ropp, P. S. (2010). *China in World History*. Oxford University Press.

Rosenberg, D., & Grafton, A. (2013). *Cartographies of time: A history of the timeline*. Princeton Architectural Press.

Roser, M. (2023). The limits of our personal experience and the value of statistics. *Our World in Data*. https://ourworldindata.org/limits-personal-experience

Roser, M., & Ortiz-Ospina, E. (2018). Literacy. In: Our World in Data.

Rosling, H., Rosling, O., & Rönnlund, A. R. (2018). *Factfulness: Ten reasons we're wrong about the world—and why things are better than you think*. Flatiron Books.

Rothstein, R. (2017). *The color of law: A forgotten history of how our government segregated America*. Liveright Publishing.

Routley, N. (2021). Mercator misconceptions: Clever map shows the true size of countries. *Visual Capitalist*. https://www.visualcapitalist.com/mercator-map-true-size-of-countries/

Rüsen, J. (2007). *Time and history: The variety of cultures*. Berghahn Books.

Saini, A. (2019). *Superior: The return of race science*. Beacon Press.

Salinas, C., Blevins, B., & Sullivan, C. C. (2012). Critical historical thinking: When official narratives collide with *other* narratives. *Multicultural Perspectives*, 14(1), 18–27. https://doi.org/10.1080/15210960.2012.646640

Sanchez, T. R., & Mills, R. K. (2005). "Telling tales": the teaching of American history through storytelling. *Social Education*, 69(5), 269.

Schnotz, W. (2002). Towards an integrated view of learning from text and visual displays. *Educational Psychology Review*, 14(1), 101–120.

Schnotz, W., Hauck, G., & Schwartz, N. H. (2022). Multiple mental representations in picture processing. *Psychological Research*, 86(3), 903–918.

Schnotz, W., Ludewig, U., Ullrich, M., Horz, H., McElvany, N., & Baumert, J. (2014). Strategy shifts during learning from texts and pictures. *Journal of Educational Psychology*, 106(4), 974.

Schnotz, W., Wagner, I., Ullrich, M., Horz, H., & McElvany, N. (2017). Development of students' text-picture integration and reading competence across grades 5–7 in a three-tier secondary school system: A longitudinal study. *Contemporary Educational Psychology*, 51, 152–169.

Schor, P. (2017). *Counting Americans: How the U.S. Census classified the nation*. Oxford University Press.

Schulten, S. (Ed.). (2022). *Emma Willard: Maps of history*. Visionary Press.

Scott, J. C. (1998). *Seeing like a state: How certain schemes to improve the human condition have failed*. Yale University Press.

Segel, E., & Heer, J. (2010). Narrative visualization: Telling stories with data. *IEEE Transactions on Visualization and Computer Graphics*, 16(6), 1139–1148.

Seixas, P. (1994). Students' understanding of historical significance. *Theory and Research in Social Education*, 22(3), 281–304.

Seixas, P. (1997). Mapping the terrain of historical significance. *Social Education*, 61, 28–31.

Seixas, P., & Morton, T. (2013). *The big six: Historical thinking concepts*. Nelson Education, Ltd.

Semega, J., & Kollar, M. (2022). *Income in the United States: 2021*. https://www.census.gov/content/dam/Census/library/publications/2022/demo/p60-276.pdf

Serafini, F. (2015). Multimodal literacy: From theories to practices. *Language Arts*, 92(6), 412–422.

Shah, P., & Hoeffner, J. (2002). Review of graphic comprehension research: Implications for instruction. *Educational Psychology Review*, 14, 47–69.

Shah, P., Mayer, R. E., & Hegarty, M. (1999). Graphs as aids to knowledge comprehension: Signaling techniques for guiding the process of graph comprehension. *Journal of Educational Psychology, 91*, 690–702. https://doi.org/10.1037/0022-0663.91.4.690

Shanahan, T., & Shanahan, C. (2008). Teaching disciplinary literacy to adolescents: Rethinking content-area literacy. *Harvard Educational Review, 78*(1), 40–59.

Shapiro, B. R., Meng, A., Rothschild, A., Gilliam, S., Garrett, C., DiSalvo, C., & DiSalvo, B. (2022). Bettering data. *Educational Technology & Society, 25*(4), 109–125.

Sharma, S. V. (2006). High school students interpreting tables and graphs: Implications for research. *International Journal of Science and Mathematics Education, 4*, 241–268.

Shemilt, D. (2009). Drinking an ocean and pissing a cupful: How adolescents make sense of history. In L. Symcox & A. Wilschut (Eds.), *The problem of the canon and the future of history teaching* (pp. 141–209). Information Age Publishing.

Shi, D. E., & Tindall, G. B. (1996). *America: A narrative history*. W.W. Norton Publishing. https://web.archive.org/web/20060405095317/http://wwnorton.com/college/history/tindall/timelinf/tranrail.htm

Shreiner, T. L. (2014). Using historical knowledge to reason about contemporary political issues: An expert-novice study. *Cognition and Instruction, 32*(4), 313–352.

Shreiner, T. L. (2018). Data literacy for social studies: Examining the role of data visualizations in K–12 textbooks. *Theory & Research in Social Education, 46*(2), 194–231. https://doi.org/https://doi.org/10.1080/00933104.2017.1400483

Shreiner, T. L. (2019). Students' use of data visualizations in historical reasoning: A think-aloud investigation with elementary, middle, and high school students. *The Journal of Social Studies Research, 43*(4), 389–404.

Shreiner, T. L. (2020). Building a data-literate citizenry: How U.S. state standards address data and data visualizations in social studies. *Information and Learning Sciences, 121*(11/12), 909–931.

Shreiner, T. L. (2023). Uncovering the discipline-specific value of data visualizations in world historical writing. *World History Connected, 20*(1).

Shreiner, T. L., & Dykes, B. M. (2021). Visualizing the teaching of data visualizations in social studies: A study of teachers' data literacy practices, beliefs, and knowledge. *Theory & Research in Social Education, 49*(2), 262–306.

Shreiner, T. L., & Guzdial, M. (2022). The information won't just sink in: Helping teachers provide technology-assisted data literacy instruction in social studies. *British Journal of Educational Technology, 53*(5), 1134–1158.

Shreiner, T. L., & Martell, C. C. (2022). Making race and racism invisible: a critical race analysis of data visualizations in online curricular materials for teaching history. *Race Ethnicity and Education*, 1–21. https://doi.org/10.1080/13613324.2022.2106473

Shreiner, T. L., & Zwart, D. E. (2020). It's just different: Identifying features of disciplinary literacy unique to World History. *The History Teacher, 53*(3), 441–469.

Shulman, L. (1986). Those who understand: Knowledge growth in teaching. *Educational Researcher, 15*(2), 4–14.

Silverman, C. (2016). This analysis shows how viral fake election news stories outperformed real news on Facebook. *BuzzFeed News*. https://www.buzzfeednews

# References

.com/article/craigsilverman/viral-fake-election-news-outperformed-real-news-on-facebook

Sinclair, N., Healy, L., & Sales, C. O. R. (2009). Time for telling stories: narrative thinking with dynamic geometry. *ZDM, 41*(4), 441–452. https://doi.org/10.1007/s11858-009-0180-x

Smil, V. (2018). *Energy in world history*. Routledge.

Snow, J. (1854). *On the mode of communication of cholera*. John Churchill.

Sorapure, M., & Fauni, A. (2020). Teaching Dear Data. https://kairos.technorhetoric.net/25.1/praxis/sorapure-fauni/

Stearns, P. N. (2000). Periodization in World History teaching: Identifying the big changes. In R. E. Dunn (Ed.), *The new World History: A teacher's companion* (pp. 364–375). Bedford/St. Martin's.

Stearns, P. N. (2011). *World History: The basics*. Routledge.

Stow, W., & Haydn, T. (2012). Issues in the teaching of chronology. In J. Arthur & R. Phillips (Eds.), *Issues in history teaching* (pp. 83–97). Routledge.

Strobel, B., Lindner, M. A., Saß, S., & Köller, O. (2018). Task-irrelevant data impair processing of graph reading tasks: An eye tracking study. *Learning and Instruction, 55*, 139–147.

Swan, K. (2013). The importance of the C3 framework. *Social Education, 77*(4), 222–224.

Swenson, K. (2020, June 29). Millions track the pandemic on Johns Hopkins's dashboard. Those who built it say some miss the real story. *The Washington Post*. https://www.washingtonpost.com/local/johns-hopkins-tracker/2020/06/29/daea7eea-a03f-11ea-9590-1858a893bd59_story.html

Taurence, K., Shreiner, T., & Dykes, B. (2022, March 23). Revealing the power of data visualizations in Social Studies through slow reveal graphs. *Statistics Teacher* (Spring 2022). https://www.statisticsteacher.org/2022/03/23/slowrevealgraphs/

Tawney, R. H. (2011). *History and society: Essays by RH Tawney* (J. M. Winter, Ed.). Routledge.

Texas Education Agency. (2022). State of Texas Assessments of Academic Readiness: Grade 8 Social Studies. https://tea.texas.gov/sites/default/files/2022-staar-may-grade-8-socialstudies-releasedtest.pdf

Tønnessen, E. S. (2020). What is visual-numeric literacy, and how does it work? In M. Engebretsen & H. Kennedy (Eds.), *Data visualization in society* (p. 189). Amsterdam University Press.

Tufte, E. R. (1997). *Visual explanations: Images and quantities, evidence and narrative*. Graphics Press.

Tufte, E. R. (2001). *The visual display of quantitative information*. Graphics Press.

U.S. Census Bureau. (1909). *A century of population growth*. Government Printing Office. https://www.census.gov/library/publications/1909/decennial/century-populaton-growth.html

U.S. Census Bureau. (2022). *Educational attainment in the United States: 2021*. https://www.census.gov/data/tables/2021/demo/educational-attainment/cps-detailed-tables.html

United States Census Office & Gannett, H. (1898). *Statistical atlas of the United States, based upon the results of the eleventh census*. Government Printing Office. https://www.loc.gov/item/07019233/

University of the State of New York. (2023). *Regents Exam in Global History and Geography II*. New York State Education Department. https://www.nysedregents.org/ghg2/123/glhg2-12023-exam.pdf

van Drie, J., & van Boxtel, C. (2008). Historical reasoning: Towards a framework for analyzing students' reasoning about the past. *Educational Psychology Research in Social Education, 20*(2), 87–110. https://doi.org/10.1007/s10648-007-9056-1

Van Rossum, M. (2020). Global slavery, local ondage? Rethinking slaveries as (im)mobilizing regimes from the case of the Dutch Indian Ocean and Indonesian Archipelago worlds. *Journal of World History, 31*(4), 693–727.

VanSledright, B., & Brophy, J. (1992). Storytelling, imagination, and fanciful elaboration in children's historical reconstructions. *American Educational Research Journal, 29*(4), 837–859.

Verdi, M. P., & Kulhavy, R. W. (2002). Learning with maps and texts: An overview. *Educational Psychology Review, 14*(1), 27–46. https://doi.org/https://doi.org/10.1023/A:1013128426099

Villa Ross, C. A., Shin, H. B., & Marlay, M. C. (2021, August 18). *Pandemic impact on 2020 American Community Survey 1-year data*. Census Blog. U. S. Census Bureau. https://www.census.gov/newsroom/blogs/random-samplings/2021/10/pandemic-impact-on-2020-acs-1-year-data.html

Wardle, C., & Derakhshan, H. (2017). *Information disorder: Toward an interdisciplinary framework for research and policymaking* (Report DGI(2017)09). Council of Europe. https://rm.coe.int/information-disorder-toward-an-interdisciplinary-framework-for-researc/168076277c

Watts, D. J., Rothschild, D. M., & Mobius, M. (2021). Measuring the news and its impact on democracy. *Proceedings of the National Academy of Sciences, 118*(15). https://doi.org/10.1073/pnas.1912443118

Wells-Barnett, I. B. (1901). Lynching and the excuse for it. *The Independent, 53*(2737), 1133–1136. https://digital.lib.niu.edu/islandora/object/niu-gildedage%3A24185

Wells-Barnett, I. B. (1895). *The red record: Tabulated statistics and alleged causes of lynching in the United States*. Cavalier Classics.

Wertsch, J. V. (2004). Specific narratives and schematic templates. In P. Seixas (Ed.), *Theorizing historical consciousness* (pp. 49–62). University of Toronto Press.

Wertsch, J. V. (2008). The narrative organization of collective memory. *Ethos, 36*(1), 120–135.

WGBH Educational Foundation. (2021). *Interpreting stories and graphs*. PBS LearningMedia. https://wgvu.pbslearningmedia.org/resource/rttt12.math.graphstories/interpreting-stories-and-graphs/

Whitby, A. (2020). *The sum of the people: How the census has shaped nations, from the ancient world to the modern age*. Basic Books.

Wiegand, P. (2006). *Learning and teaching with maps*. Psychology Press.

Wilkerson, M. H., & Laina, V. (2018). Middle school students' reasoning about data and context through storytelling with repurposed local data. *ZDM, 50*, 1223–1235.

Willard, E. (1828). *A series of maps to Willard's History of the United States, or, Republic of America. Designed for schools and private libraries*. [New York] White, Gallaher, & White. https://www.loc.gov/item/2002624002/

Willard, E. (1846). The Temple of Time. In *Willard's map of time: a companion to the historic guide*. A.S. Barnes & Co. https://www.davidrumsey.com/luna/servlet/detail/RUMSEY~8~1~315043~90083688:The-Temple-of-Time#

Williams, S. (2020). *Data Action: Using Data for Public Good*. Massachusetts Institute of Technology.

Willingham, D. T. (2004). Ask the cognitive scientist the privileged status of story. *American Educator, 28*, 43–45.

Willingham, D. T. (2009). *Why don't students like school?* Jossey-Bass.

Wills, G. (2012). *Visualizing time*. Springer.

Wilschut, A. (2012). *Images of time: The role of an historical consciousness of time in learning history*. Information Age Publishing.

Wilson, P. H., & Journell, W. (2011). Lies, damn lies, and statistics: Uncovering the truth behind polling data. *Social Studies Research & Practice, 6*(1), 169–180. DOI:10.1108/SSRP-01-2011-B0014

Wineburg, S. (1991). On the reading of historical texts: Notes on the breach between school and academy. *American Educational Research Journal, 28*(3), 495–519.

Wineburg, S. (2001). *Historical thinking and other unnatural acts: Charting the future of teaching the past*. Temple University Press.

Wineburg, S. (2018). *Why learn history (when it's already on your phone)*. University of Chicago Press.

Wineburg, S., Martin, D., & Monte-Sano, C. (2011). *Reading like a historian: Teaching literacy in middle and high school history classrooms*. Teachers College Press.

Wineburg, S., & Reisman, A. (2015). Disciplinary literacy in history: A toolkit for digital citizenship. *Journal of Adolescent & Adult Literacy, 58*(8), 636–639.

Witzel, L. (2022, February 15). Did data visualization erase the woman from women's work? *Nightingale: Journal of the Data Visualization Society*. https://nightingaledvs.com/did-data-visualization-erase-the-woman-from-womens-work/

Wood, S. (1995). Developing an understanding of time—sequencing issues. *Teaching History,* (79), 11–14.

Yearwood, P. J. (2014). Continents and consequences: The history of a concept. *Journal of Global History, 9*(3), 329–356.

Yongpradit, P., Hendrickson, K., & Phillips, R. (2016). *K–12 CS Framework*. K–12 Computer Science Framework. https://k12cs.org/wp-content/uploads/2016/09/K%E2%80%9312-Computer-Science-Framework.pdf

Zukas, A. (2021). Cartography and narrative in the maps of Herman Moll's *The World Described. XVII–XVIII: Revue de la Société d'études anglo-américaines des XVIIe et XVIIIe siècles, 78*. https://doi.org/10.4000/1718.8764

# Index

*A New Chart of History* (Priestly), 98, 99
Acheson, G., 114, 115, 119, 120, 128
Action, data-informed, 92–94
Activities, for telling stories with graphs, 145–146
Addams, Jane, 81–82, 84
Adesope, O. O., 188
Africa, Moll's 1710 map of, 57, 59
Ages, historical, 97, 101, 104
Aiello, G., 28, 90
Ainsworth, S., 170
Akerman, J. R., 60, 62, 63
Al Sharif al-Idrisi, 1154 CE world map of, 63–64
Allen, J., 22
Allen, W., 28, 29, 90
Alpizar, D., 188
American Community Survey (ACS), 11
"American Dream," 111
Amit-Danhi, E. R., 29
Anderson, K. C., 117, 119
Anderson, M. J., 29, 66, 67
Andrews, R. J., 27, 135
Arias-Ferrer, L., 145
Atkinson, R. K., 188
Austen, R. A., 107
Axes (x-/y-), distorted, 35–38
Ayers, C. A., 155

Babylonian map of world and mythology, 60–62
Bain, R. B., 52, 107
Ball, D. L., 58
Balliet, R. N., 6, 7, 136
Barbeau-Dubourg, Jacques, 24
Barbour, C., 51
Barton, K. C., 100, 101, 104, 135, 146
Baseline on graphs, omitting, 35–38
Battle-Baptiste, W., 76
Baumert, J., 10
Bausmith, J. M., 115
BBC (British Broadcasting Corporation), 133
Beach, J. D., 135, 145

"Beaver Map" (Moll), 57, 58
Bednarz, R. S., 114, 115, 119, 120, 128
Bednarz, S. W., 114, 115, 116, 119, 120, 122, 128
Beeson, M. W., 155
Beezley, W. H., 107
Beliefs, influences on, 15, 21
Bender, T., 107, 109
Bentley, J. H., 104
Bergstrom, C. T., 21, 35
Bhargava, R., 4, 93, 199
Bias(es), 6, 11. *See also* Motivations
Bienen, L., 83
*The Big History Timeline*, 108, 109
Black, E., 73, 75
Blevins, B., 106, 107, 136
Bliss, L., 129
Blow, F., 98, 100, 101, 102, 103, 170, 171
Boaler, J., 87
Bond, L. F., 92, 93
Börner, K., 6, 7, 136
boyd, d., 87
Boyer, P., 127
Braun, M., 135
Breakstone, J., 22, 23, 40, 90
Bright, G. W., 136, 137, 138, 139, 140, 168, 172, 173
British Library, 57
Britt, M. A., 61
Brodbeck, D., 155
Brophy, J., 145
Brotton, J., 60, 62, 63, 63.64, 65
Brown, W., 61
Brugar, K. A., 115, 117, 121, 122, 173
Bruner, J. S., 50
Bubble graphs/plots, 9, 50, 133, 137, 183, 202; animated, 133, 134
Bubble maps, 10, 125
Budiman, A., 189, 190
Buhrman, S., 90
Bullock, C. S., 131
Buono, P., 155
Burkholder, P., 52
Bush, George H. W., 44

# Index

C3 Framework (NCSS), 45–47, 87; data-informed action projects and, 92; data production work and, 154–155; disciplinary literacy and, 51–55; states' use of, 92–93
Cairo, A., 23, 32, 35
California Dept. of Education, 47
Calvillo, D. P., 22
Cameron, W. B., 214
Campillo, M., 139, 140
Cannato, V. J., 111
Carle, J., 22, 23, 40
Carlson, J., 4
Carney, R. N., 170
Carpendale, S., 135–136
Carr, D., 105
Carroll, J. M., 200, 2006
Causes/consequences, historical, 109
Census data, U.S.; educational attainment dataset, 11–12; historical examples, 66, 67–68, 71–72; impact of, 28–29, 67; nature of, 66–67; as primary source data, 65–71
Center for the Study of the American Constitution, 121
Chaffetz, Jason (U.S. Representative), 31
Change and continuity analysis, 107
Chapman, A., 109
Charalambous, C. Y., 88
Charner-Laird, M., 51
*Chart of Biography* (Priestly), 98, 99
Charts. *See* Graphs and charts
Chick, H. L., 145
Children, geography of (community investigation), 214–215
Chronological understanding, 100, 104–105; terminology/typology, 100, 101–102, 103, 109; timelines and, 101, 102–104
CIO Bulletin, 154
Civic action, informed, 22
Civic online reasoning, 22–23
Civics instruction, 51
Civil War (U.S.), 29, 67–69, 71–72
Clark, P., 90
Clinton, Hillary, 3, 4
Coatoam, S., 51
Cohen, J. D., 139
Cohen, J. S., 139
College Board, 105
Collins, K., 34
Combs, M., 135, 145
*The Commercial and Political Index* (Playfair, 1786), 8
Common Core Standards, 45, 165
Communication, data visualization for, 3–4
Comprehension, data visualization; skills hierarchy for, 139–143; techniques for, 187–198
Concurrence (temporal concept), 102

Content knowledge, 88–89
Contextualization, historical thinking and, 91
Correll, M., 37
Corroboration, historical thinking and, 91–92
Council for Economic Education, 44, 45
COVID-19 pandemic, data examples and, 8–9, 10, 29–30
Crabtree, C., 44
Crawford, K., 87
Cribb, G., 61
Crismore, A., 6, 7
Critical, humanistic data literacy; absence in school curricula, 87–88; contextual considerations in, 91; cross-checking claims/evidence and, 91–92; data work pathways to, 151–161; document sourcing practice in, 90–91; key propositions, 86–87; teaching of, 85–94
Critique techniques, data visualization, 188–198
Croninger, R., 51
Crowley, J. E., 57
Curcio, F. R., 136, 137, 138, 139, 140, 168, 172, 173
Curricula. *See* School curricula/courses
Cyclegraph, 86

Dale, D., 3, 4
Data. *See also* Datasets; discrimination and, 71, 73–75; manipulating and visualizing, 157, 161, 199–210; power of, 87; producing, 154–155; reading for comprehension, 139–143; working with, 151–161; worldview assumptions, 87
Data collecting/collections; by Hull House residents, 82; women's perspective absent from, 213–214
Data exchanges, 5
*The Data Game:...* (Maier and Imazeki), 213
Data-informed action, 92–94
Data literacy, 3–5; critical, humanistic. *See* Critical, humanistic data literacy; for disciplinary literacy, 51–55; empowerment and, 199; instruction in. *See* Data literacy instruction; skills/skillset, 5, 15, 47; social studies and, 15; verbal literacy *vs.*, 10
Data literacy instruction; K–2nd grade, 166–169; 3rd–5th grade, 170–173, 174–175; 6th–8th grade, 173, 176–179, 180–181; 9th–12th grade, 179, 182–186; minimal manual use in, 210; rationale for, 214; recommendations for, 165–166, 183, 186
Data points, human beings as, 86
"Data revolution," UN report on, 5–6
Data stories. *See* Stories
Data Visualization for Literacy (DV4L), 201

Data visualizations; advancements in, 6.8; assumptions about, 187; census data and, 65–71; comprehension/critique techniques, 187–198; creating, tools for, 200, 203–205; in curricular/course materials, 15; of W. E. B. Du Bois, 75–78, 80, 84, 157–158, 215; evaluating. *See* Data literacy; as evidence, historical overview, 23–28; expected conventions, 37; flawed messaging and, 71–72; forms and functions, 3–4, 6–10, 14–15. *See also specific categories and types*; future directions, 14–15; handmade, 157–158; in history research journals, 53–55; human choices for, 6, 10–14; influence/persuasive nature of, 23, 29; manipulating, tools for, 201–203; misleading, 33–40; motivation and bias in, 6, 67, 69; in newspapers, 29–30; of Florence Nightingale, 26–27, 143, 157, 215; online resources for, 50; skills flexibility and, 6; in social movements, 75–84; spatiotemporal, 7–9; as tools of oppression, 71–75; value and variety of, 6, 7–8; of Emma Willard, 41–44
Datafication of society, 5, 10
Datasets; absent, 213–214; census data on educational achievement, 11–12; choosing, 201; locating/sources for, 200, 203
DataUSA, 157, 201
Davis, A. P., 29
Dawson, I., 101, 103, 104, 166, 167, 171, 176, 177
De Blij, H., 52
De Groot-Reuvekamp, M., 98, 101
De Haan, Y., 29
de la Cosa, Juan, 1500 CE world map of, 64–65
De La Paz, S., 51, 90
Dear Data project, 151–155
DeBow, J. D. B., 69
Decision-making; data as evidence for, 28–33; data visualizations influencing, 15
Delahunty, T., 52
Delaney, J., 57
Delnero, P., 62
Demack, S., 10, 67, 90
Democracy, illiteracy threat to, 5
Denbo, S., 135, 144
Deogracias, J. S., 51
Derakhshan, H., 21
Detroit Geographic Expedition, 214–215
Devezas, T., 143
deVilla, J., 38
Diakopoulos, N., 10, 87, 90
Digital Scholarship Lab and the National Community Reinvestment Coalition, 113, 129
D'Ignazio, C., 4, 71, 86, 87, 90, 91, 93, 199, 213

DiSalvo, B., 87, 155
DiSalvo, C., 87, 155
Disciplinary inquiry/literacy, data literacy for, 51–55
Disciplines, social studies. *See also individually named disciplines*; NEA Committee of Ten's recommendations for, 43–44; unique elements in, 51–52
Discrimination, data aiding, 71, 73–75
Disinformation, 21
Dixon, C., 154
Dobbs, C. L., 51
Douglass, F., 78
Downs, R., 45
Drozda, Z., 87
Du Bois, W. E. B.; data visualizations of, 75–78, 80, 84, 157–158, 215; works cited, 75–78, 79, 81
Duke, N. K., 166, 170
Dunn, R. E., 44, 107
Duration (temporal concept), 102, 103
Dykes, B. M., 48, 192

Economics, 51–52; data visualizations use in, 45
Educational attainment, 11–14
Efficiency movement/research, 85
Egea-Vivancos, A., 145
Elementary school, data literacy instruction in; K–2nd grade, 166–169; 3rd–5th grade, 170–173, 174–175
Elias, M. J., 92, 93
Eltis, D., 124
Elwood, S., 114, 127
Empowerment, data literacy and, 199
Engebretsen, M., 3, 4–5, 29
Engel, P., 39
Equal Justice Initiative, 128, 129
Error recognition/recovery, in minimal manuals, 210
Eugenics movement, 71, 75
Events. *See* Historical events/periods

"Fake news"/False information. *See* Disinformation; Misinformation; Misleading data visualizations
Fang, Z., 51
Farr, William (physician), 27
Fauni, A., 153
Federal Housing Administration (FHA), 111–112; impact of HOLC maps on, 112
Federal Reserve Economic Database (FRED), 201, 202–203
Felton, M. K., 51, 90
Finholm, C. E., 50, 98, 99, 115, 170
Flawed statistical reasoning, 72, 73–75
Flawed/tainted messaging, examples of, 71–72
"Folk geographers," 214

# Index

Ford, J. R., 200, 2006
Forman, S. E., 195, 196
Fosmire, M., 4
Franco, J., 112, 113, 128, 129
Freire, P., 199
Friel, S. N., 136, 137, 138, 139, 140, 168, 172, 173
Friendly, M., 3, 7, 8, 23, 24, 25, 26, 27, 28, 68, 98

Gaddis, J. L., 52
Galesic, M., 139, 140
Gannett, H., 70, 77, 78–80
Gannett, Henry (1846–1914), 68, 69–70, 77
Gapminder, 133, 134, 157, 201, 202
Garcia, R. J. B., 22
Garcia-Retamero, R., 139, 140
Garland, M., 22, 23, 40
Garrett, C., 155
Geographic information systems (GIS), 52, 53; tools/technologies, 128, 129, 183; webmaps/representations, 93, 179
Geography, 52; conference on, NEA recommendations from, 44
"Geography of children" (community investigation), 214–215
George, M., 61
Gersmehl, P., 116, 122
Gibbs, F. W., 52, 53
Gilbert, E., 107
Gilbert, M., 120
Gilbreth, Frank, 85
Gilbreth, Lillian (1878–1972), 85
Gillborn, D., 10, 67, 90
Gilliam, S., 155
Gillman, J. M., 74–75
Girard, B., 105
Gold, H., 36
"Golden age of graphics," 28
Goldman, S. R., 61
Goodwin, N., 52
Google products, for manipulating/creating data visualizations, 203
Grafton, A., 98, 105
Grant, S., 46, 92
Graphics. *See indiviual types of data visualizations*
Graphs and charts; comprehension signaling techniques, 135, 139–142, 173, 188; comprehension skills hierarchy, 139–143; in data literacy instruction. *See* Data literacy instruction; making sense of, 136–139; as pedagogical tools, 44; telling stories with, 133–149; types of, 136
*Graticule* (lines of latitude and longitude), 62
Gray, C., 50
Great Depression, 29, 111
Greenleaf, C., 61

Gregg, M., 115, 1117
Grossman, J., 53
Guess, A. M., 22
Gutiérrez, K., 10, 86, 87, 90
Guzdial, M., 187, 199, 200, 201, 210

Halloran, N., 114
Halloran, Neil, 144
Hansen, M., 40
Hardy, L., 154
Harris, J. M., 52
Harris, L. M., 105, 107
Harsh, J. A., 137, 139, 140, 238
Hattab, G., 135
Hauck, G., 170
Haydn, T., 98, 100, 101, 103, 104, 166, 167, 176
Healy, L., 145
Heer, J., 136, 155
Heffron, S., 45
Hegarty, M., 137
Heimlich, J., 6, 7, 136
Hendrickson, K., 87
Hergesheimer, E., 68
Herschel, J. F. W., 24
Hertzberg, H. W., 43, 44
High school, data literacy instruction in, 179, 182–186
Hill, H. C., 88
Hill, R. L., 28, 29, 90
Historical ages, 97, 101, 104
Historical causes/consequences, timelines and, 109
Historical events/periods, 103, 104; different interpretations of, 104–105; sequence of, 101–102
Historical narrative; historical significance and, 105–106; making coherent, 105; timelines and, 105, 106–107
Historical significance; change/continuity analysis and, 65–66, 107. *See also* Census data; historian's considerations for, 106; historical narrative and, 105–106; nonhistorian's interests and, 106; timelines and, 106–109
Historical thinking; heuristics, 90–92; in history teaching, 90; timelines and, 97–109
Historical time, concept of, 97
History education; "big picture" approach to, 107–109; curricular websites for, 50; disciplinary literacy and, 52–55; NEA Committee of Ten's 1894 report on, 43–44; perception of, 52; social studies and, 59; teaching of, historical thinking in, 90
History journals, data visualizations in, 53–55
Hodkinson, A., 98, 101, 102
Hoeffner, J., 88, 137, 138, 139
Hoffman, B. P., 51

Home Owners' Loan Association (HOLC), 111, 112; maps by. *See* "Residential Security" maps
Home ownership, 111–112
Hoover, Herbert, 111
Horowitz, W., 62
Horton, N. J., 136, 143, 145
Horz, H., 10, 170
Hospelhorn, E., 93
Howard, T. C., 136
Howland, B., 22
Hsi, S., 154
*Hull-House Maps and Papers* (Residents of Hull House, 1895), 82–84
Hullman, J., 10, 87, 90
Human choices, data visualizations as, 6, 10–14
Humanistic data literacy. *See* Critical, humanistic data literacy
Hunter, B., 6, 7
Hynd-Shanahan, C., 51

Illiteracy, as threat to democracy, 5
Imazeki, J., 11, 92, 213
Immigration; Laughlin report on (1922), 73–75; McCarran-Walter Act of 1952, 75
Inchoco, G. D., 30, 31
Independent Expert Advisory Group, 5, 6
Infographics. *See indiviual types of data visualizations*
Information, false/misleading. *See* Disinformation; Misinformation; Misleading data visualizations
Informed civic action, 22
Internet; civic reasoning development and, 22; information pollutants and, 21
Internet meme, "Try to impeach this," 3, 4
Intimate interests, historical significance and, 106
*Invisible Women* (Perez), 213–214
Ippolito, J., 51
Irgens, G. A., 10, 86, 87, 90
Isenberg, P., 135–136

Jackson, C., 51
Jacobson, L., 33
Jan, T., 112
Jasanoff, S., 31
Jefferson, Thomas, 111
Jiang, S., 10, 86, 87, 90, 155
Jo, I., 116, 122
Johnson, B., 87
Johnson, H., 52
Johnson, S., 2007
Johnstone, D., 87
Jones, G. M., 30, 31
Journell, W., 155
Jung, T., 118

Kahn, J., 10, 86, 87, 90, 94, 155
Kanarinka, 215
Kandel, S., 155
Karahalios, K., 38
Karrow, R. W., 60, 62, 63
Keena, A., 131
Keirn, T., 90
Kelley, Florence, 82, 84
Kennedy, H., 3, 4–5, 28, 29, 90
Kennedy, J., 155
Kennedy, J. C. G., 68, 71–72, 78, 84
Kirk, A., 29
Kirk, Andy, 200–201
Klein, L. F., 71, 86, 87, 90, 91, 213
Knaflic, C. N., 6, 7, 106
Knight, J. A., 166, 170
Knight, S., 10, 86, 87, 90
Knight Lab, 203, 204, 206, 209
Kollar, M., 89
Köller, O., 138
Kong, H., 38, 40
Kong, H.-K., 38
Kopf, D., 29, 30
Kracauer, S., 98
Kruikemeier, S., 29
Kulhavy, R. W., 124

Laina, V., 93, 173
LaMar, T., 87
Lanouette, K., 87
Lapowsky, I., 213
Latitude and longitude, lines of, 62, 64–65
Latner, M., 131
Laughlin, Harry H. (eugenicist), 73, 84; immigration report, 73–75; works cited, 73, 74, 75
Lecheler, S., 29
Lee, B., 135–136, 155
Lee, C. D., 61
Lee, C., 30, 31, 86, 93
Lee, J., 45, 46, 51, 92
Lee, P., 98, 100, 101, 102, 103, 109, 170, 171
Lee, T. B., 32
Lee, V. R., 87
Leetaru, K., 5
Leinhardt, G., 90, 91, 115, 117, 119, 1117
Levesque, E., 40
Lévesque, S., 52, 59, 66, 90, 100, 105, 106, 107
Levin, J. R., 170
Levitt, S. D., 87
Levstik, L. S., 100, 101, 104, 135, 145, 146
Lewis, L., 50
Lewis, M. W., 59
Liben, L. S., 16, 115, 116, 119, 125
Lin, L., 188
Lindner, M. A., 138

Index 243

Literacy. *See also* Data literacy *entries*; disciplinary, 51–55; illiteracy and, 5; verbal, 10
Liu, X., 29
Liu, Z., 38
Longitude and latitude, lines of, 62, 64–65
Lopez, M. L., 10, 86, 87, 90
Louie, J., 88
Ludewig, U., 10
Lupi, G., 151–152
Lybrand, H., 3, 4
Lyons, B. A., 22

Maher, T. V., 29
Maier, M. H., 11, 92, 213
Maltese, A. V., 6, 7, 136, 137, 139, 140, 238
Manipulation of data/data visualizations, 157, 161, 199–210; falsely. *See* Disinformation; Misinformation; Misleading data visualizations; minimal manuals and, 205–210; technology role in, 199–200; tools for, 201–203
Manuals, minimal, 205–210
Map orientations, Western *vs.* Islamic worldviews, 62–63
Map-reading skills, 114
Maps, 60; comprehension signaling techniques, 179; in data literacy instruction. *See* Data literacy instruction; functional evolution of, 59–60; from Hull House residents' data collection, 83, 84; national *vs.* state standards documents, 46–47; original, as primary source data, 57–59; "oughtness," 214; as pedagogical tools, 44; religious iconography on, 65; for spatial thinking/problem solving, 111–131; thinking about, 115–121; thinking through, 127–131; thinking with, 121–127; of time. *See* Temporal data visualizations; 2016 U.S. election results, 3, 4; Emma Willard and, 41–44; of world. *See* World maps; as worldviews, 57–65
Marlay, M. C., 11
Marshall, J., 10, 86, 87, 90
Martell, C. C., 136
Martin, D., 90
Martin, N. M., 166, 170
Matthews, A., 21
Mayer, R. E., 137
Mazur-Rimetz, S. A., 200, 2006
McCarran-Walter Immigration and Naturalization Act of 1952, 75
McElvany, N., 10, 170
McGann, A. J. M., 131
McGrew, S., 22, 23, 40, 90
McSwiggen, P., 52
Melendez, J. W., 93
Meng, A., 155
Meridian, determination of (1494), 64–65

Merroth, L., 90
Metoyer, S., 122
Meyer, D., 145
Michigan Dept. of Education, 48
"Micromotion studies," 85, 86
Middle school, data literacy instruction in, 173, 176–179, 180–181
Miller, C., 4
Mills, R. K., 145
Minard, Charles, 1869 figurative map of, 7–8, 9
Minimal manuals, 200, 205–210
Misinformation, 21; data visualizations examples, 3–4; presentation and prevalence, 22; spread of (example), 21
Misleading data visualizations; distorted presentation, 34–38, 39; examples, 31–33, 74; inaccurate/slanted titles or descriptions, 38, 40; omitting/hiding data in, 33–34; "Try to impeach this" meme, 3, 4
Missing datasets, 213–214
Mitchell, B., 112, 113, 128, 129
Mitchell, K., 114, 127
Mobius, M., 22
Mohan, A., 116, 117, 119, 120, 167, 168, 171. 172, 177
Mohan, L., 116, 117, 119, 120, 167, 168, 171. 172, 177
Moje, E. B., 50, 51
Moll, H., 57, 58, 59
Moll, Herman (cartographer), 57
Monmonier, M., 116, 117
Monte-Sano, C., 51, 90
Montgomery, J. M., 22
Moreland, K., 35
Morin, K. M., 62
Morris, A., 76
Morton, T., 52
Motivations, data visualizations and, 6, 67, 69, 70–71
Ms. P, 158
Murray, C., 139, 140
Myers, C., 139, 140
Myers, J. P., 15, 137

Nærland, T. U., 28
Naimipour, B., 199, 201
Nash, G. B., 44
National Association for the Advancement of Colored People (NAACP), 127–128, 129
National Center for History in the Schools., 105
National Community Reinvestment Coalition (NCRC), 112–113
National Council for the Social Studies (NCSS), 22, 45, 46, 92, 129, 155, 166, 167, 168, 172
National Education Association Committee of Ten on Secondary School Studies, 43–44
National Geographic Society, 52

National Governors Association Center for Best Practices & Council of Chief State School Officers, 45, 167, 168, 170, 171, 172, 173, 176, 177, 179, 183
National Issues Forums and the Kettering Foundation, 189
National Research Council, 52, 114, 115, 116
Native Land Digital, 123, 129
Navarro, O., 136
Nayman, S. J., 92, 93
Nelson, J. A., 52
Nelson, M. S., 4
Network visualizations, 7, 10
Networked computers, 21
New, R., 46, 92
Newman, N., 29
Newspapers, data visualizations in, 29–30
Nguyen, J., 139, 140
Nightingale, Florence, 157, 215; data visualizations of, 26–27, 143–144
Nightingale rose chart, 143–144
Nissenbaum, S., 127
Nobles, M., 67
Nokes, J. D., 52, 53, 59.91
Non-response bias, 11
Norman, R. R., 166, 170
Northwestern University Knight Lab, 204
Norton, M. B., 127
Noushad, N. F., 153
Nunes, S., 143
Nyhan, B., 22

O'Connor, C., 21
OER Projec, 108
Olivares, M. C., 10, 86, 87, 88, 90
Online data visualizations, 23
Online resources, social studies, 50
Onuoha, M., 213
Oort, F., 101
Open-access tools, 199–200, 204
Oppression; data literacy and, 5; tools of, data visualizations as, 71–75
Ortega, T., 22, 23, 40, 90
Ortiz-Ospina, E., 191, 192, 193, 194, 195
"Oughtness maps," 214
Our World in Data, 126, 141, 190–191, 193, 194, 195
Our World in Data graphs, 157; using Slow Analysis technique, 190–191; using Slow Reveal technique, 191–195
Owens, T., 53
"Own Your Own Home" campaign, 111

Parikh, T., 10, 86, 87, 90
Paris Exposition (1900), 75–76
Pawluczuk, A., 5
Pearson, P. D., 6, 7

Pearson Institute & The Associated Press-NORC Center for Public Affairs Research., 21
Peck, C. L., 106
Pedagogical content knowledge (PCK), 88
Pedagogical tools, 44, 100
Perez, C. C., 5, 87, 91, 213
Periodization/Periodization schemes, 103; disagreements over, 104–105; in textbooks, 103–104
Pfannkuch, M., 136, 143, 145
Phelps, G., 58
Philip, T. M., 10, 86, 87, 88, 90
Phillips, R., 87
Phillips, U. B., 144
Phillips, Ulrich B., 144
Pimentel, D. R., 93
Plaisant, C., 155
Playfair, W., 8, 24, 25
Playfair, William, 8, 24–25
Political science, 51
Polley, D. E., 6, 7, 136
Popa, N., 97, 100, 102
Popova, M., 153
Population, of U.S., 67, 69–70; enslaved (1860), 67, 68, 71–72
Porter, A. C., 44
Posavec, S., 151–152
Posetti, J., 21
Poynar, R., 86
Priestley, J., 98, 99
Primary source data, 55; census data as, 65–71; comprehension signaling techniques, 179; original maps as, 57–59
Problem solving, maps for, 111–131
Production of data, 154–155
Professional organizations, national standards and, 44–46
Ptolemy (90–168 CE) world map, 62–63

Qiu, L., 31, 32
Qlik, 5
Quadri, G. J., 136
Question sequencing, in surveys, 13
Quintero, D., 40
"Quota fulfillment" measure, 73–74

Radinsky, J., 93
Rapaport, A., 22, 23, 40
Reading the data, 139–143
Redlining, 112–113
Regan, M., 136, 143, 145
Reifler, J., 22
Reisman, A., 51, 52, 90
Religious iconography, on maps, 65
"Residential Security" maps, 112; legacy of, 113–114
Residents of Hull House, 84

# Index

Reynolds, E., 90
Reynolds, J. T., 107
Ribecca, S., 107
Richardson, D., 124
Riche, N. H., 135–136, 155
Rid, T., 21
Riel, J., 93
Ritchie, H., 138, 141, 142
Roberts, K. L., 115, 117, 166, 170, 173
Robinson, S., 29
Rocha, J., 86, 88, 90
Rodríguez, M. T., 143
Rogers, B., 5
Rogowitz, B., 35
Roosevelt administration, 111–112
Ropp, P. S., 107
Ros, A., 98, 101
Rosado, P., 138, 141, 142
Rosen, P., 136
Rosenberg, D., 98, 105
Roser, M., 138, 141, 142, 191, 192, 193, 194, 195, 214
Rosling, Hans (1948–2017), 133–136, 144
Rothschild, A., 87, 155
Rothschild, D. M., 22
Rothstein, R., 111, 112
Routley, N., 118
Rubel, L., 86, 88
Rüsen, J., 98
Rusert, B., 76
Rutchick, A. M., 22
Rydal Shapiro, B., 87

Saavedra, A., 22, 23, 40
Saini, A., 71
Sales, C. O. R., 145
Salinas, C., 106, 107, 136
Sanchez, T. R., 145
Saß, S., 138
Satyanarayan, A., 30, 31
Scaffolded instruction, 187–188
Schaffer, D., 52
Schnotz, W., 10, 170
School curricula/courses; critical/humanistic data literacy and, 87; national standards development for, 44; NEA Committee of Ten's 1894 report on, 43–44; online resources for, 50; verbal vs. data literacy in, 10
Schor, P., 67, 70, 72
Schuler-Brown, S., 87
Schulten, S., 41, 43
Schwartz, N. H., 170
Scott, J. C., 71
Segel, E., 136
Seguin, C., 29
Seixas, P., 52, 106, 107
Self-instruction manuals. *See* Minimal manuals

Semega, J., 89
"Sense of period," 100, 103; duration and, 103; visual images for, 104
Sequence of events/periods, 101–102
Serafini, F., 10
Shah, P., 88, 137, 138, 139
Shanahan, C., 51, 61
Shanahan, T., 51
Shapiro, B. R., 155
Sharma, S. V., 139, 140, 158
Shemilt, D., 98, 100, 101, 102, 103, 107, 109, 170, 171
Shi, D. E., 123
Shifman, L., 29
Shim, J., 153
Shin, H. B., 11
Shreiner, T. L., 10, 48, 50, 54, 66, 87, 90, 98, 99, 103, 115, 127, 135, 136, 139, 144, 145, 158, 170, 173, 179, 187, 192, 199, 200, 201, 210
Shuler, M., 195, 196
Shulman, L., 88
Signaling techniques, 135, 139–140, 141, 142, 173, 178, 179, 188
Significance; historical. *See* Historical significance; symbolic, 106
Silverman, C., 21
Sinclair, N., 145
Skills/Skillset. *See also* Historical thinking; comprehension hierarchy, 139–143; for data literacy, 5, 15, 47; flexible, 6; map-reading, 114
Slater, John Fox/Slater Fund, 77–78
Slave schedule (1650 U.S. census), 67, 68, 71–72
Slow analysis technique, 188–191
Slow reveal technique, 191–198
Smil, V., 146, 147
Smit, G., 29
Smith, C., 98, 101, 102
Smith, C. A., 131
Smith, M., 22, 23, 40, 90
Smith, T., 52
Smith-Kerker, P. L., 200, 2006
Smithson, J. L., 44
Snow, John (physician), 25–26, 27, 215; works cited, 26
Social inadequacy, Laughlin report on (1922), 73–74
Social media platforms, 21
Social movements, data visualizations in, 75–84
Social studies; *C3 Framework*, 45–47; critical, humanistic data literacy and, 87–88, 94; data literacy and, 15; data visualizations in, 15–16, 45–51; disciplinary literacy and, 51–55; "graph stories" activities in, 145–146; NEA Committee of Ten's recommendations (1894), 43–44

Social studies teachers; data stories and, 86–87, 214–215; data work resources/support for, 199–205; justice-oriented civic action projects and, 92; subject content matter and PCK of, 88–89; teaching critical, humanistic data literacy, 85–94
Society, datafication of, 5, 10
Sorapure, M., 153
Sourcing, historical thinking and, 90–91
Spatial data visualizations/location, 9, 59–60. *See also* Maps
Spatial thinking, 114; maps for, 111–131
Spatiotemporal data visualizations, 7—9
Standardized tests, 44, 46; data visualizations in, 47–49
Standards (national); Common Core, 45, 165; development initiatives/recommendations, 44; professional organizations and, 44–46
Standards (state); alignment with national standards, 44; inconsistencies in, 47–48, 98–99
Statistical reasoning, flawed, 72, 73–75
Stearns, P. N., 103, 104, 109
Step-by-step instructions. *See* Minimal manuals
Stories/Storytelling, 24, 86–87, 213–215; characteristics of, 86–87; data-informed action examples, 93; in data literacy instruction, 183; differences in, 91, 201, 203; with graphs/infographics, 8, 16, 29, 57–59, 133–149; historical narrative and, 105; as learning tool, 135, 143; Nightingale rose chart, 143–144; wrangling data and, 155–156
Storyline.JS/Storymap.JS, 203, 204, 205
Stoutenborough, J. W., 29
Stow, W., 98, 100, 101, 103, 104, 166, 167, 176
Strobel, B., 138
Sullivan, C. C., 106, 107, 136
Surveys; non-response bias in, 11; question sequencing in, 13
Sustainable development, data literacy and, 5–6
Svetina, D., 137, 140, 238
Swan, K., 45, 46, 51, 92
Swenson, K., 9, 10
Symbolic significance, 106

Tables, 7
Taking action, data-informed. *See* Data-informed action
Taurence, K., 192
Tawney, R. H., 2015
Taylor, Frederick Winslow, 85
Teachers/Teaching; data literacy. *See* Data literacy instruction; social studies. *See* Social studies teachers
Technology; ease/speed of information spread, 21; GIS tools, 128, 129, 183; role in data manipulation, 199–200; tools for data manipulation/visualization, 201–203
Temporal concepts, timelines and, 102
Temporal data visualizations, 9. *See also* Timelines; examples, 42
Terminology/Typology; in 1790–1890 census data visualizations, 6, 67, 69, 70–71; chronological understanding and, 100, 101–102, 103, 109; use in thematic maps, 120
Tests. *See* Standardized tests
Texas Education Agency, 49
Textbooks, 48, 50; alternative to, 50; timelines/periodization schemes in, 103–104
Thames, M. H., 58
Thematic maps, terminology use in, 120
Thinking. *See* Historical thinking; Spatial thinking
Time, concept of, 97
Time and motion studies, 85
Timeline.JS, 203, 204, 205; minimal manual example for, 206–210
Timelines; causes/consequences shown in, 109; change and continuity relationship in, 107; in data literacy instruction. *See* Data literacy instruction; historical thinking and, 97–109; as pedagogical tools, 100; potential of, 97–98; published, shortcomings in, 102–103; temporal concepts in, 102; in textbooks, 103–104
Tindall, G. B., 123
Tønnessen, E. S., 10
Topical data visualizations, 10
Traffic patterns, children's deaths and, 214–215
Trump, Donald, 3, 4
"Try to impeach this" meme, 3, 4
Tufte, E. R., 6, 7, 26

Ullrich, M., 10, 170
United States Census Office, 70
University of the State of New York, 49
U.S. Census Bureau, 12, 13–14, 89, 156, 157
U.S. Congress, apportionment of representatives, 28
USAFacts, 157, 201, 202
Uttal, D., 116, 119, 167

Vakil, S., 10, 86, 87, 90
Valant, J., 40
van Boxtel, C., 91, 101
Van der Nat, R., 29
van Drie, J., 91
van Ham, F., 155
Van Horne, B., 87
Van Rossum, M., 159
van Wart, S., 10, 86, 87, 90
VanSledright, B., 145
Vedlitz, A., 29

# Index

Verdi, M. P., 124
Villa Ross, C. A., 11
Visual aids, as pedagogical tools, 44, 107
Visualizing Data (website), 200

Wagner, I., 170
Wainer, H., 3, 7, 8, 23, 24, 25, 26, 27, 28, 68, 98
Wardle, C., 21
Warmington, P., 10, 67, 90
Warren, Gwendolyn, 214–215
Washington, S., 93
Watson, J. M., 145
Watson, P., 52
Watts, D. J., 22
Way, W., 87
Wayfaring maps, 60
Weatherall, J. O., 21
Weaver, C., 155
Weber, W., 29
Wells-Barnett, Ida B., 80–82, 84, 107, 115; works cited, 80, 81, 82
Wertsch, J. V., 135
West, J. D., 21, 35
WGBH Educational Foundation, 145
Whitby, A., 23, 66
Wiegand, P., 115, 116, 117
Wigen, K., 59
Wigen, K. E., 59
Wikimeida Commons, 27, 59, 61, 63, 64, 65, 99
Wild, C., 136, 143, 145
Wilkerson, M. H., 10, 86, 87, 90, 93, 173
Willard, Emma, 41–44

Williams, S., 71, 82, 92, 127
Willingham, D. T., 145
Wilschut, A., 97, 104
Wilson, P. H., 155
Wineburg, S., 22, 23, 40, 51, 52, 90, 91
Wise, A. F., 10, 86, 87, 90
Witzel, L., 85, 86
Women; absence in data collections, 213–214; housework research and, 85–86
Wong, R. M., 188
Wood, S., 104
*World History: The Basics* (Stearns), 103–104
World maps; of Al Sharif al-Idrisi (1154 CE), 63–64; Babylonian, 60–62; of Juan de la Cosa (1500 CE), 64–65; of Ptolemy, 62
"World," social concept of, 60
World Wars I and II, 29
Worldviews; data characteristics and, 87; maps as, 57–65; personal, 114; Western *vs.* Islamic, 62–63
Wrangling data, 155–157
Wright, G. C., 51

Yang, T., 30, 31
Yearwood, P. J., 59
Yongpradit, P., 87
Yoon, S. A., 153
Young, K. M., 90, 91

Zhang, Y., 29
Zukas, A., 57
Zuspan, S., 90
Zwart, D. E., 127

# About the Author

**Tamara L. Shreiner** is an associate professor in the history department at Grand Valley State University in Michigan, where she specializes in social studies education and teaches social studies methods to prospective teachers, including instruction in teaching data literacy. Previously, Shreiner was a middle and high school history teacher, spending most of her teaching career in Ann Arbor, Michigan, where she also earned her PhD at the University of Michigan. She has been researching and writing about data literacy in social studies for nearly 10 years, with over a dozen articles on the topic in journals such as *Theory & Research in Social Education, Social Education, Journal of Social Studies Research, Race Ethnicity and Education, British Journal of Educational Technology,* and *Social Studies Research and Practice*. She has also worked with teachers across the country, providing professional development on ways to implement data literacy in the social studies curriculum. When not thinking about data and data visualizations, Shreiner likes to travel and spend time outdoors with her husband, three children, and two dogs.